KENT RIDGE

KENT RIDGE
An Untold Story

Edited by

Kevin Y.L. Tan

Contributions by

Victor R. Savage, **David Higgitt**, **Hugh T.W. Tan**,
Kelvin K.P. Lim, **Tan Ming Kai**, **Alex T.K. Yee**, **Ho Chi Tim**,
Erik Holmberg, **Tan Chye Guan**, **Kevin Y.L. Tan**,
Peck Thian Guan and **Lee Fook Ngian**

With a special contribution from

Edwin Thumboo

RIDGE BOOKS
SINGAPORE

Published under the Ridge Books imprint by:

NUS Press
National University of Singapore
AS3-01-02, 3 Arts Link
Singapore 117569

Fax: (65) 6774-0652
E-mail: nusbooks@nus.edu.sg
Website: http://nuspress.nus.edu.sg

ISBN 978-981-4722-81-0 (paper)

National Library Board, Singapore Cataloguing-in-Publication Data
Name(s): Tan, Kevin, editor.
Title: Kent Ridge: an untold story / edited by Kevin Y.L. Tan; contributions by
    Edwin Thumboo, Victor R. Savage, David Higgitt, Hugh T.W. Tan, Kelvin K.P. Lim,
    Tan Ming Kai, Alex T.K. Yee, Ho Chi Tim, Erik Holmberg, Tan Chye Guan, Kevin
    Y.L. Tan, Peck Thian Guan and Lee Fook Ngian.
Description: Singapore: Ridge Books, [2019] | Includes bibliographical references
    and index.
Identifier(s): OCN 1024241996 | ISBN 978-981-47-2281-0 (paperback)
Subject(s): LCSH: Pasir Panjang (Singapore)--History. | National University
    of Singapore--History. | College campuses--Singapore--History.
Classification: DDC 959.57--dc23

0.1: The NUS campus on Kent Ridge, pp. ii–iii

0.2: The newly-built NUS campus on Kent Ridge in 1977, pp. iv–v

0.3: A 1957 map of Kent Ridge shows how little developed the area was, and therefore how attractive to the planners of independent Singapore looking for more space for education, research, industry and the port, pp. vi–vii

0.4: Campus planners and NUS scientists have been working hard to enhance the natural environment and greenery on the NUS campus, p. viii

0.5: "Absorb, commune and walk", an early-morning scene in front of the Lee Kong Chian Natural History Museum, p. xii

0.6: The Computer Centre was one of the key buildings in the plan for the new Kent Ridge campus. This photograph is from 1977, p. xvi

Typeset by: Nur Nelani Jinadasa Abdullah
Printed by: Markono Print Media Pte Ltd

Contents

Kent Ridge Park

Edwin Thumboo

These winds, just risen from the plain,
Hurrying to reach resisting trees, are old.
They swayed earth's first shadows, and yet again
Spread evening clouds on beds of gold.

Look—a sea of many islands. Ours. Then
Inland, over Park of Knowledge: each distant hill
Is neighbourly, serene. They dream of times when
History lay quiet, and no guns poised to kill.

Yet twelve Zeros, screamed out of morning light,
Blew tanks, up into hungry flames that licked our sky.
Black, acrid smoke hid stars that night.
We children watched and wondered why.

Now green harmony returns your rooted life,
We hear, at times, those dark war days, now gone.
Let's keep the peace, and deftly stave off strife,
Counting on how peoples' bravery once shone.

Morning, noon and night the elderly and young
Exercise along your slopes.
The birds, whose rolling notes are strung
Across your Ridge, make crimson, magic tropes.

Absorb, commune and walk; meditate and feel
What shrubs what flowers what fishes securely know:
The energy, the pulse, the secrets, as they heal
The sky the earth the sea below.

Between dew and sunset are the reasons
Why our islands bask in light.
Why we thrive through turbulent seasons,
As nations scout cute words for wrong and right.

Take the path of peace where others doubt and fight.
As worlds re-make, we gradually breathe as one,
Keeping a piece of daily Sun
To light us through the night.

Preface

The idea for a book about Kent Ridge was hatched more than a decade ago, in 2005, by the National University of Singapore's (NUS) Campus Green Committee. The committee, comprising academics and staff from various NUS departments, was charged with promoting a cleaner and greener campus, and encouraging the NUS community to have a greater appreciation of the natural environment.

In furtherance of this latter objective, the committee felt that its work should begin in NUS's own backyard. The aim was to get the NUS community to better appreciate the rich heritage of Kent Ridge, to which end it was proposed that a book on several lesser known facets of Kent Ridge be put together. Diverse NUS faculty were roped in to help write the various chapters and now, we present this decade of research in this book.

Kent Ridge extends from Clementi Road in the west to Pepys Road in the east. It is divided in the middle by South Buona Vista Road through the "Gap". The Gap is the saddle where South Buona Vista Road meets Kent Ridge Road and Stockport Road. NUS occupies the western portion of the Ridge, while the 47-hectare Kent Ridge Park takes up its eastern half, with Science Park I being located at the foot of its eastern face.

The Ridge is part of the Jurong Formation, which consists of a variety of sedimentary rocks. The southern slope of the Ridge is covered mainly with natural vegetation, its lower part developed for housing. The top of the Ridge is highly undulating. It is covered with natural vegetation as well as landscaped gardens in Kent Ridge Park. Designed to take advantage of the natural vegetation and elevated topography of the area, the park offers marvellous views of the southern offshore islands.

Kent Ridge is home to many indigenous plants, such as *tembusu*, *tiup-tiup* and *senduduk*. Sundry animal species—monitor lizards, crested green lizards, flying dragons, cicadas, carpenter bees, fruit bats and oriental whip snakes, among others—also find shelter here, and some 150 different species of birds have also been spotted.

The Ridge is also historically significant. Units of the Malay Regiment held off the imperial Japanese forces for two days before being overrun at Opium Hill (Bukit Chandu). The Malay Regiment stood between the Japanese troops and the military supply dumps in the Alexandra area, and the defeat on Opium Hill sealed Singapore's surrender the day after, on 15 February 1942. A World War II Interpretative Centre opened on the 60th anniversary of the city's fall, and now stands at Bukit Chandu.

Perhaps just as historically significant as the battle on Opium Hill was the construction of the NUS campus on Kent Ridge. Construction work started soon after the ground-breaking ceremony on 25 March 1972 to develop 192 hectares of hilly ground into a campus for some 8,000 students. The development of NUS at Kent Ridge changed the landscape of Pasir Panjang and its environs, bringing further development and vibrancy. More importantly, it reshaped university education in Singapore.

As chairman of the Campus Green Committee, I have had the honour of leading this book project. This project is special to me. As a child, I would spend one to two weeks of my year-end school vacation in a holiday bungalow at the junction between Clementi Road and Pasir Panjang Road. That bungalow is still there; it belongs to the Lee Rubber Company and my uncle, who was the company's property manager, used to book the premises for our family's use. I remember the kampong houses and coconut trees that lined Pasir Panjang Road and the smell of the sea in which I used to go swimming. That, alas, is no more. Land reclamation has moved the sea coast much further out, and the old seafront is now the West Coast Highway. I remember taking intertidal walks and wading through the mudflats at low tide. I also remember the excavators on the slopes of Kent Ridge and the construction work at the site of the university. Directing this project has been special to me. It has allowed me to relive my childhood days and to discover many interesting facets of the Ridge described in this book, which I had not known previously.

This book covers various aspects of Kent Ridge—its history, geology, human geography, the role it played in Battle for Singapore in World War II, its flora and fauna and the development of the NUS Campus. It is lovingly written by a group of people who not only have a deep knowledge of these subjects, but also a passion for the Ridge. It is my hope that this passion rubs off on all those who read this book too.

Peck Thian Guan

The National University of Singapore at Kent Ridge

Reflections on Changing Landscapes

Victor R. Savage

Introduction

In 1972, I remember, as an under-graduate on the Bukit Timah campus, my first introduction to the new campus of the National University of Singapore at Kent Ridge. During a talk in one of the New Lecture Theatres (NLTs) given by the architects and planners of the new campus at Kent Ridge, I realized, at that time, that the old Bukit Timah campus was seeing its last days. The talk was attended by a small group of no more than 30 interested students and faculty and everyone was given copies of the draft plans of the new campus; unfortunately, I threw them out when moving house years ago. Kent Ridge campus was a project by Dutch architects and it was meant to house a population of 8,000–10,000 students. How this has changed with time. NUS in AY2016–17 had a population of 38,596 students (undergraduates and graduates), an increase of almost four times what it was originally planned for. The new Kent Ridge campus had

its buildings up by 1977 (Phase 1) and 1980 (Phase 2), and I recall making a visit after returning from studying overseas and taking photographs of this spanking-new campus. The Arts Faculty in the Bukit Timah campus finally moved to its new home in 1981. There was excitement in the shift. And as geographers, we explored our new environment with a great sense of adventure and curiosity in the first year.

Kent Ridge

This article traces the broad processes of landscape change at Kent Ridge and its environs, its sequent occupance, its toponymy and its establishment as an educational corridor in Singapore's development. Writing this gave me a sense of déjà vu in many ways. I was personally familiar with Kent Ridge way back in 1959 and 1960 when two of my primary-school classmates lived at what was then known as Pasir Panjang Village, at the junction of Pasir Panjang (Long Sands) and Clementi Roads (named after Sir Cecil Clementi, Governor of the Straits Settlement). During the school holidays, we would together roam the hills of Kent Ridge. In 1980, it was interesting for me to visit the place again, in 1981 to shift into the new NUS campus and, in 1984, as Sub-Dean, to be actively involved in the "garden greening" of the Arts Faculty's landscapes. This is an account of a personal journey

Fig. 1.1: Clouds gather over the Engineering Faculty, built on the western end of Kent Ridge

of recollections, memories and past experiences, augmented by fieldwork and historical data.

The Alam Melayu of Pasir Panjang

Given that Kent Ridge falls between Pasir Panjang and Ayer Rajah, areas that were important Malay hubs in Singapore's early history, we need to go back farther in time to understand how they were contextualized as place names in the history of the island. Singapore is an important part of the history of the Alam Melayu (Malay World). The flowering of the thalassic kingdom of Temasek/ Singapura in the 13th–14th centuries was a brief, but significant, interlude in the history of the Alam Melayu. The kingdom of Singapura represents that important intersection between the fall of Sri Vijaya (centred in Palembang), where the port was a small outpost of the Sri Vijayan empire,[1] and the rise of the Melaka Sultanate in the 15th century. Indeed, history records that the last king, Iskander of the likely Buddhist kingdom of Temasek/Singapura, became the founder of Melaka around 1400.[2]

Given the importance of the island and port kingdom in the Alam Melayu, Singapore's early toponymy was a product of Malay references. Hence, in the rare 1604 Godinho de Eredia map of "Sincapvra" several Malay place names have already been ascribed to the island and its surrounding marine environment: Tanjon Rusa and Tamion Ruca are probably references to Changi Point; Sunebodo probably refers to Sungei Bedok, Tamion Ru, Blacan Mati island and Salat Tubro.[3] It seems likely that references to place names in early Singapore came from three sources: the port kingdoms of the far-flung Sri Vijayan Empire, the roaming and mobile Orang Laut or sea gypsies that David Sopher calls "sea nomads"[4] and the more sedentary Malay fishermen who settled along the bays and coastlines of the area. Early references to place names in Singapore largely reflected geographical features that fishermen and sea gypsies used as landmarks and reference points for navigation in this island world. Two of these early important landmarks of Singapore were Tanah Merah on the east side of the island, a reference to the red laterite rocks that could be seen from the sea, and Batu Berlayer or Lot's Wife at the west entrance to the harbour. Given that there were less mangrove-free bays, rivers and inlets on the western side of the island, the Orang Laut were not found in this area. Singapore's Orang Laut inhabited inlets, creeks, rivers and protected coastal areas, and these areas carried the same names as the sea nomads that inhabited them—Orang Seletar, Orang Kallang, Orang Punggol, Orang Tanjong Irau, Orang Gelam and Orang Selat.[5]

Unlike the Orang Laut who settled down in other areas of Singapore even before Sir Stamford Raffles arrived in 1819, the first Malay residents of the coastal Pasir Panjang area that we know about were the followers of the Temenggong Abdul Rahman who were resettled from the banks of the Singapore River (around the new Parliament House) to the area broadly defined by Masjid Jamek in the Telok Blangah area (100 hectares), in what is now the World Trade Centre-VivoCity area. After his father's death, the son of Abdul Rahman, Daing Ibrahim, developed the hillside area (Mount Faber) by growing spices and fruits. Some of Daing's followers moved further westwards along the coast, especially when the British colonial government took over the Temengong's sea-facing area for Keppel Harbour in the 1850s. The clearance of land for the new harbour also gave rise to Malay migration out of Telok Blangah. This migration also coincided with the Temenggong shifting his residence to Johor, though many of his followers did not join him.[6] Hence over the decades of the 19th and 20th centuries, the Malay community kept moving westwards along the coast as the town area expanded. It is not surprising that Pasir Panjang Road was opened up in 1850, a time when Keppel Harbour was built[7] and the Malay settlement moved incrementally westwards along the coast.

The road was laid down by John Turnbull Thomson, the then government surveyor (1841–53). By the 1950s, there were several Malay fishing villages along Pasir Panjang Road, which ended at "Pasir Panjang Village", a small Chinese retail hub at the junction of Pasir Panjang and Clementi Roads.

As the Malay residents moved into the coastal area, place names changed throughout the 19th and 20th centuries. "Pasir Panjang" was originally a reference to the Alexandra/Labrador area in the 1860s while what is now Kent Ridge was still, in the 1860s, vacant land without a name. By the late 19th century, however, all of Kent Ridge was labelled in maps as "Pasir Panjang" as part of the estate of Tan Kim Seng. The Malay influence in the coastal area is evident by the number of place names along the Pasir Panjang coastline: Ayer Nipah, Tanjong Ayer Jumba, Patah Telok, Sungei Ayer Rajah, Telok Telaga, Tanjong Mat, Sungei Labu and Kampong Sultan (at the coast opposite Pasir Panjang Hill, and east of South Buona Vista Road). One of the mysteries of the name of Ayer Rajah Road, now the Ayer Rajah Expressway or AYE, is that the road's name has nothing to do with its immediate surroundings. Ironically, the highway located on the north side of Kent Ridge derives its name from the stream called Sungei Ayer Rajah, with its source on the south side of Kent Ridge and its mouth in coastal Pasir Panjang. The Malay reference to "Ayer Rajah" or "King's water" suggests

that the water must have been used by royalty living in the area. The location of Kampong Sultan opposite Pasir Panjang Hill does suggest that Malay royalty could have resided in the Pasir Panjang area. Could this have been the location of some descendants of Temenggong Diang Ibrahim? Time unfortunately erases landscapes but the oral history of people in myths and legends does live on. What is certain is that NUS abuts a place with an important name that signals local royal tradition.

Pasir Panjang was predominantly a Malay area in the 19th century. In the early years of settlement, the Malay fishing kampongs along Pasir Panjang Road also made and sold charcoal to people in Keppel Harbour. It seems likely that the charcoal wood came from felling the Mount Faber-Kent Ridge *belukar* (secondary forest) as well as the mangrove swamps along the coasts. One former place name—Ayer Nipah—indicates that there were mangrove swamps in the area. The fishing villages in the area were linked to the central town quite early in Singapore's colonial development. Pasir Panjang area was opened up not only by the development of Pasir Panjang Road in 1850 but also the Alexandra Road development in 1864.[8]

Around the 1860s, Clementi Road was already linking Pasir Panjang to Bukit Timah but its current name came later. Unlike the other traditional Malay enclaves in Singapore, the Malays who

Fig. 1.2: This image from a Pulau Ubin mangrove serves to remind us of the pre-reclamation coastline west of the Clementi-Pasir Panjang Road junction

moved into Pasir Panjang generally bought the lands they stayed in; the Pasir Panjang area opened up with colonial land tenure area in place. In the 19th century, the Malays called the newly cut Pasir Panjang Road "Jalan Tanah Merah" (red land road) because it was made of laterite.[9] Throughout the 19th century, the entire Pasir Panjang area was clearly a Malay area and did not feature in the Chinese or Indian native names in the area at all.[10] The Malay kampong had no specific names and were generally referred to by their locations along Pasir Panjang Road. Hence there was the kampong Pasir Panjang *lima stengah* (5½ ms) which was located at the 5½ milestone (ms) from the city and, similarly, kampong Pasir Panjang *batu enam tiga suku* (6¾ ms or 10.8 km).

In many Malay kampongs, names reflected a founding village chief, major benefactor or somebody important in the kampong. Hence a secondary name of Kampong Pasir Panjang 6¾ ms was Kampong Mohamad Yusoff because a former resident, Mohamad bin Yusoff, donated (*wakaf*) his house for use as the village *surau* or small prayer house.[11] Kampong Mat Jambol is likely named after someone in the village. In the 1930s, when Kallang Airport was being constructed (built by 1938), Malays in the area were moved out, and about 30–40 families moved to Pasir Panjang. The Malay residential dominance was preserved in Pasir Panjang partly because, in 1957, the Kesatuan Melayu Singapura

(Singapore Malay Union) lobbied to have part of the area declared as a "reserved Malay area". This reserved area was the West Coast Malay Settlement covering 70 acres and comprising 127 households, all of them Malay except for three Chinese households.[12] To serve the predominantly Malay community, a Malay school called the Sekolah Melayu Pasir Panjang (Pasir Panjang Malay School), was built prior to World War II; the building was later transformed into the National Cadet Corp (NCC) Sea Training Camp.

For most of the 19th and early 20th centuries, Malays lived in kampongs scattered throughout Singapore. The percentage of Malays living in kampongs fell dramatically from 58.7 percent in 1970 to 19.5 percent by 1980, in most part due to the government's resettlement programmes and the shift of population to HDB public housing flats. Despite the dramatic reduction of Malay kampongs in Singapore by 1980, the Malay kampong in Pasir Panjang still existed up to the late 1980s. Known by its location in terms of distance from the town, the last Malay kampong existing in the mid-1980s was Kampung Pasir Panjang 6¾ ms. My student Kartini binti Yayit (1987) did probably one of the last academic studies of Kampung Pasir Panjang 6¾ ms. The Malay kampong defined the Malay organization of community living just as squatter settlements did for the Chinese and Indian communities. Just as in Pasir

Fig. 1.3: A postcard view of Pasir Panjang dating from the early 1900s. Note the white spats sported by the policeman

Panjang, Malay kampongs underscored not only a place of residence as a "centre of felt value" for its residents, but also reflected a somewhat coherent social and community unit of solidarity, kinship ties and neighbourly cooperation (*gotong royong* spirit).[13]

Insight into the Malay kampong at Pasir Panjang 6¾ ms reveals that the early settlers came to the Tanjong Pagar area, near the present Keramat Habib Noh bin Mohammed al-Habshi at Palmer Road, and were said to be descendants of the Orang Laut. Others also were followers of the Temenggong who moved from the Telok Blangah-Tanjong Pagar area when the new docks were built in

the 1860s. Hence the Malay kampong settlers in Pasir Panjang established settlements in a rather spontaneous manner by establishing villages (*buka kampong*) in areas that comprised unoccupied forested areas. The Malay villages were strung out along Pasir Panjang Road from the Batu Belayer Village (4⅓ ms Pasir Panjang Road) to the 6¾ ms Kampong Pasir Panjang. In her 1986 study of Pasir Panjang 6¾ ms village, Kartini noted there were 25 houses left with officially listed addresses housing a population of 225 persons and serviced by a *surau* (Mohamad Yusof) in the village and a mosque (Hussain Sulaiman mosque) nearby. Unlike many of the Malay kampongs, the land at Kampong Pasir Panjang 6¾ ms was owned by the villagers.[14]

One of the clues to former Malay settlements to be found in today's resettled landscape is the location of *suraus,* mosques and *keramat* (shrines) that remain despite the changes. Hence all that remains of the former Malay fishing village on Pasir Panjang Road is the mosque: Masjid Hussein Sulaiman, probably named after one of the founders of the Malay fishing village. At the 7 ms was the Pasir Panjang *keramat* called the Keramat Datuk Mulia, which was removed in the 1980s. Within the broad Pasir Panjang-Clementi area around NUS, there are at least two other mosques: Masjid Ahmad (at the end of South Buona Vista Road), that earlier marked the location of another Malay kampong, and the Clementi Mosque known as the Masjid Tentera Di-Raja reflected the days when the Malay Regiment was stationed in the Pasir Panjang area. Lower down Pasir Panjang Road, another sample of Malay influence is ironically found in the former Chinese Tua Peh Kong temple now moved to Clementi East. Here legend has it that a Malay village chief after his death was transformed into a stone and later appeared as a deity Tua Peh Kong, revered by people.[15] On the Ayer Rajah Highway side at the current sites of the university's Conservatory of Music and Lee Kong Chian Natural History Museum was the site of another Malay kampong:

Kampung Tulloch. Similarly, the site of the Faculty of Science and NUH was built on a kampong area with a western name: Kampong O'Carroll Scott.

The Feng Shui of Kent Ridge

Up to the 1960s, Kent Ridge was not a very accessible place, though it was already defined quite clearly by four roads that were developed in the early 20th century: on the east, South Buona Vista Road or "the Gap", by Ayer Rajah Road (north), Clementi Road (west) and Pasir Panjang Road (south). These four roads, in a way, bounded the hilly area of Kent Ridge. For the Chinese, any hill or mountain chain is generally seen as being favourable in terms of feng shui (literally "wind or water"), the Chinese practice of understanding landscape. Kent Ridge is no different. Hills and mountains are said to represent the veins of *qi* that represent the ground dragons.[16] In Singapore, geomancers view the island as the site of five dragons. The western area (southwest as in Kent Ridge) represents, for some Chinese geomancers, the White Tiger. The first Chinese to colonize the area was the Malacca-born merchant and public benefactor Tan Kim Seng (1805–64), who bought property that covered the whole of the Kent Ridge area probably sometime between the 1850s and 1860s. Little reference to this property is recorded in his biographical profile. It seems strange that, after his death, we find maps between 1898 and 1911 labelling the whole Pasir Panjang Ridge as Tan Kim Seng's Estate, with indications that some rubber was grown around the "Gap". He and his descendants left more of a mark in the place names of the River Valley and Kim Seng Road area. Kim Seng's Pasir Panjang estate was obviously land he hardly developed hence no place names in the area are associated with him or his descendants.

Despite the growing Chinese population and expansion on Singapore island from the mid-19th century, and despite their auspicious geomantic qualities, Kent Ridge and Pasir Panjang were not areas of early Chinese residential colonization. During the agricultural frenzy for nutmeg, pepper and gambier plantations in the 1830s, the Pasir Panjang-Ayer Rajah-Kent Ridge area seems to have been relatively untouched, at least until later in the 19th century. Pepper and gambier farms covered 10,800 hectares of Singapore's land area by 1849.[17] Over the latter half of the 19th century and the early decades of the 20th century, smallholders grew gambier, pepper, rubber and pineapple along the Ridge. Gambier was the most destructive crop in Singapore's history and a major agent of landscape change. According to Wee and Corlett (1986), due to the massive deforestation caused by gambier plantations, only 15 percent of the island remained forested by 1886. This explains why the Kent Ridge area

was a landscape of *adinandra belukar* and lalang (*imperata cyclindrica*, a pyrophyte or fire-resistant plant) by the 1920s. The presence of lalang suggests that the area must have gone through repeated clearing and burning.

One of the features of the Chinese resident community was how it colonized the surrounding hills around the Raffles town centre, not for the living but for the dead. Chinese cemeteries soon developed in the surrounding hillocks around the town and, as the town expanded, Chinese cemeteries sprouted out in hills further from the town. Why are hilly places sought after for Chinese graveyards? Feng shui is the answer. The Chinese believe that ancestral tombstones must be buried correctly so that their descendants will have a bright future.[18] The ideal grave sites are the slopes of hills, if possible facing the sea or a water body. Bukit Cina in Melaka, one of the oldest and biggest Chinese graveyards in Southeast Asia, is a very good example.[19] In the 19th century, Singapore Chinese were also known to value their graves.[20] Despite the fact that Kent Ridge would have formed an ideal site for Chinese graveyards, it never became such a location. There were Chinese graveyards along the western side of Pasir Panjang Road, but never further west than the junction of Pasir Panjang and Alexandra Road, where the famous Yeo clan cemetery and a Teochew cemetery were located (at Heap Guan San Village off Telok Blangah). Instead, the Malays had a graveyard next to Haw Par Villa. Malay villagers also had the habit of burying their dead in any vacant land along Pasir Panjang. Hence amongst the Malay villagers, the Pasir Panjang area was considered very eerie at night, because the villagers believed that ghosts roamed the area.

Kent Ridge was probably spared as a Chinese cemetery because in a space-bound community that relied mainly on horse carriages and bullock-carts for mobility, it was too far from Chinatown and the city centre. Also, Pasir Panjang Road covered a very narrow strip of land between the Ridge and the coast, which made mobility difficult given the many Malay fishing villages in the area and flooding in the rainy season. After Tan Kim Seng's estate was sold, the next large owner of land in the area was Major Hugh Ransome Stanley Zehnder, a lawyer. Zehnder bought 4 acres of land between Pasir Panjang Road and South Buona Vista Road. The house was named Greystones and the road leading to the house is named after him, till today, as Zehnder Road.

By the 1920s, the coastal area of Pasir Panjang became an attractive residential area for rich Chinese towkays (a towkay refers to a business owner, a boss). The traditional Malay fishing area thus began to see new development. Despite Tan Kim Seng's vast property area, Pasir Panjang was known to the Chinese by the Hong Heng plantation, hence its name *hong heng sua*. As in the East Coast

area, the rich Chinese built colonial-type bungalows along Pasir Panjang Road from the 1920s onwards. Essentially, the Chinese towkays bought up land from the Malay land owners on the seaside for what Roland Braddell calls "seaside residences"[21] along Pasir Panjang Road. As the Malay Pasir Panjang kampong community became less involved in fishing, there was less reluctance to sell the sea-facing residences to the Chinese. Given its orientation, the location of houses along Pasir Panjang Road—with a hill behind the homes and the sea in front—certainly provided good feng shui for their owners. Geomancer Tan Khoon Yong endorses Pasir Panjang as "the most prosperous area in Singapore's western region".[22]

Unlike Bencoolen Street, Boat Quay, Bukit Timah and the Katong areas, which were the residential areas of the rich, Pasir Panjang Road (between the gap and Clementi Road) became more a weekend holiday residential area for rich Chinese towkays. As the Chinese moved into the area many of the dead end side roads from Pasir Panjang took the names of their Chinese land and residential owners: Yew Siang Road, Chwee Chian Road, Heng Mui Keng Terrace, Guok Avenue and Neo Pee Teck Lane. Of these, the one most spatially linked to NUS is Heng Mui Keng Terrace. This road is named after the Teochew towkay Heng Mui Keng who owned property in this area; after his death, the property was distributed to his children.

Heng's son, William Heng, was a well-known practising medical doctor and paediatrician in the 1950s and 1960s; his clinic was on his own property in Wilmer Place on Armenian Street.

The development of luxury holiday bungalows of the rich Chinese began in the 1920s; some are still present in the area till now. Two bungalows in particular can be seen clearly with the backs facing the then sea but now the reclaimed land and highway. The residential area was located between two dominant Chinese "villages" or retail hubs that developed along Pasir Panjang Road: Buona Vista village (at the junction of South Buona Vista and Pasir Panjang Roads) and Pasir Panjang village (at the corner of Clementi and Pasir Panjang Roads). The outer reaches of the town's population stopped at Pasir Panjang village; here a bus service (Keppel Bus Company) from Kampong Bahru had its terminus and made the entire area accessible from the 1950s onwards. By 1957, Pasir Panjang village reflected the multiracial character of Singapore: it had a population of 534 Chinese, 170 Malays, 10 Indians and 38 people classified as "others".[23] The shops here included those that sold fish and

Fig. 1.4: This 1926 villa stands today as a reminder of "Old Pasir Panjang", along Pasir Panjang Road

other seafood, which were products of the former Malay fishing villages in the area. Indeed, one of the Chinese shops still sells fresh fish here which it obtains from fishing fleets at Tuas.

Pasir Panjang was considered a kind of a sea resort, an idea that was reinforced by developments in the early 20th century in the area. The main long beach (fronting the Malay fishing villages) was an attractive swimming area for weekend Singaporean holiday makers. This image of a weekend relaxation venue was further enhanced by the development of the Haw Par Villa Swimming Pool facing the sea, diagonally opposite the most famous landmark of the area, Haw Par Villa or the Tiger Balm Gardens. The land was acquired in 1935 and the park was completed in 1937. The park became a major Singaporean and tourist attraction. The landmark establishment of the Pasir Panjang area was owned by the brothers Aw Boon Haw (Tiger) and Aw Boon Par (Leopard), two of the wealthiest Chinese in Southeast Asia during the 1940s and 1960s. In an era when amusement parks were unheard of, the Tiger Balm Gardens was an extraordinary park crammed with interesting sights. Hardly any young Singaporean Chinese of the 1950s, 1960s and 1970s has not been to Haw Par Villa for a day's family outing. Parents felt that the moral pictorial messages and dioramic gory depictions of the ten courts of hell imparted important lessons to their children. Further along,

at the 7 ms Pasir Panjang Road, were the West Point Gardens, famous in the 1960s and 1970s for their scenes of dating couples dancing to a live band. Later the house was converted into a zoo which attracted few patrons.

Colonial City: Town, Country and the Military Landscape

Up to the 1960s, Kent Ridge remained a place that defined the outer margins of Singapore's town centre. Singapore town, defined by the boundaries of the 1822 Raffles Town Plan, marked the centre of the British colony. It was the hub of economic, political, social and cultural activities and also housed over 70 percent of the colony's population. Singapore's colonial history reflects, in part, the very slow expansion of built-up areas which reached only 52 square kilometres by 1950 with the population concentrated in the central area.[24] For much of the 19th century, Pasir Panjang was a rural area removed from the city centre, as defined by the Raffles Town Plan. Indeed, without motorized vehicles, the only way into town was by bullock-cart and horse-drawn carriage (called *kereta kuda* or *bogie* in Malay). But the Malay villages were connected with one another by boat, along the coast as well as the southern islands of Singapore. In the Pasir Panjang 6¾ ms village, the evidence of the island connection with Pasir Panjang's Malay

Fig. 1.5: Two old unused British military buildings remain on Kent Ridge, accessible from Kent Ridge Road

community was obvious as some resident households came from Pulau Tekong and Pulau Brani.[25]

British colonialism had a greater impact on the higher ground of Kent Ridge (known then as Pasir Panjang Ridge). After the British established Singapore as its military stronghold in the East, the militarization of the island took place with the setting up of air and naval bases, military forts and army barracks. The area around Alexander Road, from Ayer Rajah to Pasir Panjang, became one such military nucleus of housing, schools, hospitals, churches and shopping areas till today known as Gillman Barracks. In part of the south side of NUS are remnants of the British military buildings which still house some of the university's facilities. It is no wonder that this military stronghold was later to become one of the bitter battlefields of the Japanese invasion. As a long-time Singaporean resident, John van Cuylenburg, recollects, the "Malay Regiment received its baptism of fire on Pasir Panjang heights, where desperate fighting took place".[26] This endorsed once again the Malay relationship to Pasir Panjang. Pasir Panjang Ridge (now Kent Ridge Park) was the scene of a major battle between the Japanese 18th division and the 1st and 2nd Malay Regiment and allied forces (British, Australian, Indian) for two days (13–14 February 1942). Second Lieutenant Adnan Bin Saidi (1915–42) is now recognized as an important Malay war

hero for his exploits. After the Ridge fell into Japanese hands, the British surrendered on 15 February 1942. The landmark to the brave battle the Malay Regiment fought with the Japanese is marked by Reflections at Bukit Chandu, a World War II interpretative centre on Pepys Road that was a former colonial bungalow. Another landmark of the war years is the Pasir Panjang Pillbox, a defensive structure in which machine guns were installed to fire in any direction. The pillboxes are testimony to the allied command's erroneous belief that the Japanese would attack Singapore from the south. The pillboxes were positioned along the entire southern coastline.

As the British developed their entrepôt of Singapore, the multiracial and multiethnic population grew rapidly, but the Chinese population soon developed as the dominant population on the island colony. The bulk of the Chinese population tended to be confined within the central area. By the turn of the 20th century, with the introduction of motorized vehicles, the wealthy Chinese population began to move away from the city centre. From the 1950s, the Pasir Panjang and Kent Ridge areas fell under the administrative division of an "urban area". In the Colonial Master Plan of 1955, Pasir Panjang (covering 195.5 acres) was listed as one of 16 urban areas, with an estimated population of 9,900 persons in 1953, which was only 0.9 percent of the colony's total

Fig. 1.6: Looking north from the Ridge, towards Normanton Park, originally built for Singapore Armed Forces personnel

population of 1.12 million.[27] Despite its urban classification, the Kent Ridge-Pasir Panjang area remained relatively untouched and unimportant, and sparsely populated, reflecting more an atmosphere of "rural" Singapore. Like the other rural areas that were defined by agriculture (Chinese market gardens) and plantations (coconut, pineapple), Kent Ridge and Pasir Panjang's rural character was based on a combination of Chinese-owned rubber estates and Malay coastal fishing villages. After the gambier mania came the rubber craze which swept the island from the late 19th to the early 20th centuries. By the 1930s, some 17,604 hectares (43,500 acres) of land was under rubber cultivation in Singapore. R.E. Holttum recalls that

in 1922–23, the gap area (Buona Vista Road) was covered with rubber trees.[28] By the time of the Japanese occupation most of the rubber trees were felled but the area remained a *belukar*. On the other hand, the Malay fishing kampongs along the Pasir Panjang coast were, in the 1950s and 1960s, still very much the landmarks of the area.

The post-war years ushered in slow changes. The Malay influence in the area was reduced overnight, when Pasir Panjang Ridge was renamed Kent Ridge to honour the Duchess of Kent and her son, the Duke of Kent's visit to Kent Ridge Park in October 1952. Kent Ridge Road was also developed and ran almost parallel to Ayer Rajah and Pasir Panjang Roads, between Clementi and South

Buona Vista Roads. After the renaming of Kent Ridge, a flood of names from the British royal family baptized the area. Other royal names bestowed in the Kent Ridge area were Prince Edward Park (the area behind the Central Library), Prince Edward Point (the hill that is the current site of the Engineering Faculty) and Prince George's Park (the site of the residential hall named after it). The new names gave Kent Ridge another level of royal connotation just as the earlier Malay names denoted royal place names on Sungei Ayer Rajah and Ayer Rajah Expressway. Given its relatively untouched landscape, Kent Ridge must have factored into the equation of Singapore's new independent leaders and planners in the early 1970s to become the site of the new university and create what is now the educational corridor of the city-state.

Establishing the National University of Singapore

None of the earlier historical landscape developments around Kent Ridge prepared the area for its role as a university site, an intellectual centre, and a place of research and innovation. Unlike most of Singapore's landscape changes in the past, the last 53 years since the current government took power have been marked not by land-scape evolution but revolution. In fact,

"slow evolutionary change typifies the colonial era (1819–1958) and rapid, dramatic revolutionary change marks the independent period (1959–present)".[29] Kent Ridge was transformed overnight because of an executive decision in Singapore's cabinet in the 1970s to build the National University here. In many ways, Kent Ridge also signalled a major change in the university's history. The Bukit Timah campus was the location of three previous incarnations of the university: Raffles College, the University of Malaya and the University of Singapore. But Kent Ridge marked a new statement for the university: it became *the* premier university for Singapore hence the name National University of Singapore (NUS). The change of name was not as controversial as the fact that the government closed the Chinese-based Nanyang University (in its Jurong campus) and amalgamated it under NUS in 1980. Hence, for several years, NUS remained the only university in Singapore.

In trying to uncover the landscape changes of Kent Ridge, it seems evident that the hilly range was essentially an unbuilt secondary forested area before the university was established in the late 1970s. In 1959, I recall Kent Ridge, as an 11-year-old, as being essentially a relatively barren ridge with patches of vegetation, exposed lateritic outcrops, a lot of lalang and a rather hot, parched, sun-drenched landscape.

Fig. 1.7: This 1970s aerial view looks northwards towards Bukit Timah, with the Engineering Faculty on the left, and the old Administration Block in the right.

My most vivid recollections of the Ridge involve my fascination with the numerous pitcher plants that dotted the relatively sparse landscape.

In feng shui terms, Kent Ridge represents one of three reclining tiger hills in Singapore (the others are Caldecott Hill and Fort Canning). Given that the reclining tiger on Kent Ridge is female, geomancer Tan Khoon Yong noted that NUS would have a larger concentration of females.[30] Further, he stated that the National University Hospital (NUH) was located where the "flying snake" (the twisting South Buona Vista Road) crossed a mountain, and this was conducive for "reproduction";[31] I presume he meant that the hospital would be good for obstetrics.

The history of the university has been recounted in other works and I do not intend to go into it here.[32] My reflections deal with three aspects of campus development. One of the tragedies of the original university plan was that it did not capitalize on the natural features of the Ridge and its scenic vantages and views. The university developed on the relatively untouched north or leeward side of the

Ridge, but the architects were unable to capitalize on natural ventilation and the fresh sea breeze of the windward or southern side of the Ridge. The location of the buildings on the leeward side meant that none of them could benefit from the scenic view of the sea towards the south. This obliviousness to the scenery seems strange when the road on the east side of the campus was called South Buona Vista (in Spanish, Good View) because of its hilly strategic location overlooking the whole area: one could get panoramic views of the landscape and seascape. The Central Library was elevated above ground on stilt-like pillars, thereby missing the dense green vegetation around the library. It would have been interesting to have the library open up, by way of a glass wall, into the rich green secondary forest in front of it, facing the south side. That would have made for a pleasant and tranquil view. Our architects and planners need to take a lesson from the university library at UC Santa Cruz to understand how buildings are so effectively woven into the natural landscape.

Given its original plans to house 8,000–10,000 students, the campus infrastructure was inadequate to accommodate the rapidly expanding student and faculty population. The 1970s student plan of 10,000 students seemed large given that, in the 1972–73 academic year, the university had a teaching staff of 831 and student enrolment of 4,934.[33] But after the campus was built, the number of students rapidly increased. For example, when the Arts Faculty moved in 1981, there were two buildings (AS1 and AS2) to house all the faculty; there was no elevator in either building (they still are without elevators). The joke at that time was that the Dutch architects were used to only designing buildings for flat land, so could not gauge the importance of elevators. But the number of buildings expanded quickly in the faculty to its current eight buildings catering to a population of over 7,200 undergraduate and graduate students currently.

Buildings on the NUS campus seem to have sprouted up in a haphazard manner, somewhat like flats in an HDB estate or even a squatter settlement, where every empty space becomes a possible site for another building. Such a riot of buildings, pathways, staircases and roads is confusing to visitors who would, in my opinion, do well to hire a tour guide to navigate the corridors of the maze of buildings that constitutes, for instance, the Faculty of Engineering.

Most foreign visitors, while extolling the beauty of the NUS landscape, are frequently struck by its lack of a nerve centre, a nucleus of student activity that forms the centre in established campuses in developed countries. The NUS buildings seem to hug the contours of Kent Ridge, snaking along the leeward side of the Ridge, from National University Hospital in the east

Fig. 1.8: The Central Library up on stilts and the 1977 Administration Block, oriented to the west

to the School of Design and Environment (SDE) and the Faculty of Arts and Social Sciences (FASS) in the west. This linear format of the university increases distance between faculties and staff thus reducing personal interaction. One thinks twice about going to another faculty or office because of the time involved. I would think that traversing such distances by foot in tropical weather would not be desirable, and this leads to an increase in bus, motorcycle and car traffic on campus. The Student Centre (NUSSU) is a locational misnomer: the fact that it is perched on a ridge makes it difficult for students to gather and meet. I wonder if it was intentionally designed to prevent students from congregating.

Fig. 1.9: The walkway
between the NUS
Central Library and
the Arts Faculty offers
a view of the garden
known as "Lover's Park"

Perhaps the lack of a central campus town, a student centre, a hub for students that could liven up the campus seems, similarly, like an intentional oversight. Is it no wonder that while the Bukit Timah campus was the scene of many student demonstrations and protests, the Kent Ridge campus has not witnessed one major student demonstration in all its 28 years—a relief for university administrators, a questionable record for academic freedom seekers.

Student life hence is found, instead, in the controlled surroundings of the hostels: Raffles, Kent Ridge, Temasek, Eusoff and Prince Georges Park. Occasionally, the Forum (the void deck below the Central Library) is the scene of some students' revelry of jams and hops. The hostels, instead of being located at the centre of campus, are at its periphery (Sheares Hall, Eusoff Hall, Kent Ridge Hall, Temasek Hall, Prince Georges Park Residence) so that the campus could be construed, at times, as rather quiet, devoid of students and lacking student buzz.

In short, if one applies the concepts of imageability, that is, identifiable holistic image of the campus, and legibility, that is, ease of navigation, to NUS, the university's landscape would, in my opinion, not rank too high in either category.[34] It was possible, on the Bukit Timah campus, to move around easily, something which is not as simple on the bigger Kent Ridge campus where navigation can be confusing without signs and directions, and landscape cues. Senior professors such as Tommy Koh, Kishore Mahbubani and Wang Gungwu, who studied at the Bukit Timah campus, recall fondly its student hostels, buildings and unique places such as Pantai Valley.[35] I feel the absence, on the Kent Ridge campus, of a clock tower, an imposing central library building or a university town. The architecture of the NUS Centre for the Arts is interesting, but the other buildings at Kent Ridge appear, to me, rather bland and regimented. On the other hand, the student hostels appear to be architecturally diversified.

NUS@Kent Ridge: Growth Pole, Research Hub and Educational Corridor

Since its establishment in 1980, NUS@ Kent Ridge might be seen as a growth pole, stimulating new developments in the area such as a new condominium heartland, the Bible belt (several churches are located in Pasir Panjang), the container port and its ancillary

functions, and the educational hub. Condominiums and churches have taken the place of bungalows in the locality's large plots. Given its historic upmarket location, land along Pasir Panjang Road has remained relatively expensive. Under the former postal district system, Pasir Panjang was District 5 and was viewed by real-estate agents as an upper middle-class residential area. Along the old Pasir Panjang Road today can be found condominiums such as The Spectrum, Palm Green, Village@Pasir Panjang, Longbeach Townhouse, Ville De West, Palm View Row, Lynnsville-Townhouse, The Frangipani, Whitevillas Row, Barossa Gardens, Redwood West, Western Grove, Starpoint and Harbour View Garden. The number of condominiums has increased partly due to the growth of NUS. Several faculty and staff members have bought condominium units or rent them from their owners, due to their proximity to the university. On the west side of Clementi, towards the west coast, one can see a hub of condominium units such as Greenacres and Varsity Park which developed between 1998 and 2008.

Despite the lack of an immediate surrounding built-up public housing area, Pasir Panjang Road has become a favourable location for many churches so much so it can be called the Bible belt of Singapore. Churches in the vicinity include Church in Singapore (Christian Stewards), Singapore Bible Baptist

Church, Nazareth Bible-Presbyterian Church, The Crystal Tabernacle Church, Pasir Panjang Church of Christ, Emmanuel Evangelical Free Church, Pasir Panjang Christ Church and Norwegian Seamen's Mission. Why churches have sprung up here seems a mystery since the area is neither densely populated nor are the residents dominantly Christians. But clearly, the availability of freehold land along Pasir Panjang Road has made it an attractive location for buying property. Given that many new Christian churches were built throughout the 1960s to the 1990s, Pasir Panjang's bungalow properties became natural targets for church sites.

The beaches along Pasir Panjang's coastline, the holiday sites of seaside recreation and Malay fishing communities have all but disappeared. All of the beach expanse has been reclaimed and now, in its place, is Keppel Harbour, an extension of Singapore's port. Pasir Panjang is currently a major container port area and the location of an industrial estate, Pasir Panjang Distripark. Goods to and from peninsular Malaysia pass through the area. Clementi, a once quiet and unimportant road, has been rejuvenated with heavy container truck traffic because of the Pasir Panjang container port and the Pasir Panjang Wholesale Centre, a wholesale vegetable market. The West Coast Highway built on reclaimed land has replaced the narrow Pasir Panjang Road as a major trunk road of container and general traffic.

Together with NUS, the Singapore Polytechnic and the ITE College West (Dover), the Kent Ridge-Ayer Rajah Highway-Buona Vista zone has become a magnet for research and development and educational institutions. Science Park I came up on the east side, opposite National University Hospital; Science Park II is located between Prince George Park and Science Park Road; and Science Park III between South Buona Vista and Zehnder Roads. Around North Buona Vista Road are other important R&D and educational centres: Biopolis, Fusionopolis and the Asia campus of the well-known French business school, INSEAD. Heng Mui Keng Terrace comprises another hub of educational and research institutes: the Energy Studies Institute, Institute of Real Estate Studies, Interactive and Digital Media Institute, Institute of Southeast Asian Studies, Institute of Systems Science, Middle East Institute, Risk Management Institute and The Logistics Institute-Asia Pacific. To complete the picture of an integrated educational hub, the area is home to local and international schools and junior colleges. Fairfield Methodist Primary and Secondary Schools; Anglo-Chinese Junior College; NUS High School of Mathematics and Science and Nan Hua High School are the local institutions while United

World College of South East Asia; Waseda Shibuya Senior High School; the Japanese Primary and Supplementary Schools and Tanglin Trust School are the international.

Summing Up

Singapore has gone through several cultural and political episodes since its earliest history. It is not surprising, in this context, that names have changed. What today we call Kent Ridge was formerly known as Pasir Panjang Ridge. The area itself has also changed over time since the founding of modern Singapore in 1819. Before 1845, Kent Ridge was probably virgin territory of untapped natural rainforest. From 1845–1900, the ridge was deforested as a result of the gambier plantation mania that took Singapore by storm. Pasir Panjang Ridge, in the latter half of the 19th century, was the private property of Tan Kim Seng. However, Malay fishing villages were established in coastal Pasir Panjang before Tan Kim Seng bought his private estate. Between 1900 and 1975, Kent Ridge and the Pasir Panjang area became a mixed site of rubber plantations, British military barracks and residential areas, Chinese holiday bungalows, Malay fishing villages and zones of *belukar*. The late 1970s onwards heralded the National University of Singapore, followed by the National University Hospital. These developments triggered a sea change of landscape transformation around the new university campus. Developments rapidly took place from the 1980s to 2008: the Pasir Panjang coastal side was reclaimed and the new container port built; new condominiums were established and Christian churches mushroomed along Pasir Panjang Road. On the south and east side of the Ridge was the new University Hospital and three science parks; and on the west side was Clementi town, and the major bus and MRT link into campus from other parts of Singapore.

From the perspective of alumni who have studied at the Bukit Timah campus, it may seem that Kent Ridge is modern and functional, but lacking in character and personality. Their warm relationship to the old Bukit Timah setting reflects not only their attachment to a smaller campus but also brings to memory the meaningful relationships amongst students, given its small student population (5,000 by the late 1970s). I have observed that students at NUS nowadays rarely have friends beyond their subject majors, departments or faculty. At the Bukit Timah campus, friendship used to cut across faculties. The Student Union (NUSSU), through its many activities and meetings, served as a major nucleus in bonding students from all faculties and disciplines, as well as between those who lived in the hostels and those who were day students (Non-

Fig. 1.10: Now densely built up in some areas, especially around the busy National University Hospital on the north face of Kent Ridge, the campus retains its connections to the landscape

Hostel Organisation or NHO). The informal culture of debate, discussion and deliberation that characterizes universities seems to be missing at NUS today. There are certainly enough formal seminars, conferences and talks on campus to fill an academic year, but the informal culture of discussion amongst students and faculty members which characterized the Bukit Timah campus is missing at Kent Ridge. In an age when students seem to want to talk solely through their computers and Google their research, the challenge of the university seems to be getting students and faculty members to engage in more informal discussion of issues and ensure dialogue rather than confrontation. Hopefully, in the years ahead, NUS@Kent Ridge will be a "dynamic site for new thinking and open and vigorous debate" as well as providing the academic spirit for "responsibility of leading".[36]

Notes

1. C.M. Turnbull, *A History of Modern Singapore 1819–2005* (Singapore: NUS Press, 2009), p. 4.
2. Ibid.
3. Victor R. Savage and Brenda S.A. Yeoh, *Toponymics: A Study of Singapore Street Names* (Singapore: Eastern Universities Press, 2004), pp. 50, 82.
4. David Sopher, *The Sea Nomads* (Singapore: Singapore National Museum, 1977).
5. Mariam Mohamed Ali, "Singapore's Orang Seletar, Orang Kallang and Orang Selat: the Last Settlements", in *Tribal Communities in the Malay World: Historical, Cultural and Social Perspectives*, ed. Geoffrey Benjamin and Cynthia Chou (Singapore: Institute of Southeast Asian Studies, 2002), pp. 273–92 and, in particular, pp. 280–82. See also Turnbull, *A History of Modern Singapore 1819–2005*, pp. 23–4.
6. Kartini binti Yayit, "Vanishing Landscapes: Malay Kampungs in Singapore", BA (Hons) thesis (Singapore: Department of Geography, National University of Singapore, 1987), p. 33.
7. George E. Bogaars, "The Effect of Opening the Suez Canal on the Trade and Development of Singapore", in *Singapore 150 Years*, ed. Mubin Sheppard (Singapore: Times Books International, 1982), pp. 220–68 and, in particular, pp. 249–52.
8. Victor R. Savage, "Landscape Change: From Kampong to Global City", in *Physical Adjustments in a Changing Landscape: The Singapore Story*, ed. Avijit Gupta and John Pitts (Singapore: Singapore University Press, 1992), pp. 5–31 and, in particular, p. 12.
9. Kartini, "Vanishing Landscapes", p. 90.
10. H.T. Haughton, "Native Names of Streets in Singapore", in *Singapore 150 Years*, ed. Mubin Sheppard (Singapore: Times Books International, 1982), pp. 208–19.
11. Kartini, "Vanishing Landscapes", p. 81.
12. Ibid., p. 39.
13. Ibid.
14. Ibid., pp. 94–5.
15. Tan Khoon Yong, *The Secrets of the Five Dragons: Feng Shui and Singapore's Success* (Singapore: Times Books International, 2001), p. 36.
16. Sara Noble, *Feng Shui in Singapore* (Singapore: Graham Brash, 1997), p. 70.
17. Charles Burton Buckley, *An Anecdotal History of Old Times in Singapore*, rpt (Kuala Lumpur: University of Malaya Press, 1965) and Y.C. Wee and R.T. Corlett, *The City and the Forest: Plant Life in Urban Singapore* (Singapore: Singapore University Press, 1986).
18. Noble, *Feng Shui in Singapore*, p. 26.

19. David G. Kohl, *Chinese Architecture in the Straits Settlements and Western Malaya: Temples, Kongsis and Houses* (Kuala Lumpur: Heinemann Asia, 1984), p. 123.

20. Ibid., p. 124.

21. Roland Braddell, *The Lights of Singapore* (London: Methuen, 1935), p. 54.

22. Tan, *The Secrets of the Five Dragons*, p. 36.

23. *Yearbook of Statistics 1962* (Singapore: Department of Statistics, 1962).

24. Rory Fonseca, "Planning and Land Use", in *Singapore Society in Transition*, ed. Riaz Hassan (Singapore: Oxford University Press, 1976), pp. 221–39.

25. Kartini, "Vanishing Landscapes", pp. 101–3.

26. John Bertram van Cuylenburg, *Singapore through Sunshine and Shadow* (Singapore: Heinemann Asia, 1982), p. 107.

27. *Master Plan Written Statement* (Singapore: Government Printing Office, 1955), p. 20.

28. R.E. Holttum, "*Adinandra Belukar* – A Succession of Vegetation from Bare Ground on Singapore Island", *Malayan Journal of Tropical Geography* 3 (1954): 27–32.

29. Savage, "Landscape Change", pp. 5–31 and, in particular, p. 28.

30. Tan, *The Secrets of the Five Dragons*, p. 33.

31. Ibid.

32. Edwin Lee and Tan Tai Yong, *Beyond Degrees: The Making of the National University of Singapore* (Singapore: Singapore University Press, 1996).

33. *Singapore '73* (Singapore: Ministry of Culture, 1973), p. 183.

34. The concepts of imageability and legibility are defined by Kevin Lynch in his *The Image of the City* (Cambridge: MIT Press, 1960).

35. Vilma D'Rozario and Lye Lin Heng (eds.), *Trees of Bukit Timah Campus: A Tribute to Old Friends* (Singapore: NUS and Nature Society, 2007).

36. Wang Gungwu, "Inception, Origins, Contemplations: A Personal Perspective", in *Imagination, Openness & Courage: The National University of Singapore at 100* (Singapore: National University of Singapore, 2006), pp. 3–31 and, in particular, pp. 28–9.

The Geology of Kent Ridge

David Higgitt

Geology and Landscape

The story of Kent Ridge begins some 230 million years ago in a shallow, warm tropical sea, close to the equator. Here, in the Upper Triassic geological period, the sediments that were to become the rocks of the Jurong Formation (sedimentary rocks on the western and southern parts of Singapore) were being laid down—a process that would continue intermittently for the next 40 million years or so. It was the beginning of the age of the dinosaurs but, for the moment, archosaurs (the ancestors for modern birds, lizards and crocodilians) ruled earth. Gazing out to sea from the summit of Kent Ridge, screening out the refinery, container ports and ships on the horizon and perhaps conjuring up an image of a crocodilian ancestor, it might be supposed that the present conditions are similar to the starting point far back in time. In fact, the geological building blocks comprising Southeast Asia have remained close to the equator and experienced tropical conditions for all of the intervening time period. However, the geological history of the region is anything but unmitigated tropical tranquility. Driven by the engine of plate tectonics,

the configuration of the continents and oceans has changed drastically, and this has imparted a profound influence on Southeast Asia hence on the development of Kent Ridge.

Plate Tectonics and Palaeogeography

From the 1960s onwards, plate tectonics has provided an encompassing theory of how large-scale motions of the earth's lithosphere are accomplished. The theory incorporated the earlier idea of continental drift which had correctly identified—from the evidence of rock types, fossil sequences and the shape of coastlines—that the position and configuration of the continents had changed over geological time. However, in the absence of a plausible explanation of a mechanism capable of accomplishing such movements, the geological community initially shunned the notion of continental drift. Though the details of the driving mechanisms remain a matter of debate, ocean exploration and improved understanding of the internal structure of the earth have provided a convincing argument. The lithosphere, comprising the crust and the upper part of the mantle, is cooler and more rigid than the underlying asthenosphere. The lithosphere is broken into a series of tectonic plates which ride on the relatively fluid-like asthenosphere driven by frictional and gravitational forces. There are eight major plates and several minor plates which move relative to each other.

The interaction between plates is usually simplified into three types: convergent (or destructive) boundaries where two plates move towards each other; divergent (or constructive) boundaries where two plates move apart and new material is added to the crust; and transform (or conservative) boundaries where plates grind past each other. Needless to say, the reality of plate interactions is far more complicated than familiar textbook examples. Furthermore, each boundary between tectonic plates has a long and often complicated history that strongly influences the formation of geological materials and the evolution of the surface topography. A major challenge to geologists is to reconstruct the nature of the tectonic boundaries and the distribution of land and sea throughout the earth's history in order to explain how different rock formations and associated mineral resources were initially created. The reconstruction of past physical landscapes is referred to as palaeogeography. It requires Herculean detective work to assemble all the available evidence about the environments in which rocks were formed into a coherent framework. Aside from the academic intrigue of reconstructing the prehistoric configuration of the continents, palaeogeography is crucial in understanding the evolutionary development of plant and animal species and the likely distribution of sedimentary basins where oil and gas reserves may have developed. Thanks to its tectonic history, Southeast Asia has the greatest concentration of suitable basins which is the focus of petroleum exploration.[1] Though oil and gas have no specific part in the geology of Singapore, the petrochemical refineries viewed from Kent Ridge are witness to the significance of reserves in the wider region.

In order to explain the origin of the rocks of Kent Ridge, a brief sketch of the tectonic and palaeogeographic setting is required. It is necessary to begin by providing a broader context both spatially and temporally. I start with the wider picture of the contemporary tectonic setting of Southeast Asia, before stepping back in time, further back than the age of the Kent Ridge rocks, to consider how the appropriate conditions came about.

The current tectonic setting of Southeast Asia is dominated by the spectacular curving boundary between the Indo-Australian Plate and the Eurasian Plate. Propelled by a spreading axis (constructive margin) in the southern Indian Ocean, the Indo-Australian Plate is moving northwards at an average rate of 70 mm per year. Such a velocity may seem trivial but, given the vast exigencies of geological time, plate tectonics is capable of spectacular rearrangement of the continents and oceans. At the Sunda Trench, south of Java, the Indo-Australian Plate approaches the Eurasian Plate in a more or less perpendicular manner. The energy of the convergence between the two plates is converted into a textbook example of a destructive plate margin with the subduction of the denser oceanic crust of the Indo-Australian Plate driven below the lighter Eurasian Plate. The plate plunges northwards beneath Java to a depth of around 600 km and is an active source of major earthquakes. The partial melting of the subduction plate feeds magma to a chain of volcanoes on Java. In contrast, the two plates converge at an oblique angle off the coast of Sumatra. Consequently, the force of convergence is partitioned into two components—a perpendicular force of subduction and a trench-parallel force of motion along major transform faults. In Sumatra, this parallel component is represented by the nearly 2,000-km-long Sumatran Fault. Further north, the velocity of the Indo-Australian Plate reduces to about 15 mm per year in the Himalayan collision zone. The continental crust of India crashed into the Eurasian Plate around 60 million years ago. When two continental crusts collide, the subduction process ceases after some time because of the lower density of continental crust hence volcanic activity becomes extinct. Thus, the evolution of a convergent margin from subduction-dominant to collision-dominant can be recognized in palaeogeographic reconstructions, and

this is relevant to conditions in the Late Triassic period around Singapore.

Singapore lies far enough away from the current subduction zone to be untroubled by major earthquakes and volcanic eruptions though close enough to occasionally feel the tremors from earthquakes on both the subduction zone west of Sumatra and the Sumatran Fault. Similarly, the geology of Singapore is not directly influenced by the current plate boundary, but past tectonic events have played an important role. To comprehend the significance of past plate motions in the story of Kent Ridge, it is worth briefly considering how the configuration of continents have changed over time. The formation and subsequent break-up of supercontinents has occurred many times through the 4.6 billion years that the earth has existed, though it is only the later stages of the process that can be articulated with any confidence. In the Palaeozoic Era (600–250 million years ago), the supercontinent known as Pannotia broke up into fragments which then began to coalesce, such that by the beginning of the Permian period (about 300 million years ago), all land masses had effectively merged into one crescent-shaped supercontinent named Pangaea. Southeast Asia was a late arrival at the edge of the global landmass, an assemblage of different continental slivers that had separated from the southern land mass of Gondwanaland and drifted northwards. The first major episode saw the terrain that became North China, South China, Indo-China and the Taiwan rift across the Palaeotethys Ocean in the Devonian Period (around 400 million years ago). The second major episode was the formative event for Kent Ridge and took place in the early-to-middle Permian period, soon after the assembly of Pangaea. The Sibumasu (or Sinoburmalaya) Block broke off from northern Gondwanaland and drifted northwards to collide with the combined Indo-China and South China blocks (known collectively as Cathaysia). Sibamasu and Cathaysia welded together and the "suture" can be traced through the Malayan Peninsula, continuing northwards under the Gulf of Thailand.[2] The evidence of the very different origins of the blocks on either side of the suture comes from the sedimentary structures and fossil contents. The collision zone lay in the tropics, and the Cathaysian origin of the eastern side of the Malay Peninsula (including Singapore) was provided by the abundance of fusulinid limestone and tropical plants. Fusulinida are a particular group of formainfera (single-celled organisms) that were abundant in tropical and subtropical seas in the Carboniferous and Permian periods. Meanwhile, the Sibumasu Block began its northward journey from Gondwanaland, which was partially glaciated during the Carboniferous period. The abundant pebbly mudstones which crop out in Langkawi and Phuket are interpreted as marine glacial deposits.[3] West of the Sibumasu Block, forming the western part of Sumatra, is another terrain of Cathaysian origin known as the Woyla Block, which collided and welded onto Sibumasu at a later stage. The Sumatran Fault, the transform fault releasing some of the pressure of the contemporary plate boundary, was reactivated along this ancient suture.

But what of Kent Ridge? The interaction, as Sibumasu approached Cathaysia, set off a chain of events that led to the deposition of sediments in that shallow tropical sea mentioned at the beginning of the article. Collision between two plates, even plates described as microcontinents or continental slivers, has a major impact on the topographic expression of the earth's surface. The collision triggered the Triassic mountain-building episode, termed the Indosinian orogeny. In a similar fashion and magnitude to the contemporary Himalayas, the initial phase involved subduction and the formation of a volcanic island arc followed by collision, which resulted in crustal thickening and emplacement of granite plutons. The granites crop out from the northern Thailand-Myanmar border area as far south as Belitung island off the east coast of Sumatra, a distance of almost 3,000 km. Bukit Timah Granite, which dominates the northern and central part of Singapore, was one of the granite bodies emplaced during the orogeny, the remnant of long since-eroded mountains. And the Jurong Formation is essentially the result of the erosion of the mountains uplifted in the Indosinian orogeny. It contains a wide variety of sedimentary rocks which implies that the depositional environments changed over time, as I describe in the next section.

Almost as soon as the supercontinent of Pangaea had formed it began to break up, the Tethys Ocean opening up a rift separating the northern continent of Laurasia (basically North America and Eurasia) from the southern continent of Gondwana (South America, Africa, India, Australia and Antarctica). Gondwana itself began to split from the Late Jurassic period (150 million years ago), the separation and rapid equatorial flight of India and Australia impacting significantly the geography and biodiversity of Southeast Asia. Meanwhile, the accreted microcontinents comprising Southeast Asia have remained in a tropical location for the entire period, forming an extension of the Eurasian Plate known as Sundaland. Tectonic activity around the passive margin of Sundaland (for example, the present location of Borneo) has been both complex and eventful, but the interior of Sundaland and future location of Singapore was spared dramatic alteration and was probably above sea level for most of the last 150 million years.

The Rocks of Kent Ridge: The Jurong Formation

As mentioned earlier, the western and southern parts of Singapore are dominated by sedimentary rocks, known collectively as the Jurong Formation. In the earliest work on the general geology of Singapore, J.B. Scrivenor referred to these rocks under the general heading of "Shale and Sandstone".[4] The term "Jurong Formation" was first applied informally by C.K. Burton[5] to describe the Triassic sequence in Singapore and Southern Johor. The Jurong Formation is of Late Triassic to Early Jurassic age and consists of a wide variety of sedimentary rocks indicative of changing depositional environments. Scholars giving early accounts of the formation were frustrated by the difficulty of recognizing the different components due to a lack of exposure, intense folding and the effects of weathering. The rocks contain relatively few fossils which also makes comparison difficult. John Pitts notes that the rocks included various types of conglomerate, sandstones and mudrock, but there was much confusion relating individual outcrops into the more general sequence.[6] He points out that the start of construction on the over ground MRT would require greater attention to the engineering properties of these hitherto little studied rocks. In the subsequent three decades, understanding of the sedimentary rocks and their engineering properties has

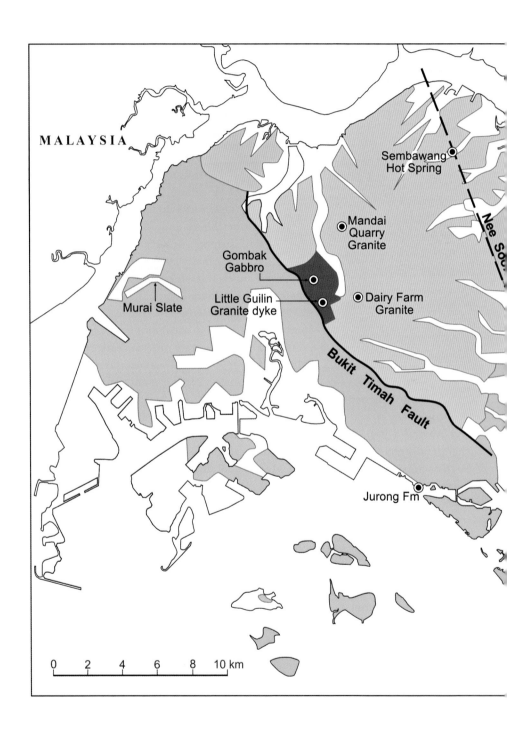

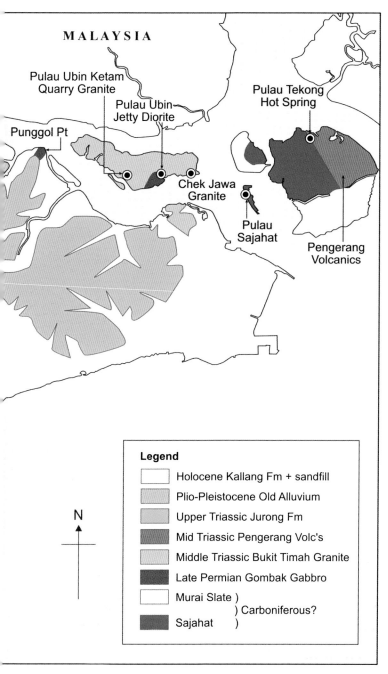

Fig. 2.1: Geological map of Singapore, modified from DSTA (2009)

been greatly improved due to borehole and tunnelling activities.

The recently updated *Geology of Singapore* proposes that the Jurong Formation is composed of seven facies.[7] "Facies" is the geological term to indicate a distinctive unit that is formed under certain environmental conditions. In a simplified setting, a vertical change in facies succession would indicate that the depositional environment was changing over time such that sediments from one type of depositional environment came to overlay older sediments from a previous depositional environment. This would be the case, for example, during a marine transgression as the sediment sequence would indicate deposition in progressively deeper water. When it comes to the Jurong Formation, the setting is far from simple and the patchy knowledge derived from outcrops and

Table 2.1: The Seven Facies of the Jurong Formation. Based on Proposed Subdivision by DSTA (2009)

Facies	Main Rock Type	Inferred Depositional Environment	Notes	Main Locality
Tengah	Muddy to medium grained sandstone	Low-energy shallow marine	Includes all other rocks of Jurong Formation not assigned to other facies	Tengah to Jurong
St John	Mudstone to muddy sandstone	Late-stage delta	Inferred as youngest in sequence	St John's to Sentosa
Rimau	Quartz sandstone and conglomerate	Shallow water marine and delta	Lithified rocks form backbone of the Southern Ridges	Kent Ridge to Mount Faber to Sentosa
Pandan	Limestone	Tidal flat to shallow marine	Limestone is not exposed at surface. Cavities exist	Pasir Panjang to Tuas (not at surface)
Ayer Chawan	Black sandstones and mudstones	Low-energy shallow marine	Includes some volcanic material	Southwestern Islands
Jong	Conglomerate and sandstone	Early-stage delta	Coarse material implies enhanced erosion of uplands	Southwestern Islands
Queenstown	Red mudstone	Ephemeral alluvial to shallow marine	Assumed to be oldest in sequence. May have been subject to subaerial weathering	Queenstown, Bukit Merah

boreholes means that much of the detail is still not resolved. Table 2.1 summarizes the characteristics of the facies and their inferred depositional environment. In keeping with geological tradition, the oldest units are listed at the bottom of the table. However, it appears that many of the facies are inter-digitated such that one unit may lie underneath another at one location, but above it at another site. This suggests that the depositional environments were rather complex and that similar sediments could have been deposited at different times. The depositional sequence implies that sediments were supplied into a back arc basin by the erosion of the recently uplifted mountains of the Indosinian orogeny.

The uncertain chronology and relationship between the facies of the Jurong Formation leaves several question marks in understanding the depositional processes and environments in which the materials accumulated. Following the collision of Sibumasu and Cathaysia, the emplacement and relatively slow uplift of the Malayan East Coast Granite (of which Bukit Timah Granite is one member) initiated erosion and transport of sediment into the back arc basin. In a consultant's report, J. Redding and J.B. Christensen suggest that the earliest rocks in the sequence may have been deposited in a non-marine environment and were subject to intense weathering before being buried by younger sediments.[8]

Engineers driving piles have often encountered rapid transitions between intact and completely weathered rock, which implies that there was periodic subsidence and emergence of the sediments during their deposition. The back arc basin was clearly highly mobile and its changing location accounts for the complicated and abrupt changes in the depositional characteristics of the rocks. The basin was, for quite a while, a low-energy marine environment, allowing the deposition of muddy fine-grained sediments in a shallow sea. Coarser-grained units in the Jong and Rimau Facies indicate higher-energy environments most likely associated with a pulse in uplift along the tectonic boundary and an invigoration of erosion rates.

The rocks which form the backbone of Kent Ridge belong to the Rimau Facies. These rocks are characteristically quartz sandstone and conglomerates which are well lithified. Being more resistant to erosion than other rocks of the Jurong Formation, the Rimau Facies are observed in the northwestern-trending ridges that form the relatively high ground of Kent Ridge Campus (75 metres); Kent Ridge Park (65 metres); Telok Blangah (90 metres); Mount Faber (100 metres) and the peaks of Mount Imbiah (62 metres) and Mount Serapong (85 metres) on Sentosa.

Direct field observation of the rocks can be a frustrating experience. Rocks at the surface are highly weathered and people have frequently moved material from its original position. Three conspicuous granite boulders near Lookout Point on Kent Ridge summit have been carried in from elsewhere, while there are several rounded coarse sandstone boulders lurking in the undergrowth lining long abandoned drains which may have once been an ornamental feature. On the NUS campus, the rocks outcrop in situ but most of the exposure has been coated in concrete to stabilize the slopes. A "conglomerate" describes a sedimentary rock which comprises rounded fragments of older rocks. In the Rimau Facies the fragments include different types of sandstone, quartz, tuff, chert, rhyolite, basic igneous pebbles and schist.[9] The inclusion of sandstone indicates that the conglomerate was, in part, derived from older facies of the Jurong Formation—most likely the Queenstown Facies which were reworked and rounded in a high-energy environment. This was probably a delta setting, with the fragments being eroded from upstream sources and rounded as they were transported by braided rivers. Rhyolite is a type of volcanic lava while tuff derives from volcanic ash. This is evidence that there was nearby volcanic activity as the Jurong Formation was being deposited: indeed, the pinkish to red colouration of much of the sandstone is most probably due to inclusion of volcanic ash. Schist is a metamorphic rock in which the mineral grains are foliated (aligned in thin layers) due to heat and pressure. The Murai Schist is one of the units of the Jurong Formation where metamorphic alteration of the original rock occurred locally around fold structures and fault lines. Inclusion of schist in the conglomerate again suggests a reworking of older Jurong Formation material. Conglomerate boulders (coarse-grained clastic sedimentary rock composed of a substantial fraction of rounded to subangular gravel-sized clasts) can be observed along the ridge east of Lookout Point where rounded quartz pebbles are the dominant constituent. More conglomerate rocks, but with a greater abundance of darker igneous pebbles, can be observed along the new link path to HortPark, where the pits dug for tree planting have thrown some fragments to the surface. Halfway up the hill, at the steepest part of the slope, a cutting reveals the weathering profile developed on a purple mudstone (Ayer Chawan Facies) which is finely laminated and is dipping at a near vertical angle.

The sandstone of the Rimau Facies is composed of up to 98 percent quartz.[10] Evidence of cross-bedding and scour features suggests that these rocks were deposited in a shallow, near-shore environment that was affected by tidal currents. Sandstone units of the Rimau Facies can be observed on the ridge west of Car Park A in Kent Ridge Park where heavy trampling has eroded the soil cover. Examples of quartz sandstone boulders are observed on the eastern side of the pond in Kent Ridge Park, diligently guarded by red ants! The dominance of quartz suggests that the source materials—rapidly eroding mountains on a nearby landmass—had been strongly leached and less stable minerals removed. The Jurong Formation came into being because of the erosion of uplifted mountains and their deposition in fluvial and near-shore environments. The sequence of uplift also had consequences for the folding and faulting of the Jurong Formation and this is briefly summarized in the following section.

Structure: Faults, Folds and Foundations

The field relations between the different facies of the Jurong Formation have been complicated by complex folding and faulting. The initial phase of uplift associated with the emplacement of the Malayan East Coast Granite was later outpaced by the uplift of the Main Range Granite to the southwest. Consequently, the back arc basin tilted to the northeast and the Jurong Formation slid in that direction, resulting in folding and deformation, as the materials essentially crumpled against the Bukit Timah Granite. Pitts described the majority of the structure to comprise open folds, but there are also isoclinal folds (where the limbs of the fold are parallel), overfolds and parasitic folds.[11] Parasitic folds are smaller features on the limbs

of larger folds but they result in huge variation in strike and dip over short distances. The coarser materials in the Jurong Formation (such as the Rimau Facies) would have been more rigid and resistant to deformation than the finer-grained material, so the tilting and compression resulted in a complicated pattern of tearing and thrusting. Most of the tear faults are relatively small and shallow, but a larger version is the Pepys Road Fault which runs directly through Kent Ridge and continues northeast along Alexandra Road. This and other northeast trending faults are thought to represent tearing as the basin tilted and material slid in this direction. The influence of the structure is apparent in the way that erosion has picked out zones of weakness. The Gap, the route by which South Buona Vista Road crosses the ridge line, is one such example.

One of the more intriguing features of the Jurong Formation, though not occurring at Kent Ridge, is the Fort Canning Boulder Bed which caused significant problems for the foundations of many buildings in the CBD of Singapore. This deposit was first encountered in the 1950s when excavations for the construction of the Asia Insurance Building discovered a deposit of huge sandstone boulders in an over consolidated clay matrix at least 135 metres thick.[12] The deposit is interpreted as an enormous submarine landslide deposit occurring at the late stages of the deposition of the Jurong

Fig. 2.2: The quartz sandstones and conglomerates which make up Singapore's Southern Ridges are visible on the NUS campus, though they have been treated and painted over. This walkway is between the School of Computing and the Central Library

Formation. However, the timing of the folding of the Jurong Formation is a matter of dispute. The conventional view is that the folding and faulting occurred contemporaneously with the deposition of the sediments.[13] An alternative view, proposed by Redding and Christiansen, is that the deformation of the Jurong Formation took place somewhat later in the Late Cretaceous period (around 100 million years ago), when the Woyla continental sliver collided with the combined Sibamasu-Indo-China block.[14] By this stage, Singapore had long been above sea level and deposition of the Jurong Formation had ceased. There were no rocks in Singapore younger than the Jurong Formation until the deposition

of the old alluvium which commenced just 2 million years ago. There is, however, evidence that faulting activity had recommenced in the Late Tertiary period, probably as a consequence of the collision of India and Eurasia. At this stage, down-faulted basins were formed into which the alluvium later accumulated, but the ground movements reactivated some of the shallow faults in the Jurong Formation. The Jurong Formation causes plenty of problems for construction, principally due to the unpredictability of material encountered around fault and fracture zones and because of rapidly changing layers from slightly weathered sandstone to highly weathered residual clay.[15] At the surface, intense tropical weathering has altered the fabric of the underlying rocks. The significance of weathering in the development of the present landscape of Kent Ridge is considered in the next section.

Under the Tropical Sun: Weathering, Sea Level and Climate Change

Despite the machinations of plate tectonics, the location of Singapore has remained firmly within the Tropics since the Mesozoic, and for much of the last 150 million years, Singapore has been above sea level and exposed to the intensity of tropical weathering. High temperature and abundant rainfall are the two main components required to produce a widespread and deep regolith. The thickness of the regolith is variable across Singapore and is typically 10–20 metres over the granite but somewhat thinner over the Jurong Formation.[16] Some of the earliest studies of weathering in Singapore were conducted by Frances Elizabeth Somerville Alexander, who initially arrived in Singapore in 1936 and worked as a consultant geologist with the Singapore Intelligence Section at the outbreak of the war. Returning to Singapore after the war, Alexander was briefly registrar of the University of Malaya before being appointed geologist to the Government of Singapore and producing the first full geological map of

the island.[17] Alexander recognized that the regolith was non-homogenous and reflected variations in the mineralogy of the underlying parent material.[18] She attributed the stratification in the regolith to the leaching and redeposition of abundant iron oxides.

At about the same time, the German geomorphologist Julius Büdel first proposed a model of "double etchplanation" which later became accepted as a key process in tropical environments.[19] The denudation (wearing down) of the landscape proceeds at a surface level where material can be "washed" down slope by the process of erosion, and at a basal weathering surface (sometimes called the weathering front) where chemical alteration of the rock mass is concentrated. In situations where the weathered material is stripped away by erosion, a distinctive bedrock topography of planation surfaces and isolated rock hills (inselbergs) can be formed. In Singapore the landforms are not as dramatic, but the nature and depth of the regolith reflects a balance between the long-term processes of weathering and accumulation of residual material versus the erosion processes operating to remove this material. The overall elevation of the land surface is reduced over a long period of time, and the thickness of overlying rocks is removed by erosion to reveal the current surface geology.

On the steep slopes of Kent Ridge, surface wash will have removed some of the soil and weathered material down slope and redeposited it as colluvium. Under intact forest cover erosion processes would have been very slow, but would have increased dramatically when humans began removing the forest to create plantations in the 19th century. There have been various attempts to measure contemporary erosion rates in Singapore. Avijit Gupta estimates that an annual sediment yield of less than 10 tonnes per kilometre[2] would be typical under forest, but would increase to 100–200 tonnes per kilometre[2] when the land was cleared.[20] Ongoing measurements under primary forest at Bukit Timah suggest that Gupta's sediment yield is in the right order of magnitude. The low nutrient status of the soils on Kent Ridge and the assemblage of *adinandra belukar* secondary forest[21] suggest that the erosion phase after clearance could have been severe. In recent years, there has been a growing concern about slope instability of the residual soil developed on the Jurong Formation. Both the NUS and NTU campuses have experienced some shallow landslides following intense rainfall events. The additional shear strength that exists in unsaturated soil due to negative pore-water pressures is lost as a result of rainwater infiltration into the soil.[22] D.G. Toll, B.H. Ong and H. Rahardjo suggest that a simple index combining the intensity of storm with the antecedent rainfall in the previous five days provides a reasonable guide to the likelihood of slope failure.[23] Such

an index could be used, for example, to predict the likelihood of future slope instability in the context of climate change. However, the landslides that occur on the Jurong Formation are generally shallow translational slides of modest dimension and in areas where the natural vegetation cover has been disturbed or the slope has been regraded. It is likely that, during the plantation phase, slope instability was common on Kent Ridge. There is some hint of some old gully forms on the northern slope where the regolith exposed by the side of trails is at least 3 metres thick. The southern slopes of Kent Ridge have been extensively modified by human activity destroying the natural slope profile.

The long period of time continuously under the tropical sun has endowed the Malay Peninsula with outstanding biodiversity with very complex trophic levels. Tectonics has again played an important role. Some similarities in the family and generic composition of tropical flora in Asia, Africa, Australia and America suggests evolution from tropical precursors in Gondwana.[24] Thus Southeast Asia—on the margin of Laurasia since the break-up of Pangaea—acquired its tropical Gondwanan taxa with the collision of India and the Eurasian Plate. The rainforest flora in Southeast Asia was therefore established some 60 million years ago. The break-up of Gondwana also signalled a dramatic change in the global climate. The isolation of Antarctica some 25 million years ago enabled a powerful westerly wind system to develop in the Southern Ocean, effectively blocking the dissipation of heat from the tropics to the South Pole. This led to the gradual refrigeration of the world's ocean and the build-up of ice on Antarctica.[25] The period of the last 2 million years, referred to by geologists as the quaternary, has been characterized by major fluctuations in the volume of ice stored in terrestrial ice caps. Relatively warm periods (like the present) have tended to be relatively short interludes (of about 10,000 years' duration) between longer episodes of cooler conditions (typically lasting 100,000 years). Although the glacial ice developed far from Singapore, the fluctuations between the glacial and interglacial period resulted in two sorts of major impact: potential changes in the vegetation structure and massive changes in global sea level. The conventional view that the tropical rainforests of Southeast Asia remained relatively stable during glacial phases is beginning to be challenged by new data.

The amount of water locked up in ice during glacial maxima caused global sea levels to fall by about 120 metres. We may imagine Kent Ridge as the last sentinel of Southeast Asia at the end of the Malay Peninsula overlooking the waters of the South China Sea, but for much of the last 2 million years this location has been faraway from the coastline. In fact, the region experienced

profound changes during glacial phases due to the extensive low gradient shelf of Sundaland, adding about 2 million kilometres to the landmass of Southeast Asia. The nearest coastline to Kent Ridge would have been the Indian Ocean beyond the current west coast of Sumatra. Heading south and east, land bridges connected the Malay Peninsula with Java and Borneo, respectively, the closest part of the South China Sea being some distance east of Natuna. The large increase in land area during periods of low sea level meant that river basins were much larger at present.

In the early phases of the quaternary, Kent Ridge stood a little higher than eastern Singapore where alluvium sheet deposits were laid down by rivers flowing eastwards across the Sunda Shelf. Most likely the Johor River transported material across Singapore before flowing into the enlarged Chao Phraya River which drained into the South China Sea. When the sea level rose, valleys were drowned and buried in fresh sediment. When the sea level fell, fluvial processes carved out new valleys. During the warmer interglacial phases the sea level may have been as much as 6 metres above what it is at present.[26] In the last episode, the rapid warming that signalled the end of the Last Glacial Maximum, the sea level rose rapidly and valleys were flooded up to about 12,000 years BP (before present). The sea level dropped temporarily during a cooler phase at about 10,000 BP but then rose again and reached about 2 metres above the present levels at about 6,000 BP, before stabilizing.[27]

In the low relief of Singapore, the Kallang Formation—marine and alluvial deposits associated with this most recent drowning phase—penetrates a surprising distance inland. During all of this excitement, Kent Ridge stood high and proud above the invading and retreating sea but there may conceivably have been a short period when the Southern Ridges formed an island with high water—or at least swamps—connecting between the Singapore River and Pandan Valley, north of Kent Ridge. Recent analysis of bathymetry (the study of oceans, and rocks and minerals on the ocean floor) suggests that even during phases of high sea level during the quaternary, Kent Ridge may not have been close to the open coast until comparatively recently. Michael I. Bird, David Taylor and Chris Hunt suggest that a connection between the Indian Ocean and the South China Sea did not come into existence until the last interglacial period (about 130,000 years ago), the initial connection resulting in the scouring out of the Singapore Deeps and a similar basin south of the Riau Islands.[28]

During the dramatic changes in sea level alternately exposing and drowning Sundaland, weathering and erosion of Kent Ridge would have proceeded. Whether the tropical rainforest remained intact throughout the quaternary is

a matter of debate and little is known specifically about the environmental change in Singapore. Geographers are able to reconstruct past environments from examining biological, physical and chemical indicators preserved in sediment, but a problem in Singapore is that very few of the depositional sites have been spared from human impact. One of the few studies of late quaternary change comes from Nee Soon freshwater swamp on the northern edge of the Central Catchments, some distance from Kent Ridge. The evidence of montane pollen types, principally represented by Podocapaceae, indicates that the Late Glacial period vegetation was rather different from the present assemblage, but David Taylor, Oh Hwee Yen, Peta G. Sanderson and John Dodson were unable to conclude categorically whether this resulted from a cooler humid climate or a seasonally dry climate.[29] It is highly probable that the vastly increased size of Sundaland during the low sea-level condition resulted in it experiencing a much drier climate than the present simply because of longer distances to moisture sources such as the ocean. An initial attempt to combine evidence from a variety of geomorphological, palynological, biogeography and climate modelling studies suggests that a "savanna corridor" existed through Sundaland during the Last Glacial period and through earlier periods of low sea level.[30] Such an open corridor would have separated the rainforest on Sumatra and Borneo, acting as a barrier for the dispersal of forest-dependent species. On the other hand, open savanna vegetation would have been important for the dispersal of another species, *Homo sapiens*. North of the equator, the evidence for the savanna corridor is sparse and sometimes conflicting but open vegetation on sandy terrain may have provided encouragement for human populations to establish and migrate from the Malay Peninsula into Borneo and Java and across to Australia between 60,000 and 45,000 years ago, when sea levels were approximately 40 metres below present. It is clear that far more work is needed to fill in the details of past environmental change, especially at a time when understanding future climate change dominates public agendas. For the time being, we have the intriguing question of whether Kent Ridge lay on the axis of ancient migration routes.

Conclusion

Kent Ridge forms part of the Southern Ridges of Singapore, a topographic feature of relatively modest elevation formed in resistant conglomerate and sandstone rocks. The development of today's landscape is dependent on a sequence of events that can be traced back to the tumultuous events of Mesozoic plate collisions, resulting in the uplift and erosion of mountain chains

and the accumulation of those eroded sediments in a sedimentary back arc basin. Even within the relatively small area of southern and western Singapore where the rocks of the Jurong Formation are found, the field relations between the different facies are complicated and there are many unanswered questions about the exact nature and sequence of events that explain how the rocks formed. However, it should always be kept in mind that Kent Ridge is but one small piece in a jigsaw of evidence that can be used to trace the geological history of the region. Rocks of similar age and characteristics to Kent Ridge are found in Johor, Bintan, Sarawak and Kelantan,[31] suggesting that the deposition occurred along an extensive belt of at least 500 kilometres.

Over time, other terrain accreted onto Southeast Asia, such that Sundaland formed a promontory on the passive margin of the Eurasian Plate. For much of the last 150 million years, the location of Kent Ridge existed near the centre of Sundaland in a tropical climate where intense chemical weathering and erosion wore down the rock, exploiting zones of weakness along the fault line and accentuating differences between relatively weak and more resistant lithology. The collision of the Indian and Eurasian plates, beginning about 60 million years ago, had a profound influence on the physical geography of Southeast Asia, setting the scene for the present configuration of plate

Fig. 2.3: The Southern Ridges are formed by the Rimau Facies of the Jurong Formation. Heavily eroded outcroppings are visible along Kent Ridge Road

boundaries. Global climate began to cool in the Tertiary period, culminating in the see-saw fluctuation of glaciation and interglacial periods that characterized the quaternary. Contrary to earlier ideas of climatic stability in low latitudes, it now seems likely that parts of Southeast Asia (including Singapore) experienced drier conditions during some of the glacial phases. Much more detailed work is required to establish the magnitude and extent of these climate changes and their influence on the geomorphological processes of erosion and sediment transport. The arrival of Europeans in the 19th century, however, signalled the beginning of major disruption to the forest cover, widespread soil erosion, slope instability and engineering intervention to reshape landscapes.

Notes

1. Robert Hall, "Hydrocarbon Basins in SE Asia: Understanding Why they are there", *Petroleum Geoscience* 15 (2009): 131–46.
2. C.S. Hutchinson, "The Geological Framework", in *The Physical Geography of Southeast Asia*, ed. Avijit Gupta (Oxford: Oxford University Press, 2005), pp. 3–23.
3. Ibid.
4. J.B. Scrivenor, "The Geology of Singapore Island: With a Geological Sketch Map", *Journal of the Malayan Branch of the Asiatic Society* 2 (1924): 1–8.
5. C.K. Burton, *Geological Survey of Malaysia, Map Bulletin No 2 — Geology and Mineral Resources: Johore Bahru-Kulai Area* (Ipoh: Ministry of Primary Industries, 1973).
6. John Pitts, "A Review of the Geology and Engineering Geology in Singapore", *Quarterly Journal of Engineering Geology* 17 (1984): 93–101.
7. Kim Woon Lee, Yingxin Zhou, Yam Khoon Tor and Juan Li, *Geology of Singapore* (Singapore: Defence Science & Technology Agency, 2009).
8. J. Redding and J.B. Christensen, *Geotechnical Feasibility Study into Rock Cavern Construction in the Jurong Formation*, report by Ove Arup & Partners International Ltd and Norconsult International A/S (1999).
9. Lee et al., *Geology of Singapore*.
10. Ibid.
11. Pitts, "A Review of the Geology and Engineering Geology in Singapore".
12. Ibid.
13. Lee et al., *Geology of Singapore*.
14. Redding and Christensen, *Geotechnical Feasibility Study into Rock Cavern Construction in the Jurong Formation*.
15. R. Krishnan, "Tunneling and Underground Projects in Singapore", in *Tunnels and Underground Structures*, ed. J. Zhao, J.N. Shirlaw and R. Krishnan (Rotterdam: Balkema, 2009), pp. 89–96.
16. G.S.P. Thomas, "Geology and Geomorphology", in *The Biophysical Environment of Singapore*, ed. Chia Lin Sien, Ausafur Rahman and Dorothy Tay B.H. (Singapore: Singapore University Press, 1991), pp. 50–88.
17. F.E.S. Alexander, "The Geology of Singapore and the Surrounding Islands", Appendix I in *Report on the Availability of Granite on Singapore and the Surrounding Islands* (Singapore: Singapore Government Press, 1950).
18. F.E.S. Alexander, "Observations on Tropical Weathering: A Study of the Movement of Iron, Aluminum and Silicon in Weathering Rocks at Singapore", *Quarterly Journal of the Geological Society* 115 (1959): 123–44.
19. Julius Büdel, "Die 'doppelten Einebnungsflächen' in den feuchten Tropen" [The

"Double Flat" Areas in the Humid Tropics], *Zeitschrift für Geomorphologie* (1957), N.F. 1, pp. 201–88.

20. Avijit Gupta, "Observations on the Effects of Urbanization and Runoff on Sediment Production in Singapore", *Singapore Journal of Tropical Geography* 3 (1982): 137–46.

21. P.J. Grubb, I.M. Turner and D.F.R.P. Burslem, "Mineral Nutrient Status of Coastal Hill Dipterocarp Forest and Adinandra Belukar in Singapore: Analysis of Soil, Leaves and Litter", *Journal of Tropical Ecology* 10, 4 (1994): 559–77.

22. John Pitts, "A Review of the Geology and Engineering Geology in Singapore", *Quarterly Journal of Engineering Geology* 17 (1984): 93–101 and D.G. Toll, B.H. Ong and H. Rahardjo, "Triaxial Testing of Unsaturated Samples on Undisturbed Residual Soil from Singapore", in *Unsaturated Soils for Asia: Proceedings of the Asian Conference on Unsaturated Soils: UNSAT-Asia 2000, Singapore 18–19 May 2000*, ed. H. Rahardjo, D.G. Toll and E.C. Leong (Rotterdam: Balkema, 2000), pp. 579–92.

23. H. Rahardjo, X.W. Li, D.G. Toll and E.C. Leong, "The Effect of Antecedent Rainfall on Slope Stability", *Geotechnical and Geological Engineering* 19 (2001): 369–97.

24. Geoffrey Hope, "The Quaternary in Southeast Asia", in *The Physical Geography of Southeast Asia*, ed. Avijit Gupta (Oxford: Oxford University Press, 2005), pp. 24–37.

25. Patrick D. Nunn, *Environmental Change in the Pacific Basin: Chronologies, Causes, Consequences* (New York: Wiley, 1999).

26. Hope, "The Quaternary in Southeast Asia".

27. Pitts, "A Review of the Geology and Engineering Geology in Singapore" and Toll et al., "Triaxial Testing of Unsaturated Samples on Undisturbed Residual Soil from Singapore".

28. Michael I. Bird, David Taylor and Chris Hunt, "Palaeoenvironments of Insular Southeast Asia During the Last Glacial Period: A Savanna Corridor in Sundaland?" *Quaternary Science Reviews* 24 (2005): 2228–42.

29. David Taylor, Oh Hwee Yen, Peta G. Sanderson and John Dodson, "Late Quaternary Peat Formation and Vegetation Dynamics in a Lowland Tropical Swamp; Nee Soon, Singapore", *Palaeogeography, Palaeoclimatology, Palaeoecology* 171 (2001): 531–8.

30. Bird et al., "Palaeoenvironments of Insular Southeast Asia during the Last Glacial Period".

31. Thomas, "Geology and Geomorphology".

The Biology of Kent Ridge

Vegetation, Plants and Animals

Hugh T.W. Tan, Kelvin K.P. Lim, Tan Ming Kai and Alex T.K. Yee

Introduction

Kent Ridge is an approximately four-kilometre-long ridge of sedimentary rock[1] hills that runs from near the junction of Clementi Road and Kent Ridge Crescent to Pepys Road in the southeast. The western portion of the ridge is occupied mostly by the Kent Ridge Campus, including an 11.9-hectare patch of forest of the National University of Singapore. The eastern portion is mostly occupied by Kent Ridge Park and terminates at Bukit Chandu, close to the museum, Reflections of Bukit Chandu, along Pepys Road. This ridge was formerly called Pasir Panjang Ridge but in 1952 it was renamed Kent Ridge, to commemorate the visit of the Duchess (mother) and Duke (son) of Kent to the British encampment at the site.[2] Before development, the ridge was sandwiched in the north by the basin of the stream, Sungei Ayer Rajah, now occupied by the Ayer Rajah Expressway, and in the

Fig. 3.1: View of the adinandra belukar at Kent Ridge Park from the north. In the foreground are the buildings of the Pasir Panjang Nursery. The palms are cultivated, just like the lawn

Vegetation and Land-use Maps of Kent Ridge

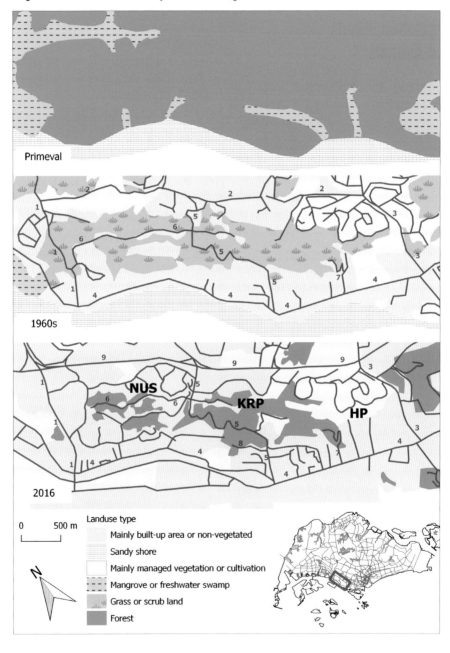

Notes to the Vegetation and Land-use Maps of Kent Ridge

Any estimations or reconstructions of the vegetation of Kent Ridge at the time of the British arrival in Singapore in the early 19th century have to be inferred from older maps and written accounts. Tony O'Dempsey's Primeval Land Cover of Singapore Island map[1] is the main source used here, supplemented by data from 1:25,000 scale topographic maps of 1945[2] and 1961[3], similar in style but at a larger scale than the 1:10,000 map reproduced in the front matter of this book. The 1960s map references the 1961 topographical map, as well as a later one drawn at 1:63,360 scale.[4] The 2016 map information was derived from OpenStreetMap[5], and the vegetation map of Yee et al.[6], and cross-checked with Google Maps[7] satellite images for cleared forest.

Legends

NUS = National University of Singapore   **KRP** = Kent Ridge Park   **HP** = HortPark

Only sealed roads are shown on the maps, and the labels are:

1 = Clementi Road	**4** = Pasir Panjang Road	**7** = Pepys Road
2 = Ayer Rajah Road	**5** = South Buona Vista Road	**8** = Zehnder Road
3 = Alexandra Road	**6** = Kent Ridge Road	**9** = Ayer Rajah Expressway

---

We are grateful to Chong Kwek Yan for providing a database of Singapore plants from which the Kent Ridge species were extracted, Jon Tan Siu Yueh for his advice on ferns, N. Sivasothi and Ng Wen Qing for kindly sharing information on the fauna of Kent Ridge, Yap Von Bing for kindly providing information on the plants of Kent Ridge, Seah Wei Wei for field assistance, and for the use of their excellent photographs, Horace Tan Hwee Huat, Ang Wee Foong, Cerlin Ng Xin Yi, Marcus Chua Aik Hwee, Tan Heok Hui, Yeo Huiqing, Yeoh Yi Shuen, Lam Weng Ngai, and Amy Choong Mei Fun. We thank the National Archives of Singapore (NAS) for hosting the historical topographic maps and the Singapore Land Authority (SLA) for permission to produce the vegetation maps based on the historical topographic maps.

1   Tony O'Dempsey, "Singapore's Changing Landscape Since c. 1800", in *Nature Contained*, ed. Timothy Barnard (Singapore: NUS Press, 2014), pp. 17–48.
2   Survey Production Centre, South East Asia, "1: 25,000 Topographic Map", *Survey Department, Federation of Malaya* (1945).
3   Chief Surveyor, Singapore, "1:25,000 Singapore", *84 Survey Squadron RE, AD Survey Far East Land Forces* (1961).
4   Chief Surveyor, Singapore, "1:63,360 Singapore Series I Edition I", *84 Survey Squadron RE, AD Survey Far East Land Forces* (1969).
5   "OpenStreetMap", OpenStreetMap contributors, no date, https://www.openstreetmap.org/#map=15/1.2893/103.7945 [accessed 5 May 2016].
6   A.T.K. Yee, Richard T. Corlett, S.C. Liew and Hugh T.W. Tan, "The Vegetation of Singapore–An Updated Map", *Gardens' Bulletin Singapore* 63, nos. 1 & 2 (2011): 205–12.
7   "Google Maps", last modified 2016, https://www.google.com.sg/maps [accessed 5 May 2016].

Fig. 3.2: The eastern end of Kent Ridge viewed from the north along Canterbury Road. The blue arrow marks the residential apartment blocks of The Peak, a condominium, which is just west of the end of the ridge. The red arrows mark the elevated boardwalk of the Canopy Walk in Kent Ridge Park. In the foreground are the buildings of the Pasir Panjang Nursery of the National Parks Board and which are part of HortPark

Fig. 3.3: The Gap, through which South Buona Vista Road runs. Stockport Road rises to the left towards Marina Hill where the DSO National Laboratories are situated, and to the right, Kent Ridge Road rises towards the National University of Singapore Kent Ridge forest area. The Gap is a natural depression in Kent Ridge and thus a logical site to place a road through the ridge. The commemorative plaque placed here indicates that, on 3 October 1952, the ridge was named Kent Ridge to honour the visit of the Duchess and Duke of Kent

Fig. 3.4: The western end of Kent Ridge, viewed from the north, at the junction of Kent Ridge Crescent and Clementi Road (beyond the right edge of the photograph) with the University Cultural Centre beyond the left edge of the photograph

south by the basin of the Sungei Nipah, which is now the site of the small canal just north of Zehnder Road. Three low hills are found south of the portion of the ridge to the west of South Buona Vista Road, the easternmost being Pasir Panjang Hill. The Pasir Panjang area is demarcated by Ayer Rajah Expressway in the north, Clementi Road in the west, Pasir Panjang Road in the south and Alexandra Road in the east.

Vegetation and Plants

Primeval Kent Ridge most likely was occupied by lowland evergreen rainforest, specifically Coastal Hill Dipterocarp Forest,[3] that would be similar to the primary forest patches found in the Bukit Timah Nature Reserve.[4] There would also have been some freshwater swamp forest along the Sungei Ayer Rajah to its north and along the Sungei Nipah, south of its central portion, whose downstream portions in turn would have transitioned into mangrove forest as it reached the sea. The southern reaches of the ridge would also have transitioned into sandy beach vegetation.

The Coastal Hill Dipterocarp Forest would have been dominated by giant trees of *seraya* (*Shorea curtisii*), a key species of this forest formation, with their greyish-green, cauliflower-like crown, *keruing* (*Dipterocarpus caudatus* ssp. *penangianus*), and other dipterocarp

species from genera such as *Anisoptera* as well as other *Dipterocarpus* and *Shorea* species.[5] Large trees from the legumes such as *kempas* (*Koompassia malaccensis*) and other families would have also formed the top of the forest canopy which would have consisted of plants from several species. Present-day Bukit Timah Nature Reserve has 1,047 species of vascular plants, and the Kent Ridge forest would have been similar[6]— this being the typical situation for tropical rainforest.

The freshwater swamp forest sites could have been similar to those of present-day Nee Soon Swamp Forest in the Central Catchment Nature Reserve, which is dominated by species that are tolerant of waterlogged soil conditions and dryland species.[7] In the wetter areas, plants growing there would have adaptations like buttresses, prop roots and breathing roots to improve stability and overcome the anoxic waterlogged soil. For instance, *Palaquium xanthochymum* (Sapotaceae) or looped breathing roots in *Xylopia fusca* (Annonaceae), and plank-like or kneed-breathing roots like those of *Lophopetalum multinervum* (Celastraceae) would be those kinds of plants.[8] The number of freshwater swamp forest plant species in Kent Ridge could also have been high as that in the Nee Soon Swamp Forest which has recorded 1,184.[9]

The name Sungei Nipah indicates the presence of the nipah palm (*Nypa*

Fig. 3.5: Leaves and two inflorescences of flower buds of gambier (*Uncaria gambir*). The leaves contain much tannin, turning brown easily when bruised. To extract the tannin, the leaves are boiled in water

Fig. 3.6: The long-stalked head inflorescence of gambier, bearing several flowers. The white stigmas are at the tips of the needle-like styles that stick out beyond the petals that are fused into a trumpet-shaped corolla

Fig. 3.7: Leafy twigs and flowers of rubber (*Hevea brasiliensis*). The leaves each have a long stalk and three shortly stalked leaflets. Rubber trees are still found growing wild in many parts of Kent Ridge

Fig. 3.8: Lily leaf orchid (*Acriopsis liliifolia*), one of the nationally Critically Endangered species in Kent Ridge. This small orchid grows on the trunks and branches of trees

fruticans) that grows best in brackish water but can also be found at the seafront. Mangrove forest was likely found at its mouth and freshwater swamp forest upstream of the nipah palm zone. Mangrove forest patches would have consisted of true mangrove species found in the intertidal zone and mangrove associates covering about 60 species,[10] including *bakau* (*Rhizophora* species), *api api* (*Avicennia* species), perepat (*Sonneratia* species), sea hibiscus (*Talipariti tiliaceum*) and others.

From the time humans first arrived to the present day, the ridge has undergone much change. Victor R. Savage has provided an excellent summary[11] of the changing landscape of Kent Ridge and the Pasir Panjang area in his chapter which we shall outline here briefly so that the present-day vegetation that has resulted from these land-use changes can be better understood:

1. Up to 1845, the forests in the present-day Kent Ridge area were likely to have been primary and untouched.[12]
2. From 1845–1900, Kent Ridge was deforested for the cultivation of gambier (*Uncaria gambir*, Rubiaceae), whose cultivation for its tannin (used primarily for tanning leather) also deforested many other parts of Singapore even earlier.
3. In the second half of the 19th century, almost all of Kent Ridge was owned by Malacca-born merchant and public benefactor Tan Kim Seng (1805–64), after whom Kim Seng Road is named. Squatters on his land grew various crops. Malay villages or kampongs were established along the sandy coast of Pasir Panjang.
4. From 1900–75, Kent Ridge and the Pasir Panjang area consisted of British army barracks[13] and a residential area, Chinese seaside bungalows, kampongs, secondary forest and rubber plantations.
5. From the late 1970s, the National University of Singapore (NUS) Kent Ridge Campus and the National University Hospital (NUH) started construction at Kent Ridge.
6. From the 1980s onwards the Pasir Panjang coastline was reclaimed, with developments that included: a new container port, expansion of the university and NUH, other research and educational institutions, condominiums, Christian churches, three science parks, Kent Ridge Park, HortPark, the Kent Ridge Mass Rapid Transit (MRT) station and the bus terminus.

Through all these land-use changes, the following main vegetation types arose:

1. Secondary forest or to use its Malay name, *belukar*
   a. Adinandra belukar
   b. Waste-woodland
2. Managed vegetation

As a basis to discuss the vegetation types, a list of the plants found in the Kent Ridge area is included (Table 3.1) in this chapter. A summary of the national status categories of the 368 vascular plant species recorded from Kent Ridge is also provided in Table 3.2.

Although there are 43 rare native species in the Presumed Nationally Extinct, Critically Endangered, Endangered and Vulnerable categories, only 24 occur as wild plants. However, some of these represent the few small populations of their species; for example, *Acriopsis liliifolia* occurs here and on Lazarus Island (Pulau Sakijang

Pelepah) only; the single tree of sea beam (*Maranthes corymbosa*) represents one of the few known wild individuals in Singapore; and there are few individuals left of *Croton oblongus* or the grass orchid (*Eulophia spectabilis*), Malayan bramble (*Rubus moluccanus* var. *angulosus*) and small-fruited archidendron (*Archidendron microcarpum*) in Singapore. Aside from the fact that the forests of Kent Ridge represent the few small areas of forest left in Singapore, these extremely rare species further emphasize that the ridge forests are worthy of conservation.

Adinandra Belukar

Adinandra belukar is an "anthropogenic (man-made) secondary forest established on degraded soil owing to poor agricultural practices and dominated by a small number of plants tolerant of the acidic and low nutrient soils, for example, tiup-tiup (*Adinandra dumosa*), tembusu (*Fagraea fragrans*), simpoh air (*Fagraea fragrans*), resam (*Dicranopteris linearis* or *Dicranopteris curranii*), etc."[14] This is a unique vegetation type found only in a 150-kilometre radius around

Fig. 3.9: Adinandra belukar in its earlier stage with plants that are shorter. The trees with the smaller leaves in the background are tiup-tiup (*Adinandra dumosa*), the plant after which adinandra belukar is named. The large-leafed plants are simpoh air (*Dillenia suffruticosa*), and the plants in the left to centre foreground with light green leaves are resam ferns (*Dicranopteris linearis*). These three species are characteristic of this vegetation type

Fig. 3.10: Adinandra belukar at a later stage in Kent Ridge Park. Most of the trunks are those of tiup-tiup trees whose stems are more or less similar sized, suggesting a common establishment date for most trees, e.g., from colonizing bare ground. The orange colour is from a green alga (*Trentepohlia* species) that grows on the trunks

Singapore,[15] including southern peninsular Malaysia in Johor and the northern portion of the Riau Archipelago in Indonesia. The name of this vegetation type is derived from the generic name of the botanical name of the dominant plant species, *Adinandra dumosa*, and Malay *belukar*, secondary forest. R.E. Holttum (1895–1990), renowned tropical botanist and former director of the Singapore Botanic Gardens, was the first to describe this vegetation type.[16] In a recently proposed updated classification scheme of secondary forest types in Singapore, adinandra belukar is

considered a native-dominated, early successional, secondary forest type.[17]

Adinandra belukar is the vegetation type that covers most of present-day Kent Ridge. It constitutes most of the 11.9-hectare forest patch in the middle of the NUS Kent Ridge Campus on the ridge proper, and a sizable portion of Kent Ridge Park. It is also found in parts of the Bukit Timah and Central Catchment nature reserves, the Western Catchment Area around the reservoirs in the west of Singapore Island, Telok Blangah Park, as well as on the islands Pulau Tekong and Pulau Ubin.

It develops after land clearing and poor agricultural practices that allow soil erosion and loss of nutrients through repeated harvesting of crops without replenishing mineral nutrients, resulting in soil that is very acidic (pH 3.3–3.9) and low in total nitrogen and total phosphorus.[18] How it arose in Kent Ridge is based on land-use history.

Although Pasir Panjang was the site of many Malay fishing villages from the 1840s onwards, the present-day Kent Ridge area was vacant land[19] until Tan Kim Seng purchased most of the ridge in the 1850s to the 1860s; evidence of this is found in maps between 1898 and 1911 which labelled the then Kent Ridge area as Tan Kim Seng's estate.[20] He apparently hardly developed the site, as is evident from the lack of place names in the Kent Ridge area, unlike the River Valley area where Kim Seng Road is presently.[21] Although Tan died in 1864, his estate in

Fig. 3.11: Flower buds, flower and young fruits of a leafy twig of tiup-tiup (*Adinandra dumosa*)

Fig. 3.12: The ripe fruit of simpoh air (*Dillenia suffrutioca*) splits open to reveal the fleshy scarlet seeds within to attract fruit-eating birds which act as dispersers of the seeds. Its oval leaf blades have the characteristically prominent secondary veins

Fig. 3.13: Flower, buds and young fruits of simpoh air (*Dillenia suffruticosa*), a characteristic species of adinandra belukar

Fig. 3.14: Ripe fruits of tembusu (*Cyrtophyllum fragrans*), a common tree of secondary forest and growing wild in the adinandra belukar, and cultivated in Kent Ridge. There are numerous planted trees in the NUS Kent Ridge Campus, many planted in 1980 when the campus was just established

Fig. 3.15: Pitcher plants grow in the adinandra belukar of Kent Ridge Park. The narrow-lidded pitcher plant (*Nepenthes ampullaria*) displaying lower pitchers is in the left foreground, and the slender pitcher plant (*Nepenthes gracilis*), displaying one upper pitcher, is in the background

Fig. 3.16: Upper pitcher of the hairy-fruited pitcher plant (*Nepenthes × trichocarpa*), a natural hybrid of *Nepenthes ampullaria* and *Nepenthes gracilis*, one of the three natural hybrids found in the adinandra belukar of Kent Ridge Park. In the background are the leaves of the resam fern (*Dicranopteris linearis*)

Fig. 3.17: Fronds of the resam fern (*Dicranopteris linearis*), a key species in the early stages of adinandra belukar

Fig. 3.18: Koster's curse (*Clidemia hirta*), an exotic weed that has found its way to the edges of adinandra belukar. It also grows in primary forests of Singapore as the only exotic species found there

Pasir Panjang, now under Kim Seng Land Company Limited, continued to exist and was occupied by squatters, as was revealed in a court case brought against the company in 1917.[22] Based on this report, vegetables and pineapple were grown by at least one squatter and at least 41 squatters grew rubber at the site. Gambier, pepper, pineapple and rubber were cultivated along the ridge by these smallholders in the latter half of the 19th century and early decades of the 20th.

Gambier (*Uncaria gambir*) and pepper (*Piper nigrum*) were, unfortunately, the crops that changed the Singapore landscape. Gambier was initially used as a masticatory to be chewed with betel nut and as a medicine; later, however, the tannin extracted from it was exported to Britain for tanning leather and dyeing cotton.[23] Pepper was a spice of great importance to flavour foods before the advent of refrigeration hence also a valuable export. To grow gambier, forest was cleared and the cuttings planted in the virgin soil.[24] To extract the tannin, the leaves had to be boiled and the firewood for this came from an area of forest about equal to the gambier plantation's. Pepper requires much soil humus, so the waste leaves from the boiling process were used to fertilize the pepper plants. Pepper is also a climber, so wooden posts had to be obtained from the nearby forest, so more trees would be felled.[25] The soil would be exhausted in 15–20 years and the area around the plantation would be bereft of firewood,

so the farmers had to move to new forest sites to start this process again, and thus abandoned plantation sites would be invaded by lalang (*Imperata cylindrica*) or adinandra belukar. Most of the gambier growers were squatters who would move freely from site to site, thus devastating the Singapore landscape.

In 1877, rubber (*Hevea brasiliensis*) arrived in Singapore as seeds sent to the Singapore Botanic Gardens from the Royal Botanic Gardens in Kew, UK. Rubber quickly became an important cash crop. By 1921, rubber plantations covered 22,200 hectares and, by 1935, almost 40 percent of the land area of Singapore Island was covered by this crop.[26] The phenomenal growth of the motorcar industry at the start of the 20th century led to the huge demand for rubber which, in turn, led to the massive cultivation of rubber in Singapore.[27] Based on a 1925 postcard of Buona Vista Road (now called South Buona Vista Road), most of the vegetation in the surrounding area had been cut down and planted with what appears to be young rubber trees. The sides of the road and steeper slopes where planting is not possible were still lined by vegetation. The southern parts that are closer to the sea had coconut cultivation. However, with the advent of World War II in 1942, the rubber plantations were abandoned and food crops such as sweet potato, tapioca and vegetables were cultivated instead because the population was starving under the

Japanese occupation.[28] The rubber plantations of Kent Ridge were felled or abandoned[29] and adinandra belukar grew in its place. However, unlike gambier, which has not persisted, rubber has, with numerous adult trees and saplings still found in many places in Kent Ridge, for instance, along Kent Ridge Road and South Buona Vista Road, in the forested areas of Kent Ridge Park and many other localities outside the ridge. Rubber has naturalized in Singapore.

The number of plant species in adinandra belukar per unit area is much less than the number in primary forest patches in the Bukit Timah Nature Reserve because the soil in Kent Ridge is very acidic and nutrient poor. Adinandra belukar is thus floristically and structurally monotonous[30] and, as seen in Table 3.1, consists of only 16 "hardcore" species.[31] The key species include the following.[32] For the trees and/ or shrubs they are: tiup-tiup (*Adinandra dumosa*), simpoh air (the Malay word *air*, meaning water, is pronounced as "ai-yer"), tembusu (*Cyrtophyllum fragrans*; *Fagraea fragrans* in the older literature), Malay gale (*Morella esculenta*; *Myrica esculenta* in the older literature), cicada tree (*Ploiarium alternifolium*), silverback (*Rhodamnia cinerea*) and rose myrtle (*Rhodomyrtus tomentosa*). The key herbaceous species are: an orchid, seraman (*Bromheadia finlaysoniana*; *Bromheadia palustris* or *Bromheadia sylvestris* in the older literature), a grass

Fig. 3.19: Burnt patch of adinandra belukar along Research Link in the NUS Kent Ridge Campus as a result of a fire on 11 February 2005

of open areas, slender eriachne (*Eriachne pallescens*), the sedge, sawgrass (*Gahnia tristis*), resam fern (*Dicranopteris linearis*), and nodding clubmoss (*Lycopodiella cernua*; *Lycopodium cernuum* in the older literature). The key climber species include *akar lampai hitam* (*Gynochthodes sublanceolata*) and the charismatic carnivorous plants, the slender pitcher plant (*Nepenthes gracilis*), narrow-lidded pitcher plant (*Nepenthes ampullaria*) and Raffles' pitcher plant (*Nepenthes rafflesiana*), and their hybrids— *Nepenthes × hookeriana* (*Nepenthes ampullaria × Nepenthes rafflesiana*), *Nepenthes × trichocarpa* (*Nepenthes gracilis × Nepenthes ampullaria*) and *Nepenthes gracilis × Nepenthes rafflesiana*.

In the absence of seed sources, adinandra belukar will be unable to proceed further in succession.[33] In the case of adinandra belukar in Kent Ridge, the seed sources from the nearest primary forest patch in Bukit Timah Nature Reserve or MacRitchie forest that is about 5–6 kilometres, so without human intervention such as planting of climax forest species and improvement of the acidic and nutrient-poor soils, such species cannot be established. Adinandra belukar also tends to catch fire, as is often observed in this vegetation type in the forest patches surrounding the reservoirs in the west of Singapore Island, in the Singapore Armed Forces Live Firing Area or in the forest patches along the Kluang-Mersing Road in the northeast of Johor state in Peninsular Malaysia. Many of the adinandra belukar species are fire-tolerant and can coppice easily after being burnt. Some species, such as the cicada tree, have wind-dispersed seeds and numerous saplings can grow densely at a newly burnt site, so much so that they can grow as an almost pure stand. On 11 February 2005, a patch of adinandra belukar about the length and width of two soccer fields in an area along Research Link of the Kent Ridge Campus at the National University of Singapore caught fire spontaneously and firefighters took about an hour to extinguish it,[34] although the site smouldered for another two weeks. The vegetation had become very dry because of a drought from January to March of that year, which saw 637 bush fires in Singapore.[35]

On the fringes of adinandra belukar forest patches, where the soils are richer because of greater human disturbance (for example, dumping of rubbish, as well as construction and garden waste) and the edge effect, there are some pioneer species that are often found growing there. These include the common acacia (*Acacia auriculiformis*), ivy tree (*Arthrophyllum diversifolium*), white-leafed fig (*Ficus grossularioides*), blue mahang (*Macaranga heynei*), *senduduk* (*Melastoma malabathricum*), common kelat (*Syzygium lineatum*), *kelat nasi nasi* (*Syzygium zeylanicum*), pink lime-berry (*Clausena excavata*) and *akar kunyit* (*Fibraurea tinctoria*). In rare situations, some kinds of mistletoe can be found parasitizing adinandra belukar trees and shrubs. These include the Malayan mistletoe (*Dendrophthoe pentandra*; *Loranthus pentantandrus* in the older literature), pink-flowered mistletoe (*Macrosolen retusus*) and oval-leafed mistletoe (*Viscum ovalifolium*). Along Kent Ridge Road, the adinandra belukar edge has many trees and shrubs grown over by the native climber, bearded smilax (*Smilax setosa*), which can smother trees to death by completely covering them and blocking off all sunlight to their leaves. The tropical American shrub Koster's curse (*Clidemia hirta*) also grows at the edge. So far it has not grown very intensively but in other countries, it has become an invasive pest species[36] and is listed by the Global Invasive Species Database as one of the 100 World's Worst Invasive Alien Species.[37] Another common exotic is the climber, yellow water lemon (*Passiflora laurifolia*), a

Fig. 3.20: Typical appearance of trema belukar. The shorter plants in the front are saplings of rough trema (*Trema tomentosa*; red arrows). The plant in the centre is blue mahang (*Macaranga heynei*), another pioneer tree species typical of trema belukar

tropical American[38] passion fruit species that naturalized after escaping from cultivation. In the undergrowth of the adinandra belukar in the NUS Kent Ridge campus forest, many seedlings of the native sea apple (*Syzygium grande*) have been observed. This may be a result of the frugivorous birds or the lesser dog-faced fruit bat (*Cynopterus brachyotis*) eating fruit from the cultivated trees on campus and dispersing the seeds in the forest as they fly through it.

Fig. 3.21: Flowers, buds and leaves of rough trema (*Trema tomentosa*)

Another form of low secondary forest in Singapore is trema belukar which is a "kind of secondary forest in Singapore and neighbouring countries that develops on undegraded soil from disturbance of primary forest such as creation of large gaps by natural tree fall and which is dominated by the pioneer tree species, lesser trema (*Trema cannabina*) or rough trema (*Trema tomentosa*)".[39] A recently proposed updated classification system for secondary forest types in

Singapore categorizes trema belukar, like adinandra belukar, as another form of "early successional native-dominated secondary forest that grows on less degraded soil".[40] In Kent Ridge there is little evidence of this vegetation type and its presence, if any, is more from the species associated with this vegetation type found usually growing at the fringes of adinandra belukar or waste-woodland vegetation, the second most common vegetation type.

Besides the two key *Trema* species, the pioneer tree and/or shrub species[41] that are found in this vegetation type include mahang species such as blue mahang (*Macaranga heynei*), white mahang (*Macaranga hypoleuca*) and three-lobed mahang (*Macaranga triloba*), fig species such as the yellow hairy fig (*Ficus aurata* var. *aurata*), common yellow-stemmed fig (*Ficus fistulosa*) and white-leafed fig (*Ficus grossularioides*), scrub Christmas tree (*Commersonia batramia*), mousedeer's delight (*Triadica cochinchinensis*; known as *Sapium discolor* in the older literature), pulai[42] (*Alstonia angustiloba*), turn-in-the-wind (*Mallotus paniculatus*) and others.

Waste-Woodland

Wasteland is "vacant urban land awaiting development"[43] so, in the tropical, perhumid climate of Singapore, there is opportunity for the growth of spontaneous secondary vegetation. Based on the recently proposed

classification of secondary forest types in Singapore, wasteland is categorized as waste-woodland. This is the vegetation type that develops on land that was cleared after the 1960s, and is dominated by non-native species through high propagule pressure from the surrounding sites.[44] Recent observations of waste-woodland have indicated that sea almond (*Terminalia catappa*), a native coastal vegetation species, is common even in inland sites.

This vegetation type tends to occur in narrow strips around buildings where construction provides the basis for its development. Although the soils are those of adinandra belukar which was cleared off, the waste materials deposited at the site, including cement which is alkaline and has calcium, a plant nutrient, make the soil less acidic and enrich it. After construction is completed, the cleared land outside the boundaries of the new building are colonized by pioneer species. The first plants to grow there are usually non-woody weeds,[45] the site being subsequently invaded by shrubs and trees.[46] These species tend to be non-native species that are naturalized in Singapore. The first plants to grow are herbaceous weeds such as the grasses, Indian goosegrass (*Eleusine indica*) and swollen windmill grass (*Chloris barbata*), composite weeds such as coat buttons (*Tridax procumbens*), cupid's shaving brush (*Emilia sonchifolia*), little ironweed (*Cyanthillium cinereum*; known as

Fig. 3.22: Wasteland vegetation along Prince George's Park. The tall trees are the exotic albizia (*Falcataria moluccana*) and the climber growing on some at the background is another exotic, the money plant (*Epipremnum aureum*). The climbers in the foreground left is paku ranu (*Stenochlaena palustris*). In the right foreground are shrubs of simpoh air (*Dillenia suffruticosa*). The red arrows indicate the ivy tree (*Arthrophyllum diversifolium*)

Fig. 3.23: Jamaican cherry (*Muntingia calabura*) flowers and young fruits. This is an exotic pioneer species of waste-woodland and urban areas. The flowers are visited by bees and the fruits eaten by native birds and bats. The ripe pink or reddish fruits are edible

Vernonia cinerea in the older literature) and white weed (*Ageratum conyzoides*); legumes such as touch-me-not (*Mimosa pudica*); and sedges such as nutgrass (*Cyperus rotundus*), Navua sedge (*Kyllinga polyphylla*; *Cyperus aromaticus* in the older literature), white kyllinga (*Kyllinga nemoralis*) and many others. In a few months' time, especially in the more fertile sites, these initial species are replaced by the larger grasses, like Guinea grass (*Panicum maximum*), fast-growing climbers like mile-a-minute (*Mikania cordata* and *Mikania micrantha*) and larger shrubby legumes like the giant false sensitive plant (*Mimosa diplotricha*; *Mimosa invisa* in the older literature) and giant sensitive plant (*Mimosa pigra*). Saplings of pioneer tree species then start appearing. These include those of legumes such as albizia (*Falcataria moluccana*; *Albizia falcataria* or *Paraserianthes falcataria* in the older literature), common acacia (*Acacia auriculiformis*) and leucaena (*Leucaena leucocephala*), African tulip

(*Spathodea campanulata*), Ceara rubber tree (*Manihot carthagenesis* ssp. *glaziovii*; *Manihot glaziovii* in the older literature), Jamaican cherry (*Muntingia calabura*) and others. Given time, a forest develops, with these trees constituting the major part of the canopy. Albizia is the most noticeable tree, towering over the others. Although considered stately and beautiful by some people and may be a tree that some native raptors nest in, its roots and wood are not strong. The tree can topple over or its branches can break easily when it reaches its relatively short lifespan of only about a decade or more. It thus poses a danger to people, especially in periods of strong wind and rain. For instance, a woman was killed by a ten-storey-tall albizia tree falling on her in Bukit Batok Nature Park on 15 May 2007;[47] therefore these large trees should be removed from areas frequented by people.

Waste-woodland in Kent Ridge also developed from abandoned kampongs that were cleared, so many cultivated species such as food crops, fruit trees and ornamental plants are found in them such as tapioca (*Manihot esculenta*), oil palm (*Elaeis guineensis*), liane-quinine (*Tinospora crispa*), banana plants (*Musa* cultivated varieties), curry leaf (*Murraya koenigii*), Jamaican cherry (*Muntingia calabura*), lantana (*Lantana camara*), money plant (*Epipremnum aureum*), dumb cane (*Dieffenbachia seguine*) and iron plant (*Dracaena fragrans*).

Managed Vegetation

Managed vegetation consists of cultivated plants as well as those that grow spontaneously, such as weeds of cultivation, epiphytes on trees and lithophytes of concrete structures such as buildings, drains and overhead bridges.

The several roads in Kent Ridge are lined by roadside planting maintained mostly by the National Parks Board (NParks) along public roads, those within the NUS campuses by the NUS Office of Facilities Management and within the grounds of the National University Hospital, by the hospital. These roadside plantings are of the same species as those in other parts of Singapore and are mostly exotic species.[48] The key species is the South American rain tree (*Samanea saman*)—as seen along Lower Kent Ridge Road—one of the most commonly cultivated trees in Singapore. Others include exotic species such as African mahogany (*Khaya grandifoliola*), angsana (*Pterocarpus indicus*), blackboard tree (*Alstonia scholaris*), brown heart (*Andira inermis*), Cuban pink trumpet tree (*Tabebuia pallida*), footstool palm (*Saribus rotundifolius*; *Livistona rotundifolia* in the older literature), MacArthur's palm (*Ptychosperma macarthurii*), mango (*Mangifera indica*), purple milletia (*Callerya atropurpurea*), rose of India (*Lagerstroemia speciosa*), saga tree (*Adenanthera pavonina*), Senegal mahogany (*Khaya senegalensis*) and trumpet tree (*Tabebuia rosea*); and native

Fig. 3.24: Streetscape along Lower Kent Ridge Road in the NUS Kent Ridge Campus. The road is lined mostly with stately rain trees (*Samanea saman*). The tree with the yellow blooms is golden shower (*Cassia fistula*). Ornamental shrubs can be seen behind that tree, and consist mostly of MacArthur's palm (*Ptychosperma macarthuri*). This scene is quite typical of streetscapes in Singapore

Fig. 3.25: The larger of the two ponds at Kent Ridge Park. Water bodies provide habitats for several animals including dragonflies and birds. The many water birds at Kent Ridge Park are recorded because of the ponds

Fig. 3.26: Flame of the Forest (*Delonix regia*) tree in full bloom in the NUS Kent Ridge Campus. Two rain trees (*Samanea saman*; one obscured partially) are behind it. They are covered with epiphytes; the most prominent are the bird's nest ferns (*Asplenium nidus*) which consist of a rosette of long, sword-shaped leaves.
Footstool palms (*Saribus rotundifolus*) are on the left. The lawn is mostly of cow grass (*Axonopus compressus*). All these species are exotics except for the epiphytes, a typical situation for cultivated areas in urban Singapore

Fig. 3.27: Several plants of niruri (*Phyllanthus debilis*), a weed of gardens and wasteland, seen here in a flower bed in Kent Ridge Campus

Fig. 3.28: Coat buttons (*Tridax procumbens*), a very common exotic weed of urban areas from the sunflower family photographed at Prince George's Park

Fig. 3.29: The oval-leafed mistletoe (*Viscum ovalifolium*; red arrow) on mempat (*Cratoxylum cochinchinense*), a native species which is grown as a street tree along Science Drive 4 at the NUS Kent Ridge Campus. Note the difference in leaf size, and shape between the mistletoe and its host

Fig. 3.30: Planting of the native plant landscaping at University Hall of the NUS Kent Ridge Campus, along Lower Kent Ridge Road in June 2011

species such as casuarina (*Casuarina equisetifolia*), mangrove tree, pong pong (*Cerbera odollam*), red lip (*Syzygium myrtifolium*; also as a hedge, topiary or shrub), sea almond (*Terminalia catappa*), sea apple (*Syzygium grande*), tembusu (*Crytophyllum fragrans*) and yellow flame (*Peltophorum pterocarpum*).

Cultivated roadside shrubs and herbs include bougainvillea (*Bougainvillea glabra* cultivated varieties), cape honeysuckle (*Tecomaria capensis*), *Ficus microcarpa* 'Golden', golden dewdrop (*Duranta erecta*), ixoras (*Ixora javanica* and several *Ixora* cultivated varieties), lantana (*Lantana camara*), Mickey Mouse plant (*Ochna kirkii*), parrot's flower (*Heliconia psittacorum*), peacock flower (*Caesalpinia pulcherrima*), Singapore daisy (*Sphagneticola trilobata*; *Wedelia trilobata* in the older literature), spider lily (*Hymenocallis speciosa*) and ti tree (*Cordyline fruticosa*).

The grass along roadsides is mostly the South American cow grass (*Axonopus compressus*) but it may also include several lawn weeds such as the greater clover-leafed desmodium (*Desmodium heterophyllum*), lesser clover-leafed desmodium (*Desmodium triflorum*), other grasses such as buffalo grass (*Paspalum conjugatum*), love grass (*Chrysopogon aciculatus*) and Bermuda grass (*Cynodon dactylon*), one-leaf clover (*Alysicarpus vaginalis*), Indian pennywort (*Centella asiatica*), fringed spiderflower (*Cleome rutidosperma*; *Cleome ciliata* in the older literature), sedges (Cyperaceae), little ironweed (*Cynthillium cinereum*), creeping ruellia (*Ruellia repens*), two-flower oldenlandia (*Oldenlandia corymbosa*), *Oldenlandia affinis* (*Oldenlandia dichotoma* in the older literature) and lavender sorrel (*Oxalis barrelieri*). Occasionally one may see the orchid, bawang hantu (*Eulophia graminea*), sprouting out of the

Fig. 3.31: Native plant landscaping at University Hall at the NUS Kent Ridge Campus, along Lower Kent Ridge Road on 13 May 2016. There are at least three layers of the canopy, a layer for the crowns of trees, a shrub or treelet layer, then an undershrub layer. The planting design does not mimic the structure of natural primary forest exactly, which makes for a very chaotic and untidy design because there are several species with only one or a few individuals each. Here the groups of individuals of the same species are clustered together for a "regimented rain forest" look, which is neater and less chaotic. University Hall is one of the best places in Singapore to observe native Singapore plant landscaping

lawn seemingly overnight, like its Malay name, meaning "ghost onion", suggests.

On the roadside, the trees include hemiparasitic mistletoes including the Malayan mistletoe (*Dendrophthoe pentandra*), common Chinese mistletoe (*Macrosolen cochinchinensis*), pink-flowered mistletoe (*Macrosolen retusus*), oval-leafed mistletoe (*Viscum ovalifolium*) and, more rarely, jointed mistletoe (*Viscum articulatum*) parasitizing the oval-leafed mistletoe, demonstrating a case of hyperparasitism.

On the trees too are found several species of mostly native epiphytes (plants that grow on other plants) including ferns such as bird's nest fern (*Asplenium nidus*), dragon's scales (*Pyrrosia piloselloides*), oak-leafed fern (*Drynaria quercifolia*), rabbit's foot fern (*Davallia denticulata*), shoestring fern (*Vittaria ensiformis*), staghorn fern (*Platycerium coronarium*) and suloi (*Pyrrosia longifolia*); button orchid (*Dischidia nummularia*); young plants of strangling figs such as the cryptogenic Benjamin fig (*Ficus benjamina*); exotic Bodhi tree (*Ficus religiosa*); native Malayan banyan (*Ficus microcarpa*); and pigeon orchid (*Dendrobium crumenatum*). These epiphytes can also grow on buildings, and several listed here can be found growing on ledges and roofs, and out of cracks of buildings, drains and other concrete structures. Many of the weeds of the lawn, mentioned here, also grow from cracks in pavements, road curbs and drains.

The main park in Kent Ridge is the 47-hectare[49] Kent Ridge Park which is part of the Southern Ridges and classified as an Arts & Heritage Park under the Parks 1 Group Parks and Park Connectors of the Park Management & Lifestyle Cluster, Parks Division of the National Parks Board. Kent Ridge Park consists of managed areas and forest. The managed areas consist of lawns, herbs, shrubs, climbers and trees, with plants similar to those mentioned above for roadsides. Institutions such as NUS also have extensive areas for cultivation. Additionally, the planting palette in such areas, which have a less harsh microclimate as compared to roads, is larger and the choices available are wide as mentioned in these references.[50,51]

Some parts of the NUS Kent Ridge campus are planted almost entirely with native species. Such native species have not been listed in Table 3.1 as they are usually only confined to these sites, unless they also occur in the forest patches in Kent Ridge or are cultivated elsewhere.

The first native landscaping site to be established was that of the NUS Native Plant Demonstration Garden at the foot of Blocks S1 and S2 near Science Drive 4. This was developed in 2007 by the staff of the NUS Department of Biological Sciences and Office of Facilities Management, and was probably the first native plant landscaping in Singapore. Native plants there include trees like bintangor bunut (*Calophyllum soulattri*;

Critically Endangered), cicada tree (*Ploiarium alternifolium*; Common), delek air (*Memecylon edule*; Endangered), kelumpang burung (*Sterculia parviflora*; Critically Endangered), nibung palm (*Oncosperma tigillarium*; Vulnerable), nyamok (*Guioa pleuropteris*; Vulnerable), perfume flower tree (*Fagraea ceilanica*; Presumed Nationally Extinct), seashore mangosteen (*Garcinia hombroniana*; Endangered); shrubs like pelir musang (*Fagraea auriculata*; Critically

Fig. 3.32: One of the more spectacular native Singapore plants, pelir musang (*Fagraea auriculata*), cultivated at University Hall. The flowers may be up to 30 centimetres across!

Endangered), sea lettuce (*Scaevola taccada*; Common) and sealing wax palm (*Cyrtostachys renda*; Presumed Nationally Extinct); herbs like crinum lily (*Crinum asiaticum*; Critically Endangered); climbers like maiden's jealousy (*Tristellateia australasiae*; Endangered), Malayan wild vine (*Cissus repens*; Critically Endangered), sandy-leafed fig (*Ficus heteropleura*; Common) and three-leaved wild vine (*Cissus trifoliata*, synonyms *Cayratia trifolia*, *Cissus trifolia*, *Cissus trifoliata*; Vulnerable); and strangler figs like strangler, brown-scurfy fig (*Ficus consociata* var. *murtoni*; Critically Endangered) and grey fig (*Ficus virens*; Critically Endangered). Most of the species here grow naturally in beach vegetation and were selected because they can tolerate the brighter, hotter and windier conditions that are found in urban sites. These plants were purchased and are not of local provenance except for the brown-scurfy fig, crinum lily, delek air, grey fig, Malayan wild vine, three-leaved wild vine, pelir musang and sandy-leafed fig.

The most prominent area for native plant landscaping is University Hall (UHall) along Lower Kent Ridge Road where the roadsides, inner courtyard and traffic island have been planted with native species of Singapore. This was implemented in 2009 by the same team as for the NUS Native Plant Demonstration Garden. The plantings here use mainly native beach vegetation species so that they can tolerate the roadside conditions

Fig. 3.33: Delek air (*Memecylon edule*), one of the native Singapore trees grown in the NUS Native Plant Demonstration Garden at the foot of Blocks S1 and S2, at Science Drive 4. This garden, established in 2007, is the first native plant garden in NUS, and possibly Singapore

better and the canopy is at least three layers with an undershrub, shrub or treelet and tree layer so as to increase the number of microhabitats available to native wildlife such as bees, birds and butterflies. Species were selected to provide nectar and pollen to attract bees, birds and butterflies, and fruit to attract birds, squirrels and tree shrews. For the pools in the inner courtyard, plants from mangrove forest and freshwater swamp forest were used.[52]

Several native plants (mostly trees and some shrubs) were planted in the area between Blocks S11 and S12 along Science Drive 4 which is adjacent to UHall. Several native tree species were also planted in the Multipurpose Sports Fields along Lower Kent Ridge Road, and beneath a grove of rain trees between Blocks AS8 and AS2 along Kent Ridge Crescent. These and the UHall plantings were implemented in 2009. The plantings at UHall, Science Drive 4, Multipurpose Sports Fields and Kent Ridge Crescent were developed for a research project done in collaboration between NUS and the National Parks Board.

The Lee Kong Chian Natural History Museum, at the junction of Kent Ridge Crescent and Conservatory Drive, also has four native plant-dominated landscaped areas and an evolution garden which consists of exotic and native species. The most obvious example of native Singapore plant landscaping is the vertical greenery at the front of the museum building which is meant to simulate the coastal rocky shore or cliff vegetation that can be observed at Labrador Nature Reserve or in the Southern Islands such as the cliffs of Lazarus Island (Pulau Sakijang Pelepah), Pulau Biola, Pulau Terkukor, and St John's Island (Pulau Sakijang Bendera). At the rear of the building, and very visible to pedestrians walking along College Link or from the higher floors of buildings in the Town Plaza of University Town, is a landscape design that simulates a section of sandy beach vegetation from the sea, beach front to dryland forest, from one end to another. In the middle of the museum

Fig. 3.34: Flowering twig of salam (*Syzygium polyanthum*), a native tree of secondary and primary forests but cultivated along Science Drive 4. The leaves are used to flavour rice because they contain aromatic oils

Fig. 3.35: Fruiting tongkat ali (*Eurycoma longifolia*), the infamous plant known for its aphrodisiac properties from compounds extracted from its long tap root. This native plant is grown at University Hall

Fig. 3.36: Front façade of the Lee Kong Chian Natural History Museum building showing the vertical greenery that represents coastal cliff vegetation of Singapore, another example of native plant landscaping

site, behind the viewing gallery is an area showing mangrove forest, transitioning to freshwater swamp forest and ending with dryland forest, to simulate a natural stream in primeval Singapore which transitions from one vegetation type to another in the same way to reflect wet to dry, and salty to freshwater conditions. Lining the driveway and porch area are attractive native shrubs and herbs. The Evolution Garden consists of representatives of key groups of plants laid out in a more or less linear sequence, from green

Fig. 3.37: Part of the Evolution Garden of the Lee Kong Chian Natural History Museum showing the monocotyledons including the banana (*Musa* species), pineapple (*Ananas comosus*), elephant ears (*Alocasia macrorrhizos*), pandan (*Pandanus* species) and, in the centre, the betel nut palm (*Areca catechu*), which would also have been grown in early Singapore

alga, bryophytes, ferns and fern allies, gymnosperms, then flowering plants. All these plantings were completed in 2015.

The secondary forest of Kent Ridge has many casual or naturalized species of plants that were cultivated but have since been abandoned and have run wild. These include rubber (*Hevea brasiliensis*), tapioca (*Manihot esculenta*), cashew nut (*Anacardium occidentale*), banana cultivated varieties (*Musa* cultivars), common bamboo (*Bambusa vulgaris*), coconut (*Cocos nucifera*),

Fig. 3.38: Forest patch that grew up from a lawn at the junction of Kent Ridge Road and Prince George's Park once mowing was stopped in the 1990s, so this forest patch is about 20 years old

woolly congea (*Congea tomentosa*), dumb cane (*Dieffenbachia seguine*), iron plant (*Dracaena fragrans*) and money plant (*Epipremnum aureum*), which can be seen climbing up the tall trunks of albizia in waste-woodland vegetation, yellow water lemon (*Passiflora laurifolia*), liane-quinine (*Tinospora crispa*), guava (*Psidium guajava*), cekur manis (*Sauropus androgynous*), seven golden candlesticks (*Senna alata*), turkey berry (*Solanum torvum*), Java plum (*Syzygium cuminum*) and rose apple (*Syzygium jambos*).

Some managed vegetation areas have been allowed to revert to forest in Kent Ridge campus. In the 1990s, the grassy slope at the junction of Prince George's Park and Kent Ridge Road was left unmown and some saplings were planted, and today, after about 20 years,

it is a patch of dense secondary forest with trees about 10 metres tall or more. From May 2011, the hill slope that was mowed regularly to the north of Kent Ridge Road from the staircase behind Block S2 westwards to the base of the water tank was also allowed to grow thick with vegetation after mowing was stopped. These actions were facilitated by the Office of Facilities Management at the request of academic staff members to increase the forest cover. Lawn mowing keeps vegetation in a subclimax condition and, once mowing becomes irregular and is stopped, succession can occur, with the seeds of forest trees growing into saplings, and ultimately developing without any effort into a forest—the natural condition of vegetation in Singapore.

Table 3.1: Checklist of the Vascular Plants of Kent Ridge

This list is based on the following references,[1] the collections of the Singapore Botanic Gardens' Herbarium (SING) and the Herbarium, Lee Kong Chian Natural History Museum, National University of Singapore (SINU), as well as personal observations. The list is in alphabetical order of the scientific name. Spontaneous or wild species have been emphasized thus the cultivated species list is incomplete because of continuous change with new introductions to and replacement at the site. Common names are mostly based on those of the National Parks Board's Flora & Fauna Web.[2] Selected synonyms have been included for the scientific names, especially those that have been used in the older literature for the convenience of the reader. The national status categories for each species is updated from *A Checklist of the Total Vascular Plant Flora of Singapore: Native, Naturalised and Cultivated Species*[3] and extracted from a data set provided by Chong Kwek Yan.

The national-status categories are in three main groups:[4]

a. Native species = Species that have originated at a particular site without human intervention, or arrived at that location without human involvement (intentional or unintentional) from an area where they originated without human involvement.
b. Exotic = non-native species = Species that are present at an area because of intentional or unintentional human involvement.
c. Cryptogenic Weed = Species that lack historical or biogeographical evidence of being non-native but are restricted to human-disturbed or -modified habitats.
(1) *Native Species* conservation status categories:[5] Common (with more than 1,000 mature individuals), Vulnerable (with more than 250 but fewer than 1,000 mature individuals and "there may or may not be any other evidence of decline, small range size, or fragmentation" of the population), Endangered (more than 50 but fewer than 250 mature individuals with no other evidence of fragmentation or decline of the population), Critically Endangered (with fewer than 50 mature individuals, or if there are more than 50 but less than 250 mature individuals, with some evidence of fragmentation or decline in the population), Extinct (nationally extinct in the wild but the species survives outside Singapore; not been recorded or collected in the last 30 years).
(2) *Non-native* = exotic species categories:[6] Cultivated Only (exotic species that can only be found under direct human care or under cultivation), Casual (exotic species that do not form self-replacing populations in the wild and rely

on repeated introductions or limited asexual reproduction to persist in the natural environment), Naturalized (exotic species that form usually sexually reproducing, self-replacing populations in the wild). Habits are the general growth form of the plant and include herbs (non-woody plants), shrubs (small woody plants including those with multiple trunks), trees (large woody plants with a single trunk), climbers (plants with weak stems and for support must climb on other structures, or creep on the ground in the absence of such structures), epiphytes (plants that only grow on other plants or grow on them and parasitize them, for example, mistletoe), stranglers (plants that grow on other plants but later smother the support plant with their strong aerial roots, for example, strangler figs). Adinandra belukar species are categorized as such based on Holttum, Sim et al.,[7] as well as our personal observations.

Notes to Table 3.1

1. Hugh T.W. Tan, "Appendix C: List of Vascular Plant Species Found on Kent Ridge", in *Kent Ridge Environs: A Proposal for Conserving Nature at the National University of Singapore Campus*, Ho Hua Chew and Clive Briffett (Singapore: Malayan Nature Society, 1991), pp. 28–30; Letchimi T. Mudaliar, "Vegetation in Kent Ridge", BSc (Hons) thesis (Singapore: National University of Singapore, 1984), pp. 121–9; Navjot S. Sodhi and Hugh T.W. Tan, "Report on the Ecosystem Study of the Proposed Site for the Nature Area at the NUS Kent Ridge Campus", internal report (Singapore: National University of Singapore, 2003), pp. 5–8; Hugh T.W. Tan, T. Morgany and Tan Kai-xin, *The History and Biology of Kent Ridge Park* (Singapore, n.d.), pp. 9, 11–22; Brandon Seah, "A Guide to the Plants of Kent Ridge", http://pasirpanjang.rafflesmuseum.net/ [accessed 28 Apr. 2016]; J.W.S. Sim, Hugh T.W. Tan and I.M. Turner, "Adinandra Belukar: An Anthropogenic Heath Forest in Singapore", *Vegetatio* 102, 2 (1992): 128–9.

2. National Parks Board, "NParks Flora & Fauna Web", National Parks Board, https://florafaunaweb. nparks.gov.sg/ [accessed 24 Apr. 2016].

3. K.Y. Chong, Hugh T.W. Tan and R.T. Corlett, *A Checklist of the Total Vascular Plant Flora of Singapore: Native, Naturalised and Cultivated Species* (Singapore: Raffles Museum of Biodiversity Research, 2009), http://lkcnhm.nus.edu.sg/nus/pdf/PUBLICATION/LKCNH%20Museum%20 Books/LKCNHM%20Books/flora_of_singapore_tc.pdf [accessed 28 Apr. 2016].

4. Ibid., p. 4.

5. G.W.H. Davison, "The Red List Categories", in *The Singapore Red Data Book: Threatened Plants and Animals of Singapore,* 2nd ed., ed. G.W.H. Davison, P.K.L. Ng and H.C. Ho (Singapore: Nature Society Singapore, 2008), p. 3.

6. Chong et al., *A Checklist of the Total Vascular Plant Flora of Singapore: Native, Naturalised and Cultivated Species*, p. 4.

7. Sim et al., "Adinandra Belukar", pp. 128–9.

S/No.	Common Name	Scientific Name	Family	National Status	Cultivated	Habit	Adinandra Belukar
1.	Common acacia	*Acacia auriculiformis*	Fabaceae	Naturalized	Yes	Tree	No
2.	Black wattle	*Acacia mangium*	Fabaceae	Naturalized	Yes	Tree	No
3.	Indian acalypha	*Acalypha indica*	Euphorbiaceae	Cryptogenic Weed	No	Herb	No
4.	Wild tea	*Acalypha siamensis*	Euphorbiaceae	Casual	Yes	Shrub	No
5.	Copperleaf	*Acalypha wilkesiana*	Euphorbiaceae	Cultivated only	Yes	Shrub	No
6.	Lily leaf acriopsis	*Acriopsis liliifolia* (synonym: *Acriopsis javanica*)	Orchidaceae	Critically Endangered	No	Epiphyte	No
7.	Saga	*Adenanthera pavonina*	Fabaceae	Naturalized	Yes	Tree	No
8.	Tiup tiup	*Adinandra dumosa*	Pentaphylacaceae	Common	Yes	Tree	Yes
9.	Christmas palm	*Adonidia merrillii* (synonym: *Veitchia merrillii*)	Arecaceae	Cultivated only	Yes	Tree	No
10.	Borneo kauri	*Agathis borneensis*	Araucariaceae	Cultivated only	Yes	Tree	No
11.	White weed	*Ageratum conyzoides*	Asteraceae	Naturalized	No	Herb	No
12.	Rain tree	*Albizia saman* (synonym: *Samanea saman*)	Fabaceae	Casual	Yes	Tree	No
13.	Allamanda	*Allamanda cathartica*	Apocynaceae	Casual	Yes	Climber	No
14.	Elephant ears	*Alocasia macrorrhizos*	Araceae	Naturalized	Yes	Herb	No
15.	Galangal	*Alpinia galanga* (synonym: *Languas galanga*)	Zingiberaceae	Casual	Yes	Herb	No
16.	Red-leafed pulai	*Alstonia angustifolia*	Apocynaceae	Common	Yes	Tree	No
17.	Pulai	*Alstonia angustiloba*	Apocynaceae	Common	Yes	Tree	No
18.	Blackboard tree	*Alstonia scholaris*	Apocynaceae	Cultivated only	Yes	Tree	No

S/No.	Common Name	Scientific Name	Family	National Status	Cultivated	Habit	Adinandra Belukar
19.	Keremak	*Alternanthera sessilis*	Amaranthaceae	Cryptogenic Weed	Yes	Herb	No
20.	One-leaf clover	*Alysicarpus vaginalis*	Fabaceae	Cryptogenic Weed	No	Herb	No
21.	Cashew nut	*Anacardium occidentale*	Anacardiaceae	Casual	Yes	Tree	No
22.	Brown heart	*Andira inermis*	Fabaceae	Casual	Yes	Tree	No
23.	King of bitters	*Andrographis paniculata*	Acanthaceae	Naturalized	Yes	Herb	No
24.	Common leechwood	*Anisophyllea disticha*	Anisophyllaceae	Common	Yes	Shrub	No
25.	Soursop	*Annona reticulata*	Annonaceae	Casual	Yes	Tree	No
26.	Anthurium	*Anthurium andraeanum*	Araceae	Cultivated only	Yes	Herb	No
27.	Bignay	*Antidesma bunius*	Phyllanthaceae	Casual	Yes	Tree	No
28.	Honolulu creeper	*Antigonon leptopus*	Polygonaceae	Casual	Yes	Climber	No
29.	Amoora	*Aphanamixis polystachya*	Meliaceae	Endangered	Yes	Tree	No
30.	New Caledonia pine	*Araucaria columnaris*	Araucariaceae	Cultivated only	Yes	Tree	No
31.	Small-fruited archidendron	*Archidendron microcarpum* (synonym: *Pithecellobium microcarpum*)	Fabaceae	Endangered	No	Tree	No
32.	Betel nut	*Areca catechu*	Arecaceae	Casual	Yes	Tree	No
33.	Hop tree	*Arfeuillea arborescens*	Sapindaceae	Cultivated only	Yes	Tree	No
34.	Ivy tree	*Arthrophyllum diversifolium*	Araliaceae	Common	Yes	Tree	No
35.	Breadfruit	*Artocarpus altilis* (synonym: *Artocarpus incisus*)	Moraceae	Casual	Yes	Tree	No

S/No.	Common Name	Scientific Name	Family	National Status	Cultivated	Habit	Adinandra Belukar
36.	Jackfruit	*Artocarpus heterophyllus*	Moraceae	Casual	Yes	Tree	No
37.	Bamboo orchid	*Arundina graminifolia*	Orchidaceae	Common	Yes	Herb	No
38.	Bird's nest fern	*Asplenium nidus*	Aspleniaceae	Common	Yes	Epiphyte	No
39.	Coromandel	*Asystasia gangetica* ssp. *gangetica* (synonym: *Asystasia coromandeliana*)	Acanthaceae	Naturalized	Yes	Herb	No
40.	Ganges primrose	*Asystasia gangetica* ssp. *micrantha* (synonym: *Asystasia intrusa*)	Acanthaceae	Naturalized	Yes	Herb	No
41.	Belimbing	*Averrhoa bilimbi*	Oxalidaceae	Casual	Yes	Tree	No
42.	Starfruit	*Averrhoa carambola*	Oxalidaceae	Casual	Yes	Tree	No
43.	Cow grass	*Axonopus compressus*	Poaceae	Naturalized	Yes	Herb	No
44.	Neem	*Azadirachta indica* (synonym: *Melia azadirachta*)	Meliaceae	Casual	Yes	Tree	No
45.	Rambai	*Baccaurea motleyana*	Phyllanthaceae	Critically Endangered	Yes	Tree	No
46.	Common bamboo	*Bambusa vulgaris*	Poaceae	Casual	Yes	Shrub	No
47.	Camwood	*Baphia nitida*	Fabaceae	Casual	Yes	Shrub	No
48.	Philippine violet	*Barleria cristata*	Acanthaceae	Cultivated only	Yes	Shrub	No
49.	White bauhinia	*Bauhinia acuminata*	Fabaceae	Cultivated only	Yes	Tree	No
50.	Kock's bauhinia	*Bauhinia kockiana*	Fabaceae	Cultivated only	Yes	Climber	No
51.	Purple bauhinia	*Bauhinia purpurea*	Fabaceae	Cultivated only	Yes	Tree	No

S/No.	Common Name	Scientific Name	Family	National Status	Cultivated	Habit	Adinandra Belukar
52.	Lipstick plant	*Bixa orellana*	Bixaceae	Cultivated only	Yes	Shrub	No
53.	Centipede fern	*Blechnum orientale*	Blechnaceae	Common	No	Herb	No
54.	Ngai camphor	*Blumea balsamifera*	Asteraceae	Cryptogenic Weed	Yes	Herb	No
55.	Bougainvillea	*Bougainvillea glabra*	Nyctaginaceae	Cultivated only	Yes	Shrub	No
56.		*Breynia racemosa* (synonym: *Breynia reclinata*)	Phyllanthaceae	Common	No	Climber	No
57.	Kernam	*Bridelia stipularis*	Phyllanthaceae	Vulnerable	No	Shrub	No
58.	Kernong	*Bridelia tomentosa*	Phyllanthaceae	Common	Yes	Tree	No
59.	Seraman	*Bromheadia finlaysoniana* (synonyms: *Bromheadia palustris*; *Bromheadia sylvestris*)	Orchidaceae	Common	No	Herb	Yes
60.	Sparrow's mango	*Buchanania arborescens*	Anacardiaceae	Common	Yes	Tree	No
61.	Short-leafed burmannia	*Burmannia coelestis*	Burmanniaceae	Common	Yes	Herb	No
62.	Peacock flower	*Caesalpinia pulcherrima*	Fabaceae	Cultivated only	Yes	Shrub	No
63.	Purple milletia	*Callerya atropurpurea* (synonym: *Milletia atropurpurea*)	Fabaceae	Casual	Yes	Tree	No
64.	Powder puff plant	*Calliandra surinamensis*	Fabaceae	Casual	Yes	Shrub	No
65.	Red powder puff plant	*Calliandra tergemina* var. *emarginata* (synonym: *Calliandra emarginata*)	Fabaceae	Cultivated only	Yes	Shrub	No

S/No.	Common Name	Scientific Name	Family	National Status	Cultivated	Habit	Adinandra Belukar
66.	Crimson bottlebrush	*Callistemon citrinus*	Myrtaceae	Cultivated only	Yes	Tree	No
67.	Bintangor laut	*Calophyllum inophyllum*	Calophyllaceae	Critically Endangered	Yes	Tree	No
68.	Papaya	*Carica papaya*	Caricaceae	Casual	Yes	Tree	No
69.	Wild tea	*Carmona retusa* (synonym: *Ehretia microphylla*)	Boraginaceae	Naturalized	Yes	Shrub	No
70.	Fishtail palm	*Caryota mitis*	Arecaceae	Common	Yes	Tree	No
71.	Golden shower	*Cassia fistula*	Fabaceae	Cultivated only	Yes	Tree	No
72.	Casuarina, ru	*Casuarina equisetifolia*	Casuarinaceae	Common	Yes	Tree	No
73.	Periwinkle	*Catharanthus roseus* (synonym: *Vinca rosea*)	Apocynaceae	Naturalized	Yes	Shrub	No
74.	Kapok	*Ceiba pentandra*	Malvaceae	Casual	Yes	Tree	No
75.	Cock's comb	*Celosia argentea*	Amaranthaceae	Casual	Yes	Herb	No
76.	Indian pennywort	*Centella asiatica* (synonym: *Hydrocotyle asiatica*)	Apiaceae	Common	Yes	Herb	No
77.	Centro	*Centrosema pubescens*	Fabaceae	Naturalized	Yes	Climber	No
78.	Pong pong	*Cerbera odollam*	Apocynaceae	Vulnerable	Yes	Tree	No
79.	White costus	*Cheilocostus speciosus* (synonym: *Costus speciosus*)	Costaceae	Common	Yes	Herb	No
80.	Swollen windmill grass	*Chloris barbata*	Poaceae	Naturalized	No	Herb	No
81.	Love grass	*Chrysopogon aciculatus*	Poaceae	Common	Yes	Herb	No
82.	Wild cinnamon	*Cinnamomum iners*	Lauraceae	Common	Yes	Tree	No

S/No.	Common Name	Scientific Name	Family	National Status	Cultivated	Habit	Adinandra Belukar
83.	White-stemmed button vine	*Cissus hastata* (synonym: *Vitis hastata*)	Vitaceae	Cryptogenic Weed	Yes	Climber	No
84.	Veldt's grape	*Cissus quadrangularis*	Vitaceae	Cultivated only	Yes	Climber	No
85.	Lemon	*Citrus limon*	Rutaceae	Casual	Yes	Tree	No
86.	Pink lime-berry	*Clausena excavata*	Rutaceae	Common	No	Shrub	No
87.	Fringed spiderflower	*Cleome rutidosperma* (synonym: *Cleome ciliata*)	Cleomaceae	Naturalized	Yes	Herb	No
88.	Chinese glory flower	*Clerodendrum chinense*	Lamiaceae	Cultivated only	Yes	Shrub	No
89.	Swaddling flower	*Clerodendrum laevifolium*	Lamiaceae	Common	Yes	Tree	No
90.	Pagoda flower	*Clerodendrum paniculatum*	Lamiaceae	Casual	Yes	Shrub	No
91.	Bleeding heart	*Clerodendrum thomsoniae*	Lamiaceae	Casual	Yes	Climber	No
92.	Tapak kerbau	*Clerodendrum villosum*	Lamiaceae	Vulnerable	Yes	Shrub	No
93.	Koster's curse	*Clidemia hirta*	Melastomataceae	Naturalized	Yes	Shrub	No
94.	Sabah snake grass	*Clinacanthus nutans*	Acanthaceae	Cultivated only	Yes	Herb	No
95.	Laurel-leaf	*Clitoria laurifolia*	Fabaceae	Naturalized	No	Shrub	No
96.	Butterfly pea	*Clitoria ternatea*	Fabaceae	Naturalized	Yes	Climber	No
97.	Coconut	*Cocos nucifera*	Arecaceae	Naturalized	Yes	Tree	No
98.	Croton	*Codiaeum variegatum*	Euphorbiaceae	Casual	Yes	Shrub	No
99.	Cocoyam	*Colocasia esculenta*	Araceae	Casual	Yes	Herb	No
100.	Climbing dayflower	*Commelina diffusa* (synonym: *Commelina nudiflora*)	Commelinaceae	Cryptogenic Weed	No	Herb	No

S/No.	Common Name	Scientific Name	Family	National Status	Cultivated	Habit	Adinandra Belukar
101.	Scrub Christmas tree	*Commersonia bartramia*	Malvaceae	Common	No	Tree	No
102.	Woolly congea	*Congea tomentosa*	Lamiaceae	Casual	Yes	Climber	No
103.	Stringbush	*Cordia cylindristachya*	Boraginaceae	Naturalized	Yes	Shrub	No
104.	Scarlet cordia	*Cordia sebestena*	Boraginaceae	Cultivated only	Yes	Tree	No
105.	Sea trumpet	*Cordia subcordata*	Boraginaceae	Critically Endangered	Yes	Tree	No
106.	Ti tree	*Cordyline fruticosa*	Asparagaceae	Casual	Yes	Shrub	No
107.	Scarlet spiral flag	*Costus woodsonii*	Zingiberaceae	Cultivated only	Yes	Herb	No
108.	Pink mempat	*Cratoxylum formosum*	Hypericaceae	Endangered	Yes	Tree	No
109.		*Croton oblongus* (synonyms: *Croton laevifolius*; *Croton griffthii*)	Euphorbiaceae	Endangered	No	Tree	No
110.	Cucumber	*Cucumis sativus*	Cucurbitaceae	Cultivated only	Yes	Climber	No
111.	Pumpkin	*Cucurbita maxima*	Cucurbitaceae	Cultivated only	Yes	Climber	No
112.	Little ironweed	*Cyanthillium cinereum* (synonym: *Vernonia cinerea*)	Asteraceae	Cryptogenic Weed	No	Herb	No
113.	Bermuda grass	*Cynodon dactylon*	Poaceae	Common	Yes	Herb	No
114.	Pacific island flatsedge	*Cyperus cyperoides*	Cyperaceae	Cryptogenic Weed	No	Herb	No
115.	Nutgrass	*Cyperus rotundus*	Cyperaceae	Cryptogenic Weed	No	Herb	No
116.	Sealing wax palm	*Cyrtostachys renda* (synonym: *Cyrtostachys lakka*)	Arecaceae	Extinct	Yes	Shrub	No

S/No.	Common Name	Scientific Name	Family	National Status	Cultivated	Habit	Adinandra Belukar
117.	Tembusu	*Cyrtophyllum fragrans* (synonym: *Fagraea fragrans*)	Gentianaceae	Common	Yes	Tree	Yes
118.	East Indian rosewood	*Dalbergia latifolia*	Fabaceae	Cultivated only	Yes	Tree	No
119.	Black rosewood	*Dalbergia oliveri*	Fabaceae	Cultivated only	Yes	Tree	No
120.	Rabbit's foot fern	*Davallia denticulata*	Davalliaceae	Common	Yes	Epiphyte	No
121.	Flame of the Forest	*Delonix regia*	Fabaceae	Cultivated only	Yes	Tree	No
122.	Pigeon orchid	*Dendrobium crumenatum*	Orchidaceae	Common	Yes	Epiphyte	No
123.	Malayan mistletoe	*Dendrophthoe pentandra* (synonym: *Loranthus pentandrus*)	Loranthaceae	Common	No	Epiphyte	No
124.	Greater clover-leafed desmodium	*Desmodium heterophyllum*	Fabaceae	Cryptogenic Weed	Yes	Herb	No
125.	Lesser clover-leafed desmodium	*Desmodium triflorum*	Fabaceae	Cryptogenic Weed	No	Herb	No
126.	Common dianella	*Dianella ensifolia*	Xanthorrhoeaceae	Common	Yes	Herb	No
127.	Resam	*Dicranopteris linearis* (synonym: *Gleichenia linearis*)	Gleicheniaceae	Common	Yes	Climber	Yes
128.	Dumb cane	*Dieffenbachia seguine* (synonyms: *Dieffenbachia maculata*; *Dieffenbachia picta*)	Araceae	Casual	Yes	Herb	No
129.	Trailing crabgrass	*Digitaria radicosa*	Poaceae	Cryptogenic Weed	No	Herb	No

S/No.	Common Name	Scientific Name	Family	National Status	Cultivated	Habit	Adinandra Belukar
130.	Simpoh air	*Dillenia suffruticosa* (synonym: *Wormia suffruticosa*)	Dilleniaceae	Common	Yes	Shrub	Yes
131.	Button orchid	*Dischidia nummularia*	Apocynaceae	Common	Yes	Epiphyte	No
132.	Narrow-leafed dracaena	*Dracaena angustifolia*	Asparagaceae	Cultivated only	Yes	Shrub	No
133.	Iron plant	*Dracaena fragrans*	Asparagaceae	Casual	Yes	Shrub	No
134.	Song of India	*Dracaena reflexa*	Asparagaceae	Cultivated only	Yes	Shrub	No
135.	Oak-leafed fern	*Drynaria quercifolia*	Polypodiaceae	Common	Yes	Epiphyte	No
136.	Golden dewdrop	*Duranta erecta*	Verbenaceae	Cultivated only	Yes	Shrub	No
137.	Durian	*Durio zibethinus*	Malvaceae	Casual	Yes	Tree	No
138.	Butterfly palm	*Dypsis lutescens*	Arecaceae	Cultivated only	Yes	Shrub	No
139.	Oil palm	*Elaeis guineensis*	Arecaceae	Casual	Yes	Tree	No
140.	Blunt-leafed oil-fruit	*Elaeocarpus pedunculatus*	Elaeocarpaceae	Common	Yes	Tree	No
141.	Elephant's foot	*Elephantopus scaber*	Asteraceae	Cryptogenic Weed	Yes	Herb	No
142.	Indian goosegrass	*Eleusine indica*	Poaceae	Naturalized	No	Herb	No
143.	Akar sulur kerang	*Embelia ribes*	Primulaceae	Common	No	Climber	No
144.	Cupid's shaving brush	*Emilia sonchifolia*	Asteraceae	Cryptogenic Weed	Yes	Herb	No
145.	Money plant	*Epipremnum aureum*	Araceae	Casual	Yes	Climber	No
146.	Slender eriachne	*Eriachne pallescens*	Poaceae	Vulnerable	No	Herb	Yes
147.	Variegated coral tree	*Erythrina variegata*	Fabaceae	Cultivated only	Yes	Tree	No

S/No.	Common Name	Scientific Name	Family	National Status	Cultivated	Habit	Adinandra Belukar
148.	Ordeal tree	*Erythrophleum suaveolens* (synonym: *Erythrophleum guineense*)	Fabaceae	Cultivated only	Yes	Tree	No
149.	Blue gum	*Eucalyptus tereticornis*	Myrtaceae	Cultivated only	Yes	Tree	No
150.	Bawang hantu	*Eulophia graminea*	Orchidaceae	Cryptogenic Weed	Yes	Herb	No
151.	Grass orchid	*Eulophia spectabilis* (synonym: *Eulophia squalida*)	Orchidaceae	Critically Endangered	Yes	Herb	No
152.	Hairy spurge	*Euphorbia hirta* (synonym: *Chamaesyce hirta*)	Euphorbiaceae	Naturalized	Yes	Herb	No
153.	Thyme-leaf spurge	*Euphorbia thymifolia* (synonym: *Chamaesyce thymifolia*)	Euphorbiaceae	Cryptogenic Weed	No	Herb	No
154.	Acuminate-leafed eurya	*Eurya acuminata*	Pentaphylacaceae	Common	No	Shrub	No
155.	Chinese croton	*Excoecaria cochinchinensis*	Euphorbiaceae	Cultivated only	Yes	Shrub	No
156.	Batai, albizia	*Falcataria moluccana* (synonyms: *Albizia falcataria*; *Paraserianthes falcataria*)	Fabaceae	Naturalized	Yes	Tree	No
157.	Akar kunyit	*Fibraurea tinctoria*	Menispermaceae	Common	Yes	Climber	No
158.	Yellow hairy fig	*Ficus aurata* var. *aurata*	Moraceae	Vulnerable	No	Tree	No
159.	Benjamin fig	*Ficus benjamina*	Moraceae	Cryptogenic Weed	Yes	Strangler	No
160.		*Ficus caulocarpa*	Moraceae	Critically Endangered	No	Strangler	No

S/No.	Common Name	Scientific Name	Family	National Status	Cultivated	Habit	Adinandra Belukar
161.	Indian rubber tree	*Ficus elastica*	Moraceae	Casual	Yes	Strangler	No
162.	Common yellow-stemmed fig	*Ficus fistulosa*	Moraceae	Common	Yes	Tree	No
163.	White-leafed fig	*Ficus grossularioides* var. *grossularioides* (synonym: *Ficus alba*)	Moraceae	Common	Yes	Tree	No
164.	Sandy leafed fig	*Ficus heterophylla*	Moraceae	Common	Yes	Climber	No
165.	Hairy fig	*Ficus hispida*	Moraceae	Naturalized	No	Tree	No
166.	Malayan banyan	*Ficus microcarpa*	Moraceae	Common	Yes	Strangler	No
167.	Creeping fig	*Ficus pumila*	Moraceae	Casual	Yes	Climber	No
168.	Climbing fig	*Ficus punctata* (synonym: *Ficus aurantiaca*)	Moraceae	Common	Yes	Climber	No
169.	Bodhi tree	*Ficus religiosa*	Moraceae	Naturalized	Yes	Strangler	No
170.	Ara jejawi	*Ficus retusa*	Moraceae	Critically Endangered	Yes	Tree	No
171.	Red stem fig	*Ficus variegata*	Moraceae	Common	No	Tree	No
172.		*Ficus vasculosa*	Moraceae	Endangered	Yes	Tree	No
173.	Grey fig	*Ficus virens*	Moraceae	Critically Endangered	Yes	Strangler	No
174.	Fern-leaf tree	*Filicium decipiens*	Sapindaceae	Cultivated only	Yes	Tree	No
175.	Pointed fimbristylis	*Fimbristylis acuminata*	Cyperaceae	Cryptogenic Weed	No	Herb	No
176.	Bracteate flemingia	*Flemingia strobilifera*	Fabaceae	Cryptogenic Weed	Yes	Shrub	No
177.	Saw-sedge	*Gahnia tristis*	Cyperaceae	Common	No	Herb	Yes
178.	Mangosteen	*Garcinia mangostana*	Clusiaceae	Casual	Yes	Tree	No

S/No.	Common Name	Scientific Name	Family	National Status	Cultivated	Habit	Adinandra Belukar
179.	Happiness tree	*Garcinia subelliptica*	Clusiaceae	Cultivated only	Yes	Tree	No
180.	Gardenia	*Gardenia jasminoides*	Rubiaceae	Cultivated only	Yes	Shrub	No
181.	Mexican lilac	*Gliricidia sepium*	Fabaceae	Casual	Yes	Tree	No
182.	Great-leafed pin-flower tree	*Glochidion superbum*	Phyllanthaceae	Common	Yes	Tree	No
183.	Soyabean	*Glycine max*	Fabaceae	Cultivated only	Yes	Herb	No
184.	Belinjau	*Gnetum gnemon*	Gnetaceae	Critically Endangered	Yes	Tree	No
185.	Caricature plant	*Graptophyllum pictum*	Acanthaceae	Cultivated only	Yes	Shrub	No
186.	Red silky oak	*Grevillea banskii*	Proteaceae	Cultivated only	Yes	Shrub	No
187.	Membrillo	*Gustavia superba*	Lecythidaceae	Cultivated only	Yes	Tree	No
188.	Bornean ru	*Gymnostoma nobile* (synonym: *Casuarina nobilis*)	Casuarinaceae	Cultivated only	Yes	Tree	No
189.	Akar lampai hitam	*Gynochthodes sublanceolata*	Rubiaceae	Common	No	Climber	Yes
190.	Fish eyes	*Gynotroches axillaris*	Rhizophoraceae	Common	Yes	Tree	No
191.	Firecracker bush	*Hamelia patens*	Rubiaceae	Cultivated only	Yes	Shrub	No
192.	Pine-leafed hedyotis	*Hedyotis pinifolia*	Rubiaceae	Vulnerable	No	Herb	No
193.	Parrot's flower	*Heliconia psittacorum*	Heliconiaceae	Casual	Yes	Herb	No
194.	Red flame	*Hemigraphis reptans* (synonym: *Hemigraphis primulifolia*)	Acanthaceae	Naturalized	Yes	Herb	No

S/No.	Common Name	Scientific Name	Family	National Status	Cultivated	Habit	Adinandra Belukar
195.	Rubber	*Hevea brasiliensis*	Euphorbiaceae	Naturalized	Yes	Tree	No
196.	Hibiscus	*Hibiscus rosa-sinensis*	Malvaceae	Casual	Yes	Shrub	No
197.	Star of Bethlehem	*Hippobroma longiflora* (synonyms: *Isotoma longiflora*; *Laurentia longiflora*)	Campanulaceae	Naturalized	Yes	Herb	No
198.		*Hopea odorata*	Dipterocarpaceae	Cultivated only	Yes	Tree	No
199.	Spider lily	*Hymenocallis speciosa*	Amaryllidaceae	Cultivated only	Yes	Herb	No
200.	Knobweed	*Hyptis capitata*	Lamiaceae	Naturalized	No	Herb	No
201.	Marsh holly	*Ilex cymosa*	Aquifoliaceae	Common	Yes	Tree	No
202.	Lalang	*Imperata cylindrica*	Poaceae	Cryptogenic Weed	Yes	Herb	No
203.	Kang kong	*Ipomoea aquatica*	Convolvulaceae	Cryptogenic Weed	Yes	Climber	No
204.	Sweet potato	*Ipomoea batatas*	Convolvulaceae	Casual	Yes	Climber	No
205.	Morning glory	*Ipomoea cairica*	Convolvulaceae	Naturalized	Yes	Climber	No
206.	Leopard lily	*Iris domestica* (synonym: *Belamcanda chinensis*)	Iridaceae	Cultivated only	Yes	Herb	No
207.	Centipede grass	*Ischaemum muticum*	Poaceae	Common	Yes	Herb	No
208.	10 men tree	*Ixonanthes reticulata*	Ixonanthaceae	Common	Yes	Tree	No
209.	Javanese ixora	*Ixora javanica*	Rubiaceae	Cultivated only	Yes	Shrub	No
210.	Jacaranda	*Jacaranda obtusifolia*	Bignoniaceae	Naturalized	Yes	Tree	No
211.	Arabian jasmine	*Jasminum sambac*	Oleaceae	Cultivated only	Yes	Climber	No

S/No.	Common Name	Scientific Name	Family	National Status	Cultivated	Habit	Adinandra Belukar
212.	African mahogany	*Khaya grandifoliola*	Meliaceae	Cultivated only	Yes	Tree	No
213.	Senegal mahogany	*Khaya senegalensis*	Meliaceae	Cultivated only	Yes	Tree	No
214.	White kyllinga	*Kyllinga nemoralis*	Cyperaceae	Cryptogenic Weed	No	Herb	No
215.	Navua sedge	*Kyllinga polyphylla* (synonym: *Cyperus aromaticus*)	Cyperaceae	Naturalized	No	Herb	No
216.	Crepe myrtle	*Lagerstroemia indica*	Lythraceae	Cultivated only	Yes	Shrub	No
217.	Rose of India	*Lagerstroemia speciosa*	Lythraceae	Cultivated only	Yes	Tree	No
218.	Indian ash tree	*Lannea coromandelica*	Anacardiaceae	Cultivated only	Yes	Tree	No
219.	Lantana	*Lantana camara*	Verbenaceae	Naturalized	Yes	Shrub	No
220.	Malayan eyebright	*Legazpia polygonoides* (synonym: *Torenia polygonoides*)	Linderniaceae	Cryptogenic Weed	Yes	Herb	No
221.	Shiny leafed licania	*Licania splendens*	Chrysobalanaceae	Common	Yes	Tree	No
222.	Grosse licuala palm	*Licuala grandis*	Arecaceae	Cultivated only	Yes	Tree	No
223.	Malaysian false pimpernel	*Lindernia crustacea*	Linderniaceae	Cryptogenic Weed	No	Herb	No
224.	Japanese honeysuckle	*Lonicera japonica*	Caprifoliaceae	Cultivated only	Yes	Climber	No
225.	Chinese fringe flower	*Loropetalum chinense*	Hamamelidaceae	Cultivated only	Yes	Shrub	No
226.	Scrambling clubmoss	*Lycopodiella cernua*	Lycopodiaceae	Common	No	Herb	Yes
227.	Climbing fern	*Lygodium circinnatum*	Schizaeaceae	Vulnerable	No	Climber	No

S/No.	Common Name	Scientific Name	Family	National Status	Cultivated	Habit	Adinandra Belukar
228.	Climbing fern	*Lygodium flexuosum*	Schizaeaceae	Common	No	Climber	No
229.	Small-leafed climbing fern	*Lygodium microphyllum*	Schizaeaceae	Common	No	Climber	No
230.	Poplar mahang	*Macaranga conifera*	Euphorbiaceae	Common	No	Tree	No
231.	Blue mahang	*Macaranga heynei* (synonym: *Macaranga javanica*)	Euphorbiaceae	Common	No	Tree	No
232.	White mahang	*Macaranga hypoleuca*	Euphorbiaceae	Common	No	Tree	No
233.	Parasol leaf tree	*Macaranga tanarius*	Euphorbiaceae	Cultivated only	Yes	Tree	No
234.	Three-lobed mahang	*Macaranga triloba*	Euphorbiaceae	Common	Yes	Tree	No
235.	Common Chinese mistletoe	*Macrosolen cochinchinensis*	Loranthaceae	Common	No	Epiphyte	No
236.	Pink-flowered mistletoe	*Macrosolen retusus*	Loranthaceae	Common	No	Epiphyte	No
237.		*Maesa ramentacea*	Primulaceae	Common	No	Shrub	No
238.	Turn-in-the-wind	*Mallotus paniculatus*	Euphorbiaceae	Common	Yes	Tree	No
239.	Mango	*Mangifera indica*	Anacardiaceae	Casual	Yes	Tree	No
240.	Ceara rubber tree	*Manihot carthagenesis* ssp. *glaziovii* (synonym: *Manihot glaziovii*)	Euphorbiaceae	Naturalized	Yes	Tree	No
241.	Tapioca	*Manihot esculenta*	Euphorbiaceae	Naturalized	Yes	Shrub	No
242.	Sea beam	*Maranthes corymbosa*	Chrysobalanaceae	Endangered	Yes	Tree	No
243.	Glam	*Melaleuca cajuputi*	Myrtaceae	Extinct	Yes	Tree	No
244.	Sea daisy	*Melanthera biflora* (synonym: *Wedelia biflora*; *Wollostonia biflora*)	Asteraceae	Common	Yes	Shrub	No

S/No.	Common Name	Scientific Name	Family	National Status	Cultivated	Habit	Adinandra Belukar
245.	Senduduk	*Melastoma malabathricum*	Melastomataceae	Common	Yes	Shrub	No
246.	Akar keremak	*Merremia tridentata* (synonym: *Xenostegia tridentata*)	Convolvulaceae	Common	No	Climber	No
247.		*Mesophlebion chylamydophorum*	Thelypteridaceae	Vulnerable	No	Herb	No
248.	Mile-a-minute	*Mikania cordata*	Asteraceae	Cryptogenic Weed	No	Herb	No
249.	Mile-a-minute	*Mikania micrantha*	Asteraceae	Naturalized	Yes	Climber	No
250.	Giant false sensitive plant	*Mimosa diplotricha* (synonym: *Mimosa invisa*)	Fabaceae	Naturalized	Yes	Shrub	No
251.	Giant sensitive plant	*Mimosa pigra*	Fabaceae	Naturalized	No	Shrub	No
252.	Touch-me-not	*Mimosa pudica*	Fabaceae	Naturalized	Yes	Shrub	No
253.	Bunga tanjong	*Mimusops elengi*	Sapotaceae	Casual	Yes	Tree	No
254.	Hill coconut	*Molineria latifolia* var. *latifolia* (synonyms: *Curculigo latifolia*; *Curculigo villosa*)	Hypoxidaceae	Vulnerable	Yes	Herb	No
255.	Malay gale	*Morella esculenta* (synonym: *Myrica esculenta*)	Myricaceae	Common	Yes	Tree	Yes
256.	Great morinda	*Morinda citrifolia*	Rubiaceae	Cryptogenic Weed	Yes	Tree	No
257.	Mengkudu akar	*Morinda umbellata*	Rubiaceae	Common	Yes	Climber	No
258.	Jamaican cherry	*Muntingia calabura*	Muntingiaceae	Naturalized	Yes	Tree	No
259.	Curry leaf	*Murraya koenigii*	Rutaceae	Casual	Yes	Shrub	No
260.	Mock orange	*Murraya paniculata*	Rutaceae	Cultivated only	Yes	Shrub	No

S/No.	Common Name	Scientific Name	Family	National Status	Cultivated	Habit	Adinandra Belukar
261.	Lotus	*Nelumbo nucifera*	Nelumbonaceae	Cultivated only	Yes	Herb	No
262.	Narrow-lidded pitcher plant	*Nepenthes ampullaria*	Nepenthaceae	Vulnerable	No	Climber	Yes
263.	Slender pitcher plant	*Nepenthes gracilis*	Nepenthaceae	Common	Yes	Climber	Yes
264.	Raffles' pitcher plant	*Nepenthes rafflesiana*	Nepenthaceae	Vulnerable	Yes	Climber	Yes
265.	Rambutan	*Nephelium lappaceum*	Sapindaceae	Critically Endangered	Yes	Tree	No
266.	Sword fern	*Nephrolepis biserrata*	Oleandraceae	Cryptogenic Weed	Yes	Herb	No
267.	Oleander	*Nerium oleander*	Apocynaceae	Cultivated only	Yes	Shrub	No
268.	Mickey Mouse plant	*Ochna kirkii*	Ochnaceae	Cultivated only	Yes	Shrub	No
269.	Basil	*Ocimum basilicum*	Lamiaceae	Cryptogenic Weed	Yes	Herb	No
270.		*Oldenlandia affinis* ssp. *affinis* (synonym: *Hedyotis dichotoma*)	Rubiaceae	Vulnerable	No	Herb	No
271.	Two-flower oldenlandia	*Oldenlandia corymbosa* (synonym: *Hedyotis corymbosa*)	Rubiaceae	Naturalized	Yes	Herb	No
272.	Snake-needle grass	*Oldenlandia diffusa* (synonym: *Hedyotis brachypoda*)	Rubiaceae	Cryptogenic weed	Yes	Herb	No
273.		*Oldenlandia tenelliflora*	Rubiaceae	Cryptogenic Weed	No	Herb	No
274.	Adder's tongue fern	*Ophioglossum reticulatum*	Ophioglossaceae	Common	No	Herb	No
275.	Mondo-grass	*Ophiopogon jaburan*	Liliaceae	Cultivated only	Yes	Herb	No

S/No.	Common Name	Scientific Name	Family	National Status	Cultivated	Habit	Adinandra Belukar
276.		*Osmoxylon lineare*	Araliaceae	Cultivated only	Yes	Shrub	No
277.	Lavender sorrel	*Oxalis barrelieri*	Oxalidaceae	Naturalized	Yes	Herb	No
278.	Akar berdara laut	*Oxyceros longiflorus* (synonym: *Randia longiflora*)	Rubiaceae	Vulnerable	No	Climber	No
279.	Akar sekentut	*Paederia foetida* (synonym: *Paederia scandens*)	Rubiaceae	Common	Yes	Climber	No
280.	White gutta	*Palaquium obovatum*	Sapotaceae	Vulnerable	Yes	Tree	No
281.	Dwarf screw pine	*Pandanus pygmaeus*	Pandanaceae	Cultivated only	Yes	Shrub	No
282.	Screw pine	*Pandanus tectorius*	Pandanaceae	Common	Yes	Shrub	No
283.	Guinea grass	*Panicum maximum* (synonym: *Megathyrsus maximus*)	Poaceae	Naturalized	No	Herb	No
284.	Buffalo grass	*Paspalum conjugatum*	Poaceae	Naturalized	No	Herb	No
285.	Kodomillet	*Paspalum scrobiculatum* var. *biscuspidatum*	Poaceae	Cryptogenic Weed	No	Herb	No
286.		*Passiflora cochinchinensis*	Passifloraceae	Cultivated only	Yes	Climber	No
287.	Love-in-a-mist	*Passiflora foetida*	Passifloraceae	Naturalized	Yes	Climber	No
288.	Golden bell apple	*Passiflora laurifolia*	Passifloraceae	Naturalized	Yes	Climber	No
289.	Giant granadilla	*Passiflora quadrangularis*	Passifloraceae	Cultivated only	Yes	Climber	No
290.	Corkystem passionflower	*Passiflora suberosa*	Passifloraceae	Naturalized	Yes	Climber	No
291.	Yellow flame	*Peltophorum pterocarpum*	Fabaceae	Critically Endangered	Yes	Tree	No

S/No.	Common Name	Scientific Name	Family	National Status	Cultivated	Habit	Adinandra Belukar
292.		*Peperomia microphylla*	Piperaceae	Cultivated only	Yes	Herb	No
293.	Shiny bush	*Peperomia pellucida*	Piperaceae	Naturalized	No	Herb	No
294.	Split-leaf philodendron	*Philodendron bipinnatifidum* (synonym: *Philodendron selloum*)	Araceae	Cultivated only	Yes	Climber	No
295.	Heart-leaf philodendron	*Philodendron hederaceum*	Araceae	Casual	Yes	Herb	No
296.	Miniature date palm	*Phoenix roebelenii*	Arecaceae	Cultivated only	Yes	Tree	No
297.	Child pick-a-back	*Phyllanthus amarus*	Phyllanthaceae	Naturalized	No	Herb	No
298.	Niruri	*Phyllanthus debilis*	Phyllanthaceae	Naturalized	No	Herb	No
299.	Ceylon myrtle	*Phyllanthus myrtifolius*	Phyllanthaceae	Cultivated only	Yes	Shrub	No
300.	Shatterstone	*Phyllanthus urinaria*	Phyllanthaceae	Naturalized	Yes	Herb	No
301.	Bladder cherry	*Physalis minima*	Solanaceae	Cryptogenic Weed	Yes	Herb	No
302.	Artillery plant	*Pilea microphylla*	Urticaceae	Naturalized	Yes	Climber	No
303.		*Pinanga polymorpha*	Arecaceae	Cultivated only	Yes	Shrub	No
304.	Betel pepper	*Piper betle*	Piperaceae	Casual	Yes	Climber	No
305.	Wild pepper	*Piper sarmentosum*	Piperaceae	Common	Yes	Climber	No
306.	Lettuce tree	*Pisonia grandis*	Nyctaginaceae	Cultivated only	Yes	Tree	No
307.	Madras thorn	*Pithecellobium dulce*	Fabaceae	Casual	Yes	Tree	No
308.	Jiring	*Pithecellobium jiringa* (synonym: *Archidendron jiringa*)	Fabaceae	Vulnerable	Yes	Tree	No
309.	Silverback fern	*Pityrogramma calomelanos*	Adiantaceae	Naturalized	No	Herb	No

S/No.	Common Name	Scientific Name	Family	National Status	Cultivated	Habit	Adinandra Belukar
310.	Common plantain	*Plantago major*	Plantaginaceae	Naturalized	Yes	Herb	No
311.	Staghorn fern	*Platycerium coronarium*	Polypodiaceae	Common	Yes	Epiphyte	No
312.	Oriental tree of life	*Platycladus orientalis* (synonym: *Thuja orientalis*)	Cupressaceae	Cultivated only	Yes	Tree	No
313.	Mexican mint	*Plectranthus amboinicus*	Lamiaceae	Cultivated only	Yes	Herb	No
314.	Cicada tree	*Ploiarium alternifolium* (synonym: *Archytaea vahlii*)	Bonnetiaceae	Common	Yes	Shrub	Yes
315.	Great white frangipani	*Plumeria obtusa*	Apocynaceae	Cultivated only	Yes	Tree	No
316.	Nosegay frangipani	*Plumeria rubra* (synonym: *Plumeria acuminata*)	Apocynaceae	Cultivated only	Yes	Tree	No
317.	Indian mast tree	*Polyalthia longifolia* var. *pendula*	Annonaceae	Cultivated only	Yes	Tree	No
318.	Seashore mempari	*Pongamia pinnata*	Fabaceae	Endangered	Yes	Tree	No
319.	Papalo	*Porophyllum ruderale*	Asteraceae	Naturalized	No	Herb	No
320.	Moss rose	*Portulaca grandiflora*	Portulacaceae	Cultivated only	Yes	Herb	No
321.	Purslane	*Portulaca oleracea*	Portulacaceae	Naturalized	Yes	Herb	No
322.	Buas buas	*Premna serratifolia*	Lamiaceae	Vulnerable	No	Climber	No
323.	Bat's laurel	*Prunus polystachya* (synonym: *Pygeum polystachyum*)	Rosaceae	Common	Yes	Tree	No
324.	Yellow-veined eranthemum	*Psederanthemum carruthersii* (synonym: *Pseuderanthemum reticulatum*)	Acanthaceae	Cultivated only	Yes	Shrub	No

S/No.	Common Name	Scientific Name	Family	National Status	Cultivated	Habit	Adinandra Belukar
325.	Guava	*Psidium guajava*	Myrtaceae	Casual	Yes	Shrub	No
326.	Sword brake fern	*Pteris ensiformis*	Pteridaceae	Cryptogenic Weed	Yes	Herb	No
327.	Chinese brake fern	*Pteris vittata*	Pteridaceae	Cryptogenic Weed	No	Herb	No
328.	Angsana	*Pterocarpus indicus*	Fabaceae	Casual	Yes	Tree	No
329.	MacArthur's palm	*Ptychosperma macarthurii*	Arecaceae	Naturalized	Yes	Tree	No
330.	Suloi	*Pyrrosia longifolia*	Polypodiaceae	Common	No	Epiphyte	No
331.	Dragon scales	*Pyrrosia piloselloides*	Polypodiaceae	Common	No	Epiphyte	No
332.	Bitterwood	*Quassia amara*	Simaroubaceae	Cultivated only	Yes	Shrub	No
333.	Rangoon creeper	*Quisqualis indica*	Combretaceae	Casual	Yes	Climber	No
334.	Traveller's palm	*Ravenala madagascariensis*	Strelitziaceae	Cultivated only	Yes	Tree	No
335.	Lady palm	*Rhapis excelsa*	Arecaceae	Cultivated only	Yes	Shrub	No
336.	Silverback	*Rhodamnia cinerea* (synonym: *Rhodamnia trinervia*)	Myrtaceae	Common	Yes	Tree	Yes
337.	Rose myrtle	*Rhodomyrtus tomentosa*	Myrtaceae	Common	Yes	Shrub	Yes
338.	Castor oil plant	*Ricinus communis*	Euphorbiaceae	Naturalized	Yes	Shrub	No
339.	Variable-leaf yellowcress	*Rorippa dubia* (synonym: *Rorippa heterophylla*)	Brassicaceae	Naturalized	No	Herb	No
340.	Cabbage palm	*Roystonea oleracea*	Arecaceae	Cultivated only	Yes	Tree	No
341.	Malayan bramble	*Rubus moluccanus* var. *angulosus*	Rosaceae	Critically Endangered	Yes	Climber	No
342.	Creeping ruellia	*Ruellia repens*	Acanthaceae	Cryptogenic Weed	No	Herb	No

S/No.	Common Name	Scientific Name	Family	National Status	Cultivated	Habit	Adinandra Belukar
343.		*Ruspolia pseuderanthemoides*	Acanthaceae	Cultivated only	Yes	Shrub	No
344.	Sugar cane	*Saccharum officinarum*	Poaceae	Casual	Yes	Herb	No
345.	Common salomonia	*Salomonia cantoniensis*	Polygalaceae	Cryptogenic Weed	Yes	Herb	No
346.	Footstool palm	*Saribus rotundifolius* (synonym: *Livistona rotundifolia*)	Arecaceae	Cultivated only	Yes	Tree	No
347.	Cekur manis	*Sauropus androgynous*	Euphorbiaceae	Common	Yes	Shrub	No
348.	Umbrella tree	*Schefflera actinophylla*	Araliaceae	Casual	Yes	Tree	No
349.	Umbrella shrub	*Schefflera arboricola*	Araliaceae	Cultivated only	Yes	Shrub	No
350.	Sialit dudok	*Scleria levis*	Cyperaceae	Cryptogenic Weed	No	Herb	No
351.	Witch's broom	*Scoparia dulcis*	Scrophulariaceae	Naturalized	No	Herb	No
352.	Rusty leafed mistletoe	*Scurrula ferruginea* (synonym: *Loranthus ferrugineus*)	Loranthaceae	Common	No	Shrub	No
353.	Seven golden candlesticks	*Senna alata* (synonym: *Cassia alata*)	Fabaceae	Naturalized	Yes	Tree	No
354.	Woolly senna	*Senna hirsuta* (synonym: *Cassia hirsuta*)	Fabaceae	Naturalized	No	Epiphyte	No
355.	Arsenic bean	*Senna occidentalis* (synonym: *Cassia occidentalis*)	Fabaceae	Naturalized	No	Shrub	No
356.	Spectacular cassia	*Senna spectabilis* (synonym: *Cassia spectabilis*)	Fabaceae	Casual	Yes	Tree	No
357.	Golden senna	*Senna surattensis*	Fabaceae	Casual	Yes	Shrub	No

S/No.	Common Name	Scientific Name	Family	National Status	Cultivated	Habit	Adinandra Belukar
358.	Cuban jute	*Sida rhombifolia*	Malvaceae	Cryptogenic Weed	No	Shrub	No
359.	Bearded smilax	*Smilax setosa* (synonym: *Smilax bracteata* var. *barbata*)	Smilacaceae	Common	No	Climber	No
360.	Turkey berry	*Solanum torvum*	Solanaceae	Naturalized	Yes	Shrub	No
361.	African tulip tree	*Spathodea campanulata*	Bignoniaceae	Naturalized	Yes	Tree	No
362.	Pacific false buttonweed	*Spermacoce exilis* (synonym: *Borreria exilis*)	Rubiaceae	Cryptogenic Weed	No	Herb	No
363.	Smooth buttonweed	*Spermacoce laevis* (synonym: *Borreria laevis*)	Rubiaceae	Naturalized	No	Herb	No
364.	Oval-leaf false buttonweed	*Spermacoce latifolia* (synonym: *Borreria alata*)	Rubiaceae	Naturalized	No	Herb	No
365.	Basil-like buttonweed	*Spermacoce ocymoides* (synonym: *Borreria ocymoides*)	Rubiaceae	Naturalized	No	Herb	No
366.	Toothed buttonweed	*Spermacoce setidens* (synonym: *Borreria setidens*)	Rubiaceae	Naturalized	No	Herb	No
367.	Singapore daisy	*Sphagneticola trilobata* (synonym: *Wedelia trilobata*)	Asteraceae	Naturalized	Yes	Herb	No
368.	Smut grass	*Sporobolus indicus*	Poaceae	Common	No	Herb	No
369.	Indian snakeweed	*Stachytarpheta indica*	Verbenaceae	Naturalized	Yes	Herb	No
370.	Jamaican snakeweed	*Stachytarpheta jamaicensis*	Verbenaceae	Naturalized	No	Herb	No
371.	Paku ranu	*Stenochlaena palustris*	Blechnaceae	Common	No	Climber	No

S/No.	Common Name	Scientific Name	Family	National Status	Cultivated	Habit	Adinandra Belukar
372.	Asiatic witchweed	*Striga asiatica*	Orobanchaceae	Cryptogenic Weed	No	Herb	No
373.	False lime	*Suregada multiflora*	Euphorbiaceae	Critically Endangered	Yes	Tree	No
374.	Broad-leafed mahogany	*Swietenia macrophylla*	Meliaceae	Casual	Yes	Tree	No
375.	Cinderella weed	*Synedrella nodiflora*	Asteraceae	Naturalized	No	Herb	No
376.	Arrowhead vine	*Syngonium podophyllum*	Araceae	Naturalized	Yes	Climber	No
377.	Java plum	*Syzygium cumini* (synonym: *Eugenia cumini*)	Myrtaceae	Naturalized	Yes	Tree	No
378.	Sea apple	*Syzygium grande* (synonym: *Eugenia grandis*)	Myrtaceae	Common	Yes	Tree	No
379.	Rose apple	*Syzygium jambos* (synonym: *Eugenia jambos*)	Myrtaceae	Casual	Yes	Tree	No
380.	Common kelat	*Syzygium lineatum* (synonym: *Eugenia lineata*)	Myrtaceae	Common	Yes	Tree	No
381.	Jambu bol	*Syzygium malaccense* (synonym: *Eugenia malaccensis*)	Myrtaceae	Casual	Yes	Tree	No
382.	Red lip	*Syzygium myrtifolium* (synonym: *Syzygium campanulatum*)	Myrtaceae	Extinct	Yes	Tree	No
383.	Salam	*Syzygium polyanthum* (synonym: *Eugenia polyantha*)	Myrtaceae	Vulnerable	Yes	Tree	No

S/No.	Common Name	Scientific Name	Family	National Status	Cultivated	Habit	Adinandra Belukar
384.	Kelat nasi nasi	*Syzygium zeylanicum* (synonyms: *Eugenia spicata; Eugenia zeylanica*)	Myrtaceae	Common	Yes	Shrub	No
385.	Cuban pink trumpet tree	*Tabebuia pallida*	Bignoniaceae	Cultivated only	Yes	Tree	No
386.	Trumpet tree	*Tabebuia rosea*	Bignoniaceae	Casual	Yes	Tree	No
387.	Great nosegay	*Tabernaemontana corymbosa*	Apocynaceae	Endangered	Yes	Shrub	No
388.		*Taenitis blechnoides*	Pteridaceae	Common	Yes	Climber	No
389.	Tamarind	*Tamarindus indica*	Fabaceae	Casual	Yes	Tree	No
390.	Cape honeysuckle	*Tecoma capensis* (synonym: *Tecomaria capensis*)	Bignoniaceae	Cultivated only	Yes	Shrub	No
391.	Yellow bells	*Tecoma stans*	Bignoniaceae	Cultivated only	Yes	Shrub	No
392.	Sea almond	*Terminalia catappa*	Combretaceae	Common	Yes	Tree	No
393.	Hedge row tetracera	*Tetracera indica*	Dilleniaceae	Common	Yes	Climber	No
394.	Miracle berry	*Thaumatococcus danielli*	Marantaceae	Casual	Yes	Herb	No
395.	Black-eyed Susan	*Thunbergia alata*	Acanthaceae	Naturalized	Yes	Climber	No
396.	Fragrant thunbergia	*Thunbergia fragrans*	Acanthaceae	Naturalized	Yes	Climber	No
397.	Blue skyflower	*Thunbergia grandiflora*	Acanthaceae	Casual	Yes	Climber	No
398.	Laurel-leafed thunbergia	*Thunbergia laurifolia*	Acanthaceae	Critically Endangered	Yes	Climber	No
399.	Liane-quinine	*Tinospora crispa*	Menispermaceae	Casual	Yes	Climber	No
400.	Purple heart	*Tradescantia pallida*	Commelinaceae	Cultivated only	Yes	Herb	No

S/No.	Common Name	Scientific Name	Family	National Status	Cultivated	Habit	Adinandra Belukar
401.	Moses-in-the-cradle	*Tradescantia spathacea* (synonym: *Rhoeo spathacea*)	Commelinaceae	Casual	Yes	Herb	No
402.	Lesser trema	*Trema cannabina*	Cannabaceae	Common	No	Shrub	No
403.	Greater trema	*Trema tomentosa* (synonym: *Trema orientalis*)	Cannabaceae	Common	No	Shrub	No
404.	Mousedeer's delight	*Triadica cochinchinensis* (synonym: *Sapium discolor*)	Euphorbiaceae	Common	Yes	Tree	No
405.	Coat buttons	*Tridax procumbens*	Asteraceae	Naturalized	Yes	Herb	No
406.	Forenoon yellow flag	*Trimezia martinicensis*	Iridaceae	Naturalized	Yes	Herb	No
407.	Maiden's jealousy	*Tristellateia australasiae*	Malpighiaceae	Endangered	Yes	Climber	No
408.	Orange turnera	*Turnera aurantiaca*	Passifloraceae	Cultivated only	Yes	Herb	No
409.	West Indian holly	*Turnera ulmifolia*	Passifloraceae	Naturalized	Yes	Herb	No
410.	Threelobed typhonium	*Typhonium trilobatum*	Araceae	Naturalized	No	Herb	No
411.	Congo jute	*Urena lobata*	Malvaceae	Cryptogenic Weed	No	Shrub	No
412.	Jointed mistletoe	*Viscum articulatum*	Santalaceae	Common	No	Epiphyte	No
413.	Oval-leafed mistletoe	*Viscum ovalifolium*	Santalaceae	Common	No	Epiphyte	No
414.	Five-leafed chaste tree	*Vitex negundo*	Lamiaceae	Critically Endangered	Yes	Shrub	No
415.	Malayan teak	*Vitex pinnata* (synonym: *Vitex pubescens*)	Lamiaceae	Common	Yes	Tree	No
416.	Shoestring fern	*Vittaria ensiformis*	Pteridaceae	Common	No	Epiphyte	No

S/No.	Common Name	Scientific Name	Family	National Status	Cultivated	Habit	Adinandra Belukar
417.	Seashore tubeflower	*Volkameria inerme* (synonym: *Clerodendrum inerme*)	Lamiaceae	Common	Yes	Climber	No
418.	Water jasmine	*Wrightia religiosa*	Apocynaceae	Casual	Yes	Shrub	No
419.	Oriental false hawksbeard	*Youngia japonica*	Asteraceae	Naturalized	No	Herb	No
420.	Manila grass	*Zoysia matrella*	Poaceae	Common	Yes	Herb	No

Table 3.2: National Status Categories of the Vascular Plants of Kent Ridge

The definition of each category is provided in the caption for Table 3.1.

S/No.	National Status Category	No. of Species	Remarks
1.	Native species	142	The native species include those that are spontaneous and/or cultivated.
1a.	Presumed Nationally Extinct	3	The three species—*Cyrtostachys renda*, *Melaleuca cajuputi* and *Syzygium myrtifolium*—are extinct in the wild in Singapore and those cultivated in Kent Ridge are from non-local provenance.
1b.	Critically Endangered	15	Of the 15 species, only *Acriopsis lillifolia*, *Eulophia spectabilis*, *Ficus caulocarpa*, *Ficus virens* and *Rubus moluccanus* var. *angulosus* grow as wild plants. The rest are cultivated in Kent Ridge from plants of non-local provenance.
1c.	Endangered	9	Of the nine species, only *Archidendron microcarpum*, *Croton oblongus*, *Ficus vasculosa* and *Maranthes corymbosa* occur as wild plants. The remainder are cultivated in Kent Ridge from plants of non-local provenance.
1d.	Vulnerable	17	Of the 17 species, all are represented by wild plants except for *Cerbera odollam*, *Premna serratifolia* and *Syzygium polyanthum*, which are cultivated from plants of non-local provenance. *Molineria latifolia* and *Palaquium obovatum* consist of wild and cultivated specimens, the latter from plants of non-local provenance.

S/No.	National Status Category	No. of Species	Remarks
1e.	Common	98	Common species are found in many parts of Singapore. Most grow wild.
2.	Exotic species	237	The exotic species include those that are cultivated and/or spontaneous. This list is not exhaustive, and species are removed and replaced constantly by landscaping contractors or home gardeners where they are cultivated.
2a.	Cultivated only	92	Cultivated-only species are those that grow best with human maintenance and have not yet demonstrated that they can grow outside cultivation.
2b.	Casual	64	Casual species are cultivated species that have only spread close to where they have been cultivated.
2c.	Naturalized	81	Many naturalized species were previously introduced deliberately for cultivation or accidentally, then have run wild.
3.	Cryptogenic weed species	41	Cryptogenic weeds are weeds of cultivated areas and grow best in open areas that were largely absent in primeval Singapore where most of the country was under the canopy of dense forest.
	TOTAL	420	

Animals

In primeval Singapore, as mentioned, the primary forest that occurred in Kent Ridge would have consisted mostly of lowland evergreen rainforest. In particular, it would have included Coastal Hill Dipterocarp Forest that would be similar to the primary forest patches found in the Bukit Timah Nature Reserve, some freshwater swamp forest along the Sungei Ayer Rajah, and Sungei Nipah whose downstream portions in turn would have transitioned into mangrove forest as they reached the sea. The southern reaches of the ridge would also have had sandy beach vegetation. The animals then would have been likely to be what would be observed in similar forest types currently in Peninsular Malaysia, which is at the least only about 700 metres from the shores of Singapore Island across the Johor Strait. These would include the now extinct tiger[53] (*Panthera tigris*) and leopard (*Panthera pardus*; now extinct but with unverified sightings on Pulau Tekong in the 1990s[54]) and their prey such as the still extant wild pig[55] (*Sus scrofa*), red barking deer (*Muntiacus muntjak*) and sambar deer (*Rusa unicolor*)—the latter two were extinct at one time, but now wild specimens are likely escapees from captivity.[56]

Tigers were apparently very common here as there were tiger incidents reported in the Pasir Panjang area in the newspapers between 1845 and 1910.[57] Other animals would have included those extant today such as bats, birds of prey, two kinds of civet (*Arctogalidia trivirgata* and *Paradoxurus hermaphroditus*), frogs, the leopard cat (*Prionailurus bengalensis*), lizards, snakes including the reticulated python (*Malayopython reticulatus*; the largest snake in present-day Singapore) and the water monitor (*Varanus salvator*), and numerous invertebrates, especially ants, beetles and spiders.[58] Malayan porcupines (*Hystrix brachyura*) were also likely present as they were regarded as pests that attacked cultivated rubber trees before 1917.[59]

Present-day Kent Ridge is an urban matrix of secondary forest (mainly adinandra belukar and waste-woodland forest), parks, residential housing, buildings of various institutions and a university campus, and is a mixture of wild, semi-wild and managed vegetation. The animals seen here too are those associated with such habitats. However, although there are several groups of animals that occur in Kent Ridge, data that are available include those listed as follows:

1. Invertebrates: insects (butterflies and moths; crickets, grasshoppers and katydids; dragonflies and damselflies), spiders, millipedes and molluscs
2. Vertebrates: Amphibians and reptiles, birds, fish and mammals

Butterflies

The list of butterflies of Kent Ridge in Table 3.3 is based on a survey[60] carried out in 2003 in Kent Ridge Park, the NUS Kent Ridge Campus forest area and peripheral areas of the forest patch; it has since been updated with supplementary observations.

Butterflies are charismatic and highly visible organisms, but are also especially valuable as ecological indicators owing to their dependence of specific food plants for their caterpillars and nectar-producing plants for the adults. The presence of many butterfly species is a reflection of the diversity and state of health of the plants in the various habitats.

Thirteen butterfly species have been recorded in Kent Ridge (Table 3.3). All are native to Singapore and nationally Common. Five species are common at Kent Ridge Park, NUS Kent Ridge campus forest and its peripheral areas, and these are the species that occur in all urban areas of Singapore possibly owing to the availability of the caterpillar food plants: the common grass yellow (*Eurema hecabe*), common

Fig. 3.39: Striped albatross (*Appias libythea*)

Fig. 3.40: Lemon emigrant (*Catopsilia pomona*) female

Fig. 3.41: Lemon emigrant (*Catopsilia pomona*) male

Fig. 3.42: Orange emigrant (*Catopsilia scylla*)

Fig. 3.43: Painted jezebel (*Delias hyparete*)

Fig. 3.44: Common palmfly (*Elymnias hypermnestra*)

Fig. 3.45: King crow (*Euploea phaenareta*)

Fig. 3.46: Common grass yellow (*Eurema hecabe*)

Fig. 3.47: Peacock pansy (*Junonia almanac*)

Fig. 3.48: Chocolate pansy (*Junonia hedonia*)

Fig. 3.49: Dingy bush brown (*Mycalesis perseus*)

Fig. 3.50: Common Mormon (*Papilio polytes*)

Fig. 3.51: Short-banded sailor (*Phaedyma columella*)   Fig. 3.52: Less grass blue (*Zizina otis*)

Table 3.3: Butterflies of Kent Ridge

All species are native. The national conservation status categories follow those of second edition of *The Singapore Red Data Book*.[1]

S/No.	Common Name	Scientific Name	Family	National Conservation Status
1.	Striped albatross	*Appias libythea*	Pieridae	Common
2.	Lemon emigrant	*Catopsilia pomona*	Pieridae	Common
3.	Orange emigrant	*Catopsilia scylla*	Pieridae	Common
4.	Painted jezebel	*Delias hyparete*	Pieridae	Common
5.	Common palmfly	*Elymnias hypermnestra*	Nymphalidae	Common
6.	King crow	*Euploea phaenareta*	Nymphalidae	Common
7.	Common grass yellow	*Eurema hecabe*	Pieridae	Common
8.	Peacock pansy	*Junonia almana*	Nymphalidae	Common
9.	Chocolate pansy	*Junonia hedonia*	Nymphalidae	Common
10.	Dingy bush brown	*Mycalesis perseus*	Nymphalidae	Common
11.	Common Mormon	*Papilio polytes*	Papilionidae	Common
12.	Short-banded sailor	*Phaedyma columella*	Nymphalidae	Common
13.	Lesser grass blue	*Zizina otis*	Lycaenidae	Common

Note to Table 3.3

1. Davison, "The Red List Categories", p. 3; Khew Sin Khoon, "Butterflies: Checklist of Singapore Butterflies", in *The Singapore Red Data Book: Threatened Plants and Animals of Singapore*, 2nd ed., ed. Davison et al. (Singapore: Nature Society Singapore, 2008), pp. 250–8.

palmfly (*Elymnias hypermnestra*), lemon emigrant (*Catopsilia pomona*), lesser grass blue (*Zizina otis*) and striped albatross (*Appias libythea*). All the other recorded species are common in Singapore, except for the peacock pansy (*Junonia almana*), which is considered rare. However, this is a species of open grassland and not found in forests. None of the species are unique to Kent Ridge and the butterfly fauna there is a subset of those found in the Central Catchment Nature Reserve of Singapore.[61]

Crickets, Grasshoppers and Katydids

This account of the diversity of the insect order Orthoptera (grasshoppers, crickets and katydids) is based on surveys conducted in 2011 at Kent Ridge Park[62] and also specimens in the Zoological Reference Collection of the Lee Kong Chian Natural History Museum (Table 3.4).

Being abundant and diverse,[63] orthopterans are important drivers of ecosystem processes and play numerous ecological roles (herbivory, nutrient recycling and even predation of smaller insects). In Singapore, most species can be found in secondary forest.[64] In fact, owing to the sensitivity of orthopterans to their floristic environment, they are potentially useful ecological indicators of vegetation types in Singapore.

At least 29 species of orthopterans have been recorded at Kent Ridge, of which 17 are grasshoppers, 7 are

crickets and 5 are katydids. It is likely that more species of these insects remain to be found, particularly those of the suborder Ensifera.[65] Most species recorded in Kent Ridge can be seen in other parts of Singapore, including the meadow katydids (*Conocephalus* species) and paddy/rice grasshoppers

Fig. 3.53: Ground crickets such as the *Velarifictorus aspersus* (Orthoptera: Gryllidae) can be commonly heard chirping around Kent Ridge at night. Body length ca. 1.5 cm

Fig. 3.54: Hump-backed cricket *Rhaphidophora* species (Orthoptera: Rhaphidophoridae) is a wingless cricket (even as an adult) and can be found in moist environments such as dead logs or small crevices in the forest understorey. Body length ca. 3 cm

Fig. 3.56: *Traulia azureipennis* (Orthoptera: Acrididae) is a forest grasshopper with striking black and white colouration. Body length ca. 2.5 cm

Fig. 3.55: Javanese grasshopper (*Valanga nigricornis*, Orthoptera: Acrididae), a common grasshopper of urban areas

Fig. 3.57: The grasshopper *Phlaeoba infumata* (Orthoptera: Acrididae) is the less common of the two *Phlaeoba* species found in Singapore. Body length ca. 2 cm

(*Oxya* species) that inhabit grassy areas. Other species, such as the hump-backed cricket (*Rhaphidophora* species) and pygmy grasshoppers such as *Thoradonta nodulosa*, tend to be found in the forest area. Orthopterans form a significant part of the night soundscape as males of different species produce different forms of calls to attract conspecific females. Meadow katydids chirp softly,[66] the jangkrik (*Teleogryllus* species) trills[67] and ground crickets of the genus *Gymnogryllus* produce a loud and resonant buzz.[68]

Fig. 3.58: *Xenocatantops humilis* (Orthoptera: Acrididae), one of the most common grasshoppers in Singapore, is brown with white lateral stripes when they reach adulthood unlike the colouration and patterns of the nymphs pictured here. Body length (of nymph) ca. 0.5 cm

Fig. 3.59: Cone-headed katydid *Conocephalus maculatus* (Orthoptera: Tettigoniidae) female adult feeding on grasses. They are also known to be predatory of small insect pests. Body length ca. 1 cm

Fig. 3.60: *Conocephalus melaenus* (Orthoptera: Tettigoniidae) is one of the two meadow katydids. This is a nymph which is distinctly red and can be commonly seen around Kent Ridge. Body length ca. 1 cm

Table 3.4: Orthoptera (Grasshoppers, Crickets and Katydids) of Kent Ridge

All species are native to Singapore. The national conservation status categories follow those of the second edition of *The Singapore Red Data Book*.[1]

S/No.	Common Name	Scientific Name	Suborder: Family	National Conservation Status
1.		*Aiolopus thalassinus tamulus*	Caelifera: Acrididae	Common
2.		*Gastrimargus marmoratus*	Caelifera: Acrididae	Common
3.		*Gonista cf. bicolor*	Caelifera: Acrididae	Vulnerable
4.	Smaller rice grasshopper	*Oxya hyla intricata*	Caelifera: Acrididae	Common
5.	Lesser paddy grasshopper	*Oxya japonica japonica*	Caelifera: Acrididae	Common
6.		*Phlaeoba antennata*	Caelifera: Acrididae	Common
7.		*Phlaeoba infumata*	Caelifera: Acrididae	Common
8.		*Pseudoxya diminuta*	Caelifera: Acrididae	Common
9.		*Stenocatantops splendens*	Caelifera: Acrididae	Common
10.		*Traulia azureipennis*	Caelifera: Acrididae	Common
11.	Javanese grasshopper	*Valanga nigricornis*	Caelifera: Acrididae	Common
12.	Brown grasshopper	*Xenocatantops humilis*	Caelifera: Acrididae	Common
13.	Monkey grasshopper	*Erianthus species*	Caelifera: Chorotypidae	Common
14.	Tobacco grasshopper	*Atractomorpha psittacina*	Caelifera: Pyrgomorphidae	Common
15.	Pygmy grasshopper	*Coptotettix species*	Caelifera: Tetrigidae	Common
16.	Pygmy grasshopper	*Scelimeninae species*	Caelifera: Tetrigidae	Common
17.	Pygmy grasshopper	*Thoradonta nodulosa*	Caelifera: Tetrigidae	Vulnerable
18.	Silent cricket	*Euscyrtus concinnus*	Ensifera: Gryllidae	Common
19.	Ground cricket	*Gymnogryllus species*	Ensifera: Gryllidae	Common
20.		*Homoeoxipha lycoides*	Ensifera: Trigonidiidae	Common

Table 3.4 (cont'd)

21.		*Nisitrus vittatus*	Ensifera: Gryllidae	Common
22.	Jangkrik	*Teleogryllus species*	Ensifera: Gryllidae	Common
23.	Ground cricket	*Velarifictorus aspersus*	Ensifera: Gryllidae	Common
24.	Hump-backed cricket	*Rhaphidophora species*	Ensifera: Rhaphidophoridae	Common
25.	Cone-headed katydid, meadow katydid	*Conocephalus maculatus*	Ensifera: Tettigoniidae	Common
26.	Cone-headed katydid, meadow katydid	*Conocephalus melaenus*	Ensifera: Tettigoniidae	Common
27.		*Ducetia malayana*	Ensifera: Tettigoniidae	Common
28.	White-footed katydid	*Holochlora species*	Ensifera: Tettigoniidae	Common
29.		*Phaneroptera brevis*	Ensifera: Tettigoniidae	Common

Note to Table 3.4

1. Davison, "The Red List Categories", p. 3; Dennis H. Murphy, Cheong Loong Fah, Wang Luan Keng and Samantha Ang, "Springtails, Peripatus and Insects (to Moths)", in *The Singapore Red Data Book: Threatened Plants and Animals of Singapore*, 2nd ed., ed. Davison et al. (Singapore: Nature Society Singapore, 2008), p. 248.

Fig. 3.61: *Ducetia malayana* (Orthoptera: Tettigoniidae) is a species of bush-katydids and is known to visit flowers. They can be found commonly among grassy areas. Body length ca. 2.5 cm

Dragonflies and Damselflies

Dragonflies and damselflies are colourful and important insects in the ecosystem.[69] As ferocious predators, both as flying adults and aquatic larvae, they are known to prey upon disease-carrying mosquitoes and midges. The presence of the larvae of some species has been used as a biological indicator for good water quality in waterbodies. Singapore has an impressive record of 117 species of Odonata.[70] As such, dragonflies and damselflies can be flagship insects for freshwater ecosystem conservation in Singapore.

Twenty-eight kinds of dragonflies and five kinds of damselflies have been recorded from Kent Ridge (Table 3.5). All are native and nationally Common, except three species are

Fig. 3.62: Common parasol (*Neurothemis fluctuans*). This could be the most common species of dragonfly in Singapore. It can be found at most freshwater bodies, such as the ponds in Kent Ridge Park

Table 3.5: Odonata (Dragonflies and Damselflies) of Kent Ridge

All species are native to Singapore. The national conservation status categories follow those in the second edition of *The Singapore Red Data Book*.[1] This list of the insect order Odonata (dragonflies and damselflies) of Kent Ridge is extracted from the book *Dragonflies of Our Parks and Gardens*.[2]

S/No.	Common Name	Scientific Name	Suborder: Family	National Conservation Status
1.	Emperor	*Anax guttatus*	Anisoptera: Aeshnidae	Common
2.	Dingy duskhawker	*Gynacantha subinterrupta*	Anisoptera: Aeshnidae	Common
3.	Pond cruiser	*Epophthalmia vittigera*	Anisoptera: Corduliidae	Common
4.	Common flangetail	*Ictinogomphus decoratus*	Anisoptera: Gomphidae	Common
5.	Trumpet tail	*Acisoma panorpoides*	Anisoptera: Libellulidae	Common
6.	Pond adjutant	*Aethriamanta gracilis*	Anisoptera: Libellulidae	Common
7.	Grenadier	*Agrionoptera insignis*	Anisoptera: Libellulidae	Common
8.	Blue dasher	*Brachydiplax chalybea*	Anisoptera: Libellulidae	Common
9.	Sultan	*Camacinia gigantea*	Anisoptera: Libellulidae	Critically Endangered
10.	Common scarlet	*Crocothemis servilla*	Anisoptera: Libellulidae	Common
11.	Black-tipped percher	*Diplacodes nebulosa*	Anisoptera: Libellulidae	Common
12.	Water monarch	*Hydrobasileus croceus*	Anisoptera: Libellulidae	Common

Table 3.5 (cont'd)

13.	Scarlet grenadier	*Lathrecista asiatica*	Anisoptera: Libellulidae	Common
14.	Common parasol	*Neurothemis fluctuans*	Anisoptera: Libellulidae	Common
15.	Spine-tufted skimmer	*Orthetrum chrysis*	Anisoptera: Libellulidae	Common
16.	Common blue skimmer	*Orthetrum glaucum*	Anisoptera: Libellulidae	Common
17.	Variegated green skimmer	*Orthetrum sabina*	Anisoptera: Libellulidae	Common
18.	Scarlet skimmer	*Orthetrum testaceum*	Anisoptera: Libellulidae	Common
19.	Banded skimmer	*Pseudothemis jorina*	Anisoptera: Libellulidae	Critically Endangered
20.	Common redbolt	*Rhodothemis rufa*	Anisoptera: Libellulidae	Common
21.	Bronze flutterer	*Rhyothemis obsolescens*	Anisoptera: Libellulidae	Critically Endangered
22.	Yellow-barred flutterer	*Rhyothemis phyllis*	Anisoptera: Libellulidae	Common
23.	Sapphire flutterer	*Rhyothemis triangularis*	Anisoptera: Libellulidae	Common
24.	White-barred duskhawk	*Tholymis tillarga*	Anisoptera: Libellulidae	Common
25.	Saddlebag glider	*Tramea transmarina*	Anisoptera: Libellulidae	Common
26.	Crimson dropwing	*Trithemis aurora*	Anisoptera: Libellulidae	Common
27.	Indigo dropwing	*Trithemis festiva*	Anisoptera: Libellulidae	Common
28.	Scarlet basker	*Urothemis signata*	Anisoptera: Libellulidae	Common
29.	Variable wisp	*Agriocnemis femina*	Zygoptera: Coenagrionidae	Common
30.	Ornate coraltail	*Ceriagrion cerinorubellum*	Zygoptera: Coenagrionidae	Common
31.	Common bluetail	*Ischnura senegalensis*	Zygoptera: Coenagrionidae	Common
32.	Short-tail	*Onychargia atrocyana*	Zygoptera: Coenagrionidae	Common
33.	Blue sprite	*Pseudagrion microcephalum*	Zygoptera: Coenagrionidae	Common

Notes to Table 3.5
1. Davison, "The Red List Categories", p. 3; Murphy et al., "Springtails, Peripatus and Insects (to Moths)", pp. 248–9.
2. Robin Ngiam, *Dragonflies of Our Parks and Gardens* (Singapore: National Parks Board, 2011), pp. 104–5.

nationally Critically Endangered: banded skimmer (*Pseudothemis jorina*), bronze flutterer (*Rhyothemis obsolescens*) and sultan (*Camacinia gigantean*). Different odonate communities are found in the large and smaller ponds in Kent Ridge Park.[71] Most species here are nationally Common and can be found in urban Singapore ponds.

Spiders

Spiders are important predatory arthropods that prey on insects, some of which, such as houseflies, are considered pests. According to a 2008 study, 28 species from 15 families of spiders were recorded in the Kent Ridge area.[72] The batik golden web spider

Fig. 3.63: Golden web spider female (*Nepila maculata*) at the centre of its web

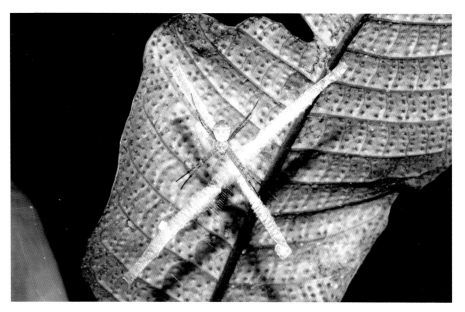

Fig. 3.64: *Argiope versicolor* (Arachnida: Araneidae), also known as the multicoloured St. Andrew's Cross spider, positioned itself in the characteristics shape of a cross. Body length ca. 2 cm

Fig. 3.65: The yellow-lined epeus, *Epeus flavobilineatus* (Arachnida: Araneidae) is one of the jumping spiders that can be found in Kent Ridge. Body length ca. 1 cm

(*Nephila antipodiana*) is probably the most conspicuous species and is among the largest orb-weavers.[73] Another prominent group is that of the jumping spiders (family *Salticidae*), which includes the fighting spider (*Thiania bhamoensis*) and the relatively larger mangrove jumper (*Ligurra latidens*). These spiders do not spin webs but capture prey with the aid of their highly specialized eyes.[74] Because the 2008 study was a rapid assessment, a greater diversity of spiders in Kent Ridge may be expected with more intensive exploration.

Table 3.6: Spiders of Kent Ridge

This data is from a report.[1] All species are native to Singapore. The national conservation status categories follow those of the second edition of *The Singapore Red Data Book*.[2] This checklist of the spiders of Kent Ridge is based on a survey in 2008.

S/No.	Common Name	Scientific Name	Suborder: Family	National Conservation Status
1.		*Araneus mitificus*	Araneomorphae: Araneidae	Common
2.	Multicoloured St. Andrew's Cross spider	*Argiope versicolor*	Araneomorphae: Araneidae	Common
3.	Red tent spider	*Cyrtophora unicolor*	Araneomorphae: Araneidae	Common
4.	Batik golden web spider	*Nephila antipodiana*	Araneomorphae: Araneidae	Common
5.	Golden web spider	*Nephila maculata*	Araneomorphae: Araneidae	Common
6.	Malabar spider	*Nephilengys malabarensis*	Araneomorphae: Araneidae	Common
7.	Ant-mimicking sac spider	*Castianeira* species	Araneomorphae: Clubionidae	Common
8.	Stout sac spider	*Clubiona* species	Araneomorphae: Clubionidae	Common
9.		*Cupiennus salei*	Araneomorphae: Ctenidae	Common
10.	Ogre-faced spider	*Dinopis spinosa*	Araneomorphae: Dinopidae	Common
11.	Wolf spider	*Lycosidae* species	Araneomorphae: Lycosidae	Common
12.	Lynx spider	*Oxyopes birmanicus*	Araneomorphae: Oxyopidae	Common
13.		*Perenethis unifasciata*	Araneomorphae: Pisauridae	Common
14.		*Cosmophasis umbratica*	Araneomorphae: Salticidae	Common
15.	Yellow-lined epeus	*Epeus flavobilineatus*	Araneomorphae: Salticidae	Common
16.	Mangrove jumper	*Ligurra latidens*	Araneomorphae: Salticidae	Common

Table 3.6 (cont'd)

17.	Common housefly catcher	*Plexippus petersi*	Araneomorphae: Salticidae	Common
18.	Fighting spider	*Thiania bhamoensis*	Araneomorphae: Salticidae	Common
19.	Brown spitting spider	*Scytodes fusca*	Araneomorphae: Scytodidae	Common
20.	Domestic huntsman spider	*Heteropoda venatoria*	Araneomorphae: Sparassidae	Common
21.	Big-bellied tylorida	*Tylorida ventralis*	Araneomorphae: Tetragnathidae	Common
22.		*Achaearanea mumdulum*	Araneomorphae: Theridiidae	Common
23.	Silver comb-footed spider	*Argyrodes argentatus*	Araneomorphae: Theridiidae	Common
24.	Whip spider	*Argyrodes flagellum*	Araneomorphae: Theridiidae	Common
25.	Red silver spider	*Argyrodes flavescens*	Araneomorphae: Theridiidae	Common
26.	Bird-dung crab spider	*Phrynarachne* species	Araneomorphae: Thomisidae	Common
27.	Humped spider	*Zosis geniculatus*	Araneomorphae: Uloboridae	Common
28.	Spotted ground spider	*Storena cinctipes*	Araneomorphae: Zodariidae	Common

Notes to Table 3.6

1. Dexiang Chen, *Fauna of Kent Ridge: Spider Diversity and the Identification of Common Spiders* (Singapore: National University of Singapore, 2008), p. 18.
2. Davison, "The Red List Categories", p. 3; Joseph Koh and David J. Court, "Class Arachnida (Phylum Arthropoda: Subphylum Chelicerata)", in *The Singapore Red Data Book: Threatened Plants and Animals of Singapore*, 2nd ed., ed. Davison et al. (Singapore: Nature Society Singapore, 2008), p. 259.

Fig. 3.66: The mangrove spider, *Ligurra latidens* (Arachnida: Araneidae) is among the largest jumping spiders found in Kent Ridge. It can also be found in mangrove forest, as its common name implies. Body length ca. 1.5 cm

Miscellaneous Invertebrates

In addition to the various groups of invertebrates mentioned above, for which surveys have been conducted, Kent Ridge also is home to many other species such as molluscs which consist of slugs and snails, insects such as shield bugs, mantises and moths.

Fig. 3.67: Tropical leather leaf slug (*Laevicaulis alte*). Slugs are essentially snails without shells. This species is commonly found in urban environments, but is active mainly at night, and thus infrequently noticed by people. The 4-cm example shown here was photographed in January 2016 on a wall of a building in Kent Ridge Campus

Fig. 3.69: Ocellated shield bug (*Cantao ocellatus*). A female guards a brood of nymphs that had hatched from a cluster of eggs beneath her. This species of bug has been observed to feed on the fruits of turn-in-the-wind (*Mallotus paniculatus*). The photograph was obtained along Kent Ridge Road in October 2011

Fig. 3.68: African land snail (*Achatina fulica*). This species is native to Africa but has been introduced to many other parts of the world. In Singapore, it seems to be the most commonly seen snail in urban areas. The featured individual was photographed on a grass lawn in Kent Ridge Campus in October 2011

Fig. 3.70: Stick mantis (*Euchomenella heteroptera*). Praying mantises are predatory insects that carry their first pair of limbs raised and folded such that they appear to be in prayer. Many species have evolved to blend in with their surroundings so that they can creep unnoticed up to their prey, which usually consists of smaller insects. This one, resembling a dried twig, was found on the Kent Ridge Campus in July 2004

Fig. 3.71: Swallowtail moth (*Lyssa zampa*). This moth is seasonally common in Singapore, and is one of the largest lepidopteran in the region. It resembles a butterfly, but is nocturnally active and tends to rest with its wings spread open. The pictured individual was found on a wall of a concrete building in Kent Ridge Campus in May 2005

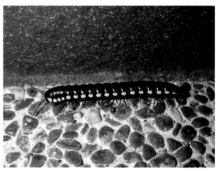

Fig. 3.73: Millipede (*Anoplodesmus saussurii*). About 3 cm in length, this is a very common land arthropod at Kent Ridge. It can usually be found on soil and feeds on decaying plant matter. It is believed to be an introduced species that is native to India and Sri Lanka

Amphibians and Reptiles

This data on amphibians and reptiles are primarily based on a 2003 survey[75] of Kent Ridge Park, the NUS Kent Ridge campus forest area and peripheral areas of the forest patch, and a report,[76] and updated with supplementary observations (such as by Kelvin K.P. Lim) since. The former survey was mostly based on records from the Zoological Reference Collection of the Lee Kong Chian Natural History Museum and personal observations of experts.

Amphibians and reptiles are collectively known as herpetofauna, or informally as "herptiles". Eight amphibians (frogs and toads) and 27 reptiles (lizards, snakes, turtles), so totalling 35 herptile species, have been recorded (Tables 3.7 and 3.8). Although Kent Ridge consists primarily of secondary forest and managed

Fig. 3.72: Black dwarf honeybee (*Apis andreniformis*). One of several species of honeybees in Singapore. This small hive and its occupants was found at NUS campus on a small tree in between buildings in April 2014

Fig. 3.74: *Microhyla heymonsi* (Microhylidae) is known as the dark-sided chorus frog because of the ventral half of the abdomen has a dark brown horizontal band. Body length ca. 2.5 cm

Fig. 3.75: Four-lined tree frog (*Polypedates leucomystax*). This species does not live on trees, but among shrubs, bushes and grass around bodies of freshwater. The tips of its fingers and toes are expanded to resemble suction discs, and these enable the frog to cling to vertical surfaces. At Kent Ridge, it can sometimes be found inside buildings

Fig. 3.76: Banded bullfrog, *Kaloula pulchra*. The picture shows a pair spawning in a puddle in the sports field at the NUS Kent Ridge Campus. The male is clinging on to his mate with his "hands" under her "arm-pits". Note the string of eggs being laid in the water by the female. They were photographed after a rainy spell one morning in December 2006

vegetation, this diversity of herptiles is a rather respectable number considering the vegetation is not as pristine as the primary forest fragments in the Bukit Timah and Central Catchment nature reserves.

As expected, most of the species are not forest-specific and are frequently associated with urban areas. Most of the herpetofaunal species are common, and even the rarer species are not threatened with extinction in Singapore or the Southeast Asian region.

Three species of agamid lizard occur in Kent Ridge. The most common and noticeable one is the non-native changeable lizard (*Calotes versicolor*), which appears to have displaced the native green crested lizard (*Bronchocela cristatella*) in exposed environments. The green crested lizard is largely restricted to wooded areas. Where the two species are found together, the changeable lizard appears to be more bold and aggressive than its native counterpart. In gardens and belukar, the Sumatran flying dragon (*Draco sumatranus*) is quite common and may be observed gliding from tree to tree on a pair of large skin folds supported by extensions of the ribs. The skin folds are brightly coloured but are folded out of sight when the lizard is stationary. The cryptic colouration of its dorsum enables the flying dragon to camouflage against the bark of trees.

There are five species of gecko, all of which can be observed on the walls of buildings, especially near lamps which attract their insect prey at night. The two skinks are diurnal species and may be observed basking in sunlit areas on the forest floor or on footpaths. The garden supple skink (*Lygosoma bowringi*) is less commonly observed because it is smaller and tends to burrow into the leaf litter. The largest lizard is the Malayan water monitor (*Varanus salvator*); a few large ones can often be seen ambling at the edge of, or swimming slowly in, the ponds of Kent Ridge Park. This species is both a carrion feeder and a predator of small animals. It can be observed flicking its forked tongue in and out of its mouth to taste the air for edible items.

Two of the 14 snake species recorded from Kent Ridge are known to be highly venomous—the equatorial spitting cobra (*Naja sumatrana*) and the banded Malayan coral snake (*Calliophis intestinalis*). The cobra is easily identified by its solid jet-black body. The coral snake is recognized by its brown dorsum with a narrow, bright red stripe from the head down to the tail. When harassed, the coral snake often flips its body over to reveal its startling black-and-white checkered underside, which serves as warning colouration to other animals. The equatorial spitting cobra appears to be relatively common at Kent Ridge, having been observed at bus stops in the NUS campus; it occasionally creeps into gardens, and even enters buildings. As its name implies, this snake spits its venom instinctively at the eyes of animals that threaten it, be they humans, dogs or cats.

Fig. 3.77: Mourning gecko (*Lepidodactylus lugubris*). Of the five species of gecko that inhabit buildings in Kent Ridge, this is the smallest species. It is quite common, and this example was found in Kent Ridge Campus in February 2012

Fig. 3.78: Sumatran flying dragon (*Draco sumatranus*). The dorsal surface of the flying dragon is mottled with various shades of brown and grey, offering this small lizard good camouflage against the bark of tree trunks on which it may be seen scampering about and snacking on ants. The male has a distinctive yellow throat flag that he erects to attract mates. This female was photographed on the NUS Kent Ridge Campus in August 2009

Fig. 3.79: The largest lizard in Kent Ridge, the Malayan water monitor (*Varanus salvator*). Its forked tongue "tastes" the air to find carrion or prey. It enables it to determine where the target is

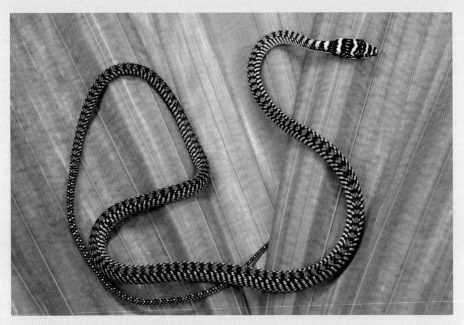

Fig. 3.80: Paradise gliding snake, *Chrysopelea paradisi*. Measuring no longer than 20 cm in length, this young example was discovered in June 2009 on a staircase within a building on the NUS Kent Ridge Campus. This species feeds primarily on lizards, and individuals occasionally enters buildings probably to hunt geckoes. This species is unique because it can glide from tree to tree

Fig. 3.81: Reticulated python (*Malayopython reticulatus*). Look hard at this photograph, for it shows a snake that is well concealed against the background. Reticulated pythons may rely on this camouflage to ambush passing rats or birds on which they feed. This juvenile of about one metre was found at the Kent Ridge Campus in October 2003. This species is the largest carnivore now extant in Singapore as adults can reach up to 4–5 metres in length

Fig. 3.82: Banded Malayan coral snake (*Calliophis intestinalis*). A venomous but usually unaggressive snake that lives in leaf litter. It is recognized by the red mid-dorsal stripe, and when disturbed, will curl its tail to reveal the red and black underside. This is a message to potential predators that it is venomous and should be left alone. This example was found in a garden on Kent Ridge Campus in September 2005

Table 3.7: Amphibians of Kent Ridge Park, NUS Kent Ridge Campus Forest Area and the Periphery of the Latter

The nomenclature and classification largely follows that of Nick Baker and Kelvin K.P. Lim.[1] The national conservation status categories follow those of the second edition of *The Singapore Red Data Book*.[2]

S/No.	Common Name	Scientific Name	Family	Native or Exotic	National Conservation Status
1.	Asian toad	*Duttaphrynus melanostictus* (synonym: *Bufo melanostictus*)	Bufonidae	Native	Common
2.	Crab-eating frog	*Fejervarya cancrivorus* (synonym: *Rana cancrivora*)	Dicroglossidae	Native	Common
3.	Field frog	*Fejervarya limnocharis* (synonym: *Rana limnocharis*)	Dicroglossidae	Native	Common
4.	Common greenback frog	*Hylarana erythraea* (synonym: *Rana erythraea*)	Ranidae	Native	Common
5.	Four-lined tree frog	*Polypedates leucomystax*	Rhacophoridae	Native	Common
6.	Banded bull-frog	*Kaloula pulchra*	Microhylidae	Exotic	-
7.	Painted chorus frog	*Microhyla butleri*	Microhylidae	Native	Common
8.	Dark-sided chorus frog	*Microhyla heymonsi*	Microhylidae	Native	Common

Notes to Table 3.7

1. Nick Baker and Kelvin K.P. Lim, *Wild Animals of Singapore: A Photographic Guide to Mammals, Reptiles, Amphibians and Freshwater Fishes* (Singapore: Draco Publishing & Nature Society, 2012), pp. 158–9.
2. Davison, "The Red List Categories", p. 3; Kelvin K.P. Lim, "Fishes, Amphibians and Reptiles", in *The Singapore Red Data Book: Threatened Plants and Animals of Singapore*, 2nd ed., ed. Davison et al. (Singapore: Nature Society Singapore, 2008), p. 264.

Table 3.8: Reptiles of Kent Ridge

The nomenclature and classification largely follows that of Nick Baker and Kelvin K.P. Lim.[1] The national conservation status categories follow those of the second edition of *The Singapore Red Data Book*.[2]

S/No.	Common Name	Scientific Name	Family	Native or Exotic	National Conservation Status
	Lizards and skinks				
1.	Green crested lizard	*Bronchocela cristatella*	Agamidae	Native	Common
2.	Changeable lizard	*Calotes versicolor*	Agamidae	Exotic	
3.	Sumatran flying dragon	*Draco sumatranus* (also as: *Draco volans*)	Agamidae	Native	Common
4.	Four-clawed gecko	*Gehyra mutilata*	Gekkonidae	Native	Common
5.	Spotted house gecko	*Gekko monarchus*	Gekkonidae	Native	Common
6.	Spiny-tailed house gecko	*Hemidactylus frenatus*	Gekkonidae	Native	Common
7.	Flat-tailed house gecko	*Hemidactylus platyurus* (synonym: *Cosymbotes platyurus*)	Gekkonidae	Native	Common
8.	Mourning gecko	*Lepidodactylus lugubris*	Gekkonidae	Native	Common
9.	Many-lined sun skink	*Eutropis multifasciata* (synonym: *Mabuya multifasciata*)	Scincidae	Native	Common
10.	Garden supple skink	*Lygosoma bowringi* (synonym: *Riopa bowringi*)	Scincidae	Native	Common
11.	Malayan water monitor	*Varanus salvator*	Varanidae	Native	Common

S/No.	Common Name	Scientific Name	Family	Native or Exotic	National Conservation Status
	Snakes				
1.	Oriental whip snake	*Ahaetulla prasina*	Colubridae	Native	Common
2.	Paradise gliding snake	*Chrysopelea paradisi*	Colubridae	Native	Common
3.	Common Malayan racer	*Coelognathus flavolineatus* (synonym: *Elaphe flavolineata*)	Colubridae	Native	Endangered
4.	Striped bronzeback	*Dendrelaphis caudolineatus*	Colubridae	Native	Common
5.	Red-necked bronzeback	*Dendrelaphis kopsteini* (also as: *Dendrelaphis formosus*)	Colubridae	Native	Vulnerable
6.	Painted bronzeback	*Dendrelaphis pictus*	Colubridae	Native	Common
7.	House wolf snake	*Lycodon capucinus* (also as: *Lycodon aulicus*)	Colubridae	Native	Common
8.	Striped kukri snake	*Oligodon octolineatus*	Colubridae	Native	Common
9.	Banded Malayan coral snake	*Calliophis intestinalis* (synonym: *Maticora intestinalis*)	Elapidae	Native	Vulnerable
10.	Equatorial spitting cobra	*Naja sumatrana* (also as: *Naja naja sputatrix*)	Elapidae	Native	Common
11.	Puff-faced water snake	*Homalopsis buccata*	Homalopsidae	Native	Vulnerable
12.	Reticulated python	*Malayopython reticulatus* (synonym: *Python reticulatus*)	Pythonidae	Native	Common
13.	Brahminy blind snake	*Ramphotyphlops braminus*	Typhlopidae	Native	Common
14.	Sunbeam snake	*Xenopeltis unicolor*	Xenopeltidae	Native	Common

S/No.	Common Name	Scientific Name	Family	Native or Exotic	National Conservation Status
	Turtles and Tortoises				
1.	Red-eared slider	*Trachemys scripta elegans*	Emydidae	Exotic	Common
2.	Malayan box terrapin	*Cuora amboinensis*	Geoemydidae	Native	Common

Notes to Table 3.8

1. Baker and Lim, *Wild Animals of Singapore*, pp. 159–61.
2. Davison, "The Red List Categories", p. 3; Lim, "Fishes, Amphibians and Reptiles", pp. 246–64. *Draco volans* is still a valid name so is not really a synonym of *Draco sumatranus*, but previous workers have misapplied this name to individuals now identified as *Draco sumatranus*.

Another potentially dangerous snake is the reticulated python (*Malayopython reticulatus*). Although not venomous, it kills its prey by constriction. It hunts by using heat sensing pits in the front of its head and is an ambush predator. In the mid-1980s, a 5-metre-long python was found stuck in a drain at the foot of a building in Kent Ridge Campus.[77] It was removed by staff of the Singapore Civil Defence Force (the then Singapore Fire Brigade). Large pythons can kill dogs or cats by constricting, then swallowing them whole. When under threat, this snake bites viciously, causing severe lacerations with its multiple rows of inward-facing, needle-like teeth on both jaws. Pythons are often found in the sewers of Singapore where they hunt for rats, and may emerge unexpectedly from a toilet bowl; a former national athlete was unfortunate to have his scrotum lacerated by such a python![78]

The paradise tree snake (*Chrysopelea paradisi*), like the flying dragon, is capable of gliding from tree to tree. It becomes airborne by launching itself from high branches, then flattening its body such that it traps a cushion of air beneath to slow its descent, slithering sinuously as it falls downwards.

Two species of turtle have been recorded from Kent Ridge. The introduced red-eared slider (*Trachemys scripta elegans*), which is native to the USA, is usually seen in the ponds at Kent Ridge Park. The species is frequently released into the wild by people whose enthusiasm for their pet is outlived by this turtle, or by Buddhists practising life release. The Malayan box terrapin (*Cuora amboinensis*) is known to be native to Singapore, but specimens encountered in urban areas are likely to be life-released specimens that are imported from overseas.

Birds

At least 201 species of bird have been recorded thus far from the Kent Ridge area (Table 3.9). The birds of Kent Ridge can be broadly classified into two groups: residents and migrants. Resident birds live and nest in Singapore, and consist of two subgroups based on their origins: native (resident, 81 species; resident or migrant, 10 species; resident and possibly migratory, 2 species; resident or non-breeding visitor, 1 species; resident or possibly non-breeding visitor, 1 species) and non-native, naturalized alien (introduced, 15 species; introduced or migrant, 1 species; possibly introduced, 1 species). Some species that are resident in the region do not roost or nest in Singapore, but make occasional visits from their primary habitats nearby to feed. Those that come over from Malaysia and Indonesia are classified as non-breeding visitors (non-breeding visitor, 2 species; possibly non-breeding visitor, 1 species; migrant or non-breeding visitor, 3 species; migrant or possibly non-breeding visitor, 1 species; resident or non-breeding visitor, 1 species; resident or possibly non-breeding visitor, 1 species). Escapees (18 species) refer to non-native birds that have been artificially introduced to the area either by escaping from captivity or having been deliberately liberated by their owners. Many of these lone individuals tend to perish after some time. However, those that have been freed in some numbers and managed to establish stable local populations by being able to occupy suitable niches and reproduce naturally, become naturalized aliens. Migrant birds (non-native species) stop at Singapore to spend the winter months (migrant, 62 species; migrant or non-breeding visitor, 3 species; migrant or possibly non-breeding visitor, 1 species; introduced resident or migrant, 1 species; resident or migrant, 10 species; resident or possibly migrant, 2 species) or pass through to their wintering grounds elsewhere (passage migrant, 1 species) at certain times of the year. They tend not to breed in Singapore, and are only present particularly during the northern-hemisphere winter, usually from August to May in the following year. Many bird species thus spend their winter in Kent Ridge, or use this as a stopover point on their migration along the East Asian-Australasian flyway.[79] Vagrants (non-native species), not represented on the list, are birds that show up in Singapore because they have strayed outside of their regular distribution but appear in an apparently wild state.

Of the 95 resident native species, 11 are nationally Critically Endangered, 8 are nationally Endangered, 3 are nationally Vulnerable, and the remaining 73 are nationally Common. The presence of these 22 rare species serves to emphasize the importance of Kent Ridge as an area of conservation concern; that 6 of these are water birds—black-crowned nigh heron

Fig. 3.83: Asian koel (*Eudynamys scolopaceus*). This bird has a very loud call, and is a member of the cuckoo family. The Asian koel is known to be a brood parasite of the house crow, and is credited for helping to keeping the population of that pest bird in Singapore under control. The male koel is shown here

Fig. 3.84: White-bellied sea-eagle (*Haliaeetus leucogaster*). This large bird lives largely along the coast, and can often be seen soaring in the sky over Kent Ridge. It feeds largely on fish that it snatches with its talons from the surface of the water

Fig. 3.85: Pink-necked green pigeon, Treron vernans. This male was photographed in March 2007 incubating an egg in a nest built on a simpoh air (*Dillenia suffruticosa*) shrub next to a building in the Science Faculty of the NUS Kent Ridge Campus. The female was also observed sharing incubation duty

Fig. 3.86: Oriental white-eye (*Zosterops palpebrosus*). This species is popularly kept as a song bird in Singapore. The wild population of the Oriental white-eye is believed to be derived from escaped individuals imported for the pet trade. This photograph shows a parent bird incubating eggs in its nest which is suspended from tree branches in Kent Ridge Campus in March 2007

(*Nycticorax nycticorax*), great-billed heron (*Ardea sumatrana*), grey heron (*Ardea cinerea*), grey-headed fish eagle (*Haliaeetus ichyaetus*), lesser whistling duck (*Dendrocygna javanica*) and purple heron (*Ardea purpurea*)—indicates the value of the two ponds in Kent Ridge Park. The birds may be spotted in large bodies of water such as these ponds that offer refuge in the form of dense vegetation at their edges. The lesser whistling duck (*Dendrocygna javanica*) is known to make occasional visits to the ponds. As the name suggests, this brown bird does not quack but makes shrill whistling calls.

Chickens on Kent Ridge are not domestic poultry from someone's yard. Once believed to be extinct in Singapore, the red jungle fowl (*Gallus gallus*), like the wild pig, has recently recolonized the island nation, with some birds having flown across the Johor Strait from Malaysia to Singapore, where they also now reproduce. The wild fowl can be differentiated from its domesticated counterpart by its slender appearance, ability to fly, large white ear patch, blackish legs and crow which has a distinctly abrupt ending. This species tends to favour densely vegetated areas, the birds foraging for food on the ground that is exposed by scratching the leaf litter with their feet.

In the mornings, the grass fields in the NUS Kent Ridge campus may be dotted with large white birds. Many of these are individuals of the eastern cattle egret (*Bubulcus coromandus*). These are possibly the most conspicuous members of the heron family at Kent Ridge. They feed on small creatures such as frogs, lizards and insects, which they may flush out of hiding by walking among the grass. Eastern cattle egrets are supposed to be migratory in Singapore. However, birds have been noted to be present all year in the campus. A resident species, the striated heron (*Butorides striata*), tends to be found near water bodies and in canals, skulking along the edges and stabbing its long, sharp beak at small fish on which it feeds.

Neither chicken nor duck, the white-breasted waterhen (*Amaurornis phoenicurus*) is a species of rail that is fairly common in Kent Ridge. Resembling a black-and-white chicken with large, greenish-yellow feet, this resident species inhabits grassy areas, often near a water body. Its call is a series of harsh croaks. The chicks are fluffy and entirely black.

Two species of raptor are found all year round in Kent Ridge; both are associated with coastal areas. The white-bellied sea eagle (*Haliaeetus leucogaster*) is the largest resident raptor in Singapore. It can sometimes be observed circling over Kent Ridge, uttering its characteristic honking calls. It feeds on fish and marine snakes, snatching these with its talons from the surface of the sea. A smaller raptor, the brahminy kite (*Haliastur indus*), is a bright chestnut colour, with white head and breast.

It also feeds on fish, but does not shy away from scavenging for offal. Most of the other raptors seen at or around Kent Ridge are migrants that show up during the northern-hemisphere winter. They tend to gather in large numbers, spiralling in the sky as they ride the thermals during hot afternoons. Such congregations usually consist of several species, the most common being the Japanese sparrowhawk (*Accipiter gularis*), crested honey-buzzard (*Pernis ptilorhynchus*) and black baza (*Aviceda leuphotes*). The peregrine falcon (*Falco peregrinus*) used to be classified with the raptors, but is now believed to be more closely related to parrots;[80] this migrant preys on other birds, such as pigeons, and is known to be the fastest bird in the air, reaching a diving speed of more than 200 miles per hour[81] (about 321.9 km/hour).

The rock pigeon (*Columba livia*) is a familiar semi-domestic bird that nests in buildings, and is often an unwelcome guest at cafeterias on the NUS Kent Ridge campus. However, it has wild relatives that are not as closely associated with humans. The spotted dove *Spilopelia chinensis* (synonym: *Streptopelia chinensis*) has a distinctive black collar that is speckled with white. The smaller zebra dove (*Geopelia striata*) is grey, with fine blackish lines. Both birds are usually seen strutting about on the ground in built-up areas, particularly in carparks. In contrast, the pink-necked green pigeon (*Treron vernans*) is found largely in trees. It likes to roost gregariously on exposed branches and flocks often descend on roadside palm trees to gorge on the fruit, alongside its larger black-and-white relative, the pied imperial pigeon (*Ducula bicolor*).

Cuckoos are known famously for their brood-parasitic tendencies. Many species lay eggs in the nests of other birds, and have their young raised by unsuspecting parents of another species. A large number of cuckoos in Singapore are migratory. Among the cuckoos in Singapore, the Asian koel (*Eudynamys scolopacea*) is perhaps the most familiar. The male is black with red eyes while the female is brown with dark streaks. It occurs in Singapore as both migrant and resident and plays a significant role in controlling the population of the much-despised house crow by being its brood parasite. However, the koel itself is not a popular bird. It has a strong tendency to call before sunrise, and its loud, monotonous song is especially detested by those who are not early risers.

Of the three species of owl recorded from Kent Ridge, the spotted wood owl (*Strix seloputo*) is the largest. In Kent Ridge, it has been found in the day roosting in large trees while at dusk, it calls before embarking on hunting sessions; its call sounds vaguely like a loud, low-pitched bark. Its much smaller relative, the Sunda scops owl (*Otus lempiji*), inhabits areas of denser vegetation. The migratory oriental scops owl (*Otus sunia*) is similar in appearance but is distinguishable by its yellow (instead of brown) eyes.

Owls are not the only nocturnal birds at Kent Ridge. The characteristic "choink-choink" call of the large-tailed nightjar (*Caprimulgus macrurus*) can be heard in suburban areas at night. This bird often sits on lawns or on exposed perches, making the occasional aerial foray to hawk for insects. During the day, it sits motionless among leaf litter where its brown, black and white plumage enables it to blend in with dead foliage.

Swiftlets are small, lithe birds that superficially resemble swallows. *Aerodramus* species are often seen hawking for insects in open areas at dawn or dusk, or before approaching rain. These birds produce the edible nest much esteemed in East Asia as a health and beauty tonic. Swiftlets nest in colonies in dark and high places like caves and abandoned buildings. Their nests are made of the birds' saliva plastered to the walls. Swiftlets have tiny legs and are unable to perch on branches, but cling to their nest or rock walls when at rest. They are also adept at flying about in dark places using echolocation.

The oriental dollarbird (*Eurystomus orientalis*) is a blackish-blue bird with a red bill, and is often seen sitting alone on exposed branches at the top of trees. It is named after the large round white patch (resembling a dollar coin) on the underside of the wing which is evident when the bird is in flight. Both migratory and resident individuals of this species occur in Singapore.

Two species of resident kingfisher are often observed in Kent Ridge. Despite the name, they do not hunt and feed solely on fish. The white-throated kingfisher (*Halcyon smyrnensis*) tends to frequent open grassy spaces where it hunts lizards, frogs and large insects. The blue-and-white collared kingfisher (*Todiramphus chloris*) inhabits coastal areas and its call, like a maniacal laugh, is often heard at dawn. The small and colourful oriental dwarf kingfisher (*Ceyx erithaca*) is a migrant; a dead individual has been collected in Kent Ridge campus.

Bee-eaters, recognized by their slender, slightly curved beaks and long pointed tails, often hawk for insects in the sky. The two native Singaporean species are migratory. The blue-tailed bee-eater (*Merops philippinus*) is more commonly seen, especially during the northern hemisphere winter migration season.

A mention must be made of the oriental pied hornbill (*Anthracoceros albirostris*) which is sometimes seen in Kent Ridge. It is a large and conspicuous bird with a distinctive large beak and casque. Although it feeds on fruit, it is also a voracious predator on small animals, including other birds. Like the red jungle-fowl, this hornbill was believed to be extinct in Singapore until two decades ago when birds started to fly over from Johor and re-established a breeding population in Singapore.

A call which consists of a continuous series of "took-took-took" from treetops indicates the presence of the coppersmith barbet (*Megalaima haemacephala*). This small and colourful bird, with hair at the base of its thick bill, inhabits open parkland and nests in holes in trees.

Continuous drumming sounds coming from trees indicate the presence of woodpeckers. Woodpeckers use their strong, straight bills to punch holes in tree trunks and branches from which they extract grubs. The more common species in Kent Ridge is the small, white-and-brown Sunda pygmy woodpecker (*Dendrocopos moluccensis*) and the considerably larger, yellow-coloured common flameback (*Dinopium javanense*). Both can occasionally be seen on roadside trees, clinging to tree trunks or creeping over the branches.

Parrots are easily recognized by their large round heads; short, broad, curved beaks; and feet with two digits facing forwards and two backwards. They tend to be noisy and their calls can be screechy and harsh. The long-tailed parakeet (*Psittacula longicauda*) usually travels in large flocks around wooded areas. Its congener, the red-breasted parakeet (*Psittacula alexandri*), is distinguished by its pinkish (instead of green) breast. The latter is a non-native species that has established large populations all over Singapore. The diminutive blue-crowned hanging parrot (*Loriculus galgulus*) tends to be found singly or in pairs, and has a shrill metallic ringing call. It has the unusual habit of hanging upside down from its perch. The Tanimbar corella or Goffin's cockatoo (*Cacatua goffiniana*) is a large white non-native parrot that has become naturalized in Singapore. The species is native to the Maluku Islands in Indonesia.

The golden-bellied gerygone (*Gerygone sulphurea*) is a small brown-and-yellow bird which is cryptic and difficult to see despite being quite common in urban areas. However, its very distinct melodious, high-pitched wheezy call often gives its presence away.

The common iora (*Aegithina tiphia*) and pied triller (*Lalage nigra*) are small resident birds that frequent urban gardens, and may be seen on trees at Kent Ridge. The former is coloured yellow and black, and the latter is easily recognized by its black-and-white plumage. Comparatively larger in size, the black-naped oriole (*Oriolus chinensis*), also a common resident in urban parks, is unmistakable in its bright yellow plumage and red bill.

During the northern-hemisphere winter months, the migratory brown shrike (*Lanius cristatus*) can often be observed perched on fences and shrubs in open spaces. It hunts for large insects and small vertebrates such as lizards. Shrikes are known to impale their victims on thorns or barbed wire on which the prey can be torn apart.

The greater racket-tailed drongo (*Dicrurus paradiseus*) is essentially a bird of lowland rainforest and is occasionally sighted in the wooded areas of Kent Ridge. It is iridescent black with red eyes, and has a pair of outer tail feathers that are long and filamentous with a curled racket-like end. It is a noisy bird with a varied repertoire that includes mimicking the calls of other birds.

The brown-and-white Malaysian pied fantail (*Rhipidura javanica*) is a resident of secondary and mangrove forests, and can be observed in the wooded areas of Kent Ridge. An adult male trying to attract a mate performs a dance in which he fans open his tail feathers like a peacock and hops about frantically.

No bird is more despised than the house crow (*Corvus splendens*). This large grey-and-black bird often raids rubbish bins and is considered a pest. A concerted effort to control its previously large numbers in the 1990s appears to be successful, as it is no longer common in the country. The house crow is an introduced species from India, but its cousin, the black large-billed crow (*Corvus macrorhynchos*), is native to Singapore and can also be found in Kent Ridge, but is relatively uncommon and keeps to wooded areas. It also seems less likely to scavenge on garbage.

Two species of bulbul are common residents in Kent Ridge. The yellow-vented bulbul (*Pycnonotus goiavier*) has a white head with a black eye streak. It makes a bubbly call, and frequents urban parkland. In contrast, the olive-winged bulbul (*Pycnonotus plumosus*), which has greenish wings and red eyes,

tends to favour the shadier environs of the forest.

The Pacific swallow (*Hirundo tahitica*) is a common resident bird that can be seen swooping through the air over grass fields. It has a pair of long, tapering wings and a prominent reddish head and throat. At rest, it often perches on telegraph cables. Its migratory cousin, the barn swallow (*Hirundo rustica*), flies in from the north just before winter. It is distinguished from the Pacific swallow by a blackish band across the breast and often a pair of tail streamers.

The Arctic warbler (*Phylloscopus borealis*) can be recognized by its long black-and-white eye stripe. It is a common migrant that usually escapes attention because it is small and tends to stay on treetops. In contrast, its relative, the resident common tailorbird (*Orthotomus sutorius*), is active nearer the ground, skulking about among shrubbery and feeding on insects. It is hardly unusual in appearance. However, its nest is a most interesting construct: it is a cup of dried plant material within a cradle formed by leaves sewn together with fine threads of plant fibre.

Essentially a forest specialist, the pin-striped tit-babbler (*Macronus gularis*) can be seen in the denser wooded areas of Kent Ridge, where it travels in small groups. It has yellow underparts with dark brown streaks on the throat and breast. The white-crested laughingthrush (*Garrulax leucolophus diardi*) is a large brown bird with a white head and

Fig. 3.87: White-crested laughingthrush (*Garrulax leucolophus*). An introduced bird that is native to southern China and Indochina. It is gregarious and travels in small parties, flying from bush to bush and foraging for insects and fallen fruits on the ground

underside. It is native to southeast Myanmar to southwest Yunnan, Indo-china and peninsular Thailand,[82] and is a popular cage bird because of its loud, distinctive, melodious call. Groups of this bird can be seen in the forested areas of Kent Ridge, foraging for insects on the forest floor.

The oriental white-eye (*Zosterops palpebrosus*) is a diminutive green bird with a distinct white ring around its eyes. It is a popular songbird, and although the species is native to Singapore, part of the population could consist of escaped or released pet birds imported from elsewhere. It is known to nest in Kent Ridge, and the hatchlings grow rapidly, fledging in less than two weeks.

The Asian glossy starling (*Aplonis panayensis*) is a noisy metallic black bird with red eyes that moves about in large flocks. Its relatives include two species of myna that are perhaps the most conspicuous birds on campus. The Javan myna (*Acridotheres javanicus*) and the ironically uncommon common myna (*Acridotheres tristis*) strut boldly about the buildings and lawns. They are a notorious nuisance in cafeterias throughout the NUS Kent Ridge campus. They home in on food left unattended, snatching morsels, stepping onto plates and defecating on the contents, and generally messing up tables. Along with rock pigeons and the Eurasian tree sparrow, these birds are so aggressive and relentless in their raids that some NUS canteens have erected wire netting

around the building to prevent birds from entering. Other canteens have installed spikes on overhead structures and surfaces to discourage birds from perching around the diners.

During the northern-hemisphere winter, the Siberian thrush (*Geokichla sibirica*) makes the long journey south to escape the cold weather. While passing through Singapore, some individuals, unaware of glass windows on buildings that reflect the sky, crash into these and die instantly. One such victim was collected in the NUS Kent Ridge Campus in November 2013.

The oriental magpie robin (*Copsychus saularis*) has a noticeable black-and-white pattern, but is even more conspicuous because of its melodious call for which it was widely trapped and reared in cages. This practice could have contributed in part to its uncommon occurrence in Singapore. However, there seems to be a thriving population at Kent Ridge.

Often seen perched on exposed branches, the Asian brown flycatcher (*Muscicapa dauurica*) makes forays into the immediate area to catch insects in flight, and then returns to the same perch. This nondescript bird is one of many species of small migratory birds that make an appearance in Singapore during the northern winter months.

The scarlet-backed flowerpecker (*Dicaeum cruentatum*) is a small, compact bird whose male is black on top, with a striking red crown and back. It feeds on the fruit of the mistletoe (for example,

Fig. 3.88: Spotted wood owl (*Strix seloputo*). Recognized as a nationally Critically Endangered species in Singapore, this large nocturnal bird has been encountered roosting in large trees at certain parts of the NUS Kent Ridge Campus. This individual is one of two birds photographed at Kent Ridge campus in March 2015

Dendrophthoe pentandra, *Macrosolen cochinchinensis* and *Viscum ovalifolium*) and helps spread this hemiparasitic plant around. Mistletoe seeds are sticky, and cause the flowerpecker's faeces to be sticky as well. As a consequence, it wipes its vent on tree branches each time it defecates. Mistletoe seeds thus lodged germinate on the branch.

Of the four species of sunbirds recorded from Kent Ridge, the olive-backed sunbird (*Cinnyris jugularis*) is probably the most common. It makes a nest of plant matter that resembles a pear with a hole at the side. The nest is often suspended from branches, railings or cables, sometimes in areas with high human traffic. Flitting from flower to flower, the sunbird inserts its long, curved bill into the centre of blossoms to feed on their nectar.

Frequently seen in built-up areas, Eurasian tree sparrows (*Passer montanus*) often join mynas and pigeons in raiding cafeterias or food centres. This species is a human commensal and is usually not found in wooded areas. With its short, conical beak, the scaly-breasted munia (*Lonchura punctulata*) looks like a sparrow. However, it has a short tail and a plain brown back, and inhabits exposed locations with long grass, often travelling in small flocks and feeding on grass seeds. Lawns and fields of short grass are the preferred habitat for the paddyfield pipit (*Anthus rufulus*). Even though it is exposed and actively foraging, this small, brown-streaked resident bird is so well camouflaged in the grass that it easily escapes detection.

Table 3.9: Birds of Kent Ridge

Nomenclature and classification follow those adopted by D.L. Yong, K.C. Lim and T.K. Yee.[1] R—resident (native), I—introduced resident (non-native), M—migrant (non-native), P—passage migrant (non-native), N—non-breeding visitor (non-native), Es—escapee or released from captivity (with no established local population; non-native). Abundance in Singapore: 1—very rare, 2—rare, 3—uncommon, 4—common, 5—very common, ?—unknown, NA—not applicable. Only native species have a national conservation status category. The national conservation status categories follow those of the second edition of *The Singapore Red Data Book*.[2] The checklist of present-day birds was compiled from a survey in 2003,[3] surveys from 1991 to 1996,[4] a website on the birds of the NUS Kent Ridge Campus[5] and more recent records and publications.[6]

S/No.	Common Name	Scientific Name	Family	Nativeness and Abundance	National Conservation Status
1.	Japanese sparrowhawk	*Accipiter gularis*	Accipitridae	M, 4	
2.	Chinese sparrowhawk	*Accipiter soloensis*	Accipitridae	M, 3	
3.	Crested goshawk	*Accipiter trivirgatus*	Accipitridae	R, 3	Critically Endangered
4.	Besra	*Accipiter virgatus*	Accipitridae	M, 2	
5.	Crested myna	*Acridotheres cristatellus*	Sturnidae	I, 1	
6.	Javan myna, white-vented myna	*Acridotheres javanicus*	Sturnidae	I, 5	
7.	Black-winged myna, black-winged starling	*Acridotheres melanopterus* (synonym: *Sturnus melanopterus*)	Sturnidae	Es, NA	
8.	Common myna	*Acridotheres tristis*	Sturnidae	R, 4	Common
9.	Black-browed reed warbler	*Acrocephalus bistrigiceps*	Acrocephalidae	M, 3	
10.	Oriental reed warbler	*Acrocephalus orientalis*	Acrocephalidae	M, 4	
11.	Common sandpiper	*Actitis hypoleucos*	Scolopacidae	M, 5	
12.	Common iora	*Aegithina tiphia*	Aegithinidae	R, 5	Common
13.	Germain's swiftlet, edible-nest swiftlet	*Aerodramus germaini* (also as: *Collocalia fuciphaga; Aerodramus fuciphagus*)	Apodidae	R, 5	Common
14.	Black-nest swiftlet	*Aerodramus maximus* (synonym: *Collocalia maxima*)	Apodidae	R, 3	Common
15.	Crimson sunbird	*Aethopyga siparaja*	Nectariniidae	R, 4	Common
16.	Daurian starling, purple-backed starling	*Agropsar sturninus* (synonym: *Sturnus sturninus*)	Sturnidae	M, 4	
17.	Common kingfisher	*Alcedo atthis*	Alcedinidae	M, 4	
18.	White-breasted waterhen	*Amaurornis phoenicurus*	Rallidae	R/M, 5	Common

S/No.	Common Name	Scientific Name	Family	Nativeness and Abundance	National Conservation Status
19.	Yellow-fronted parrot	*Amazona orchocephala*	Psittacidae	Es, NA	
20.	Oriental pied hornbill	*Anthracoceros albirostris*	Bucerotidae	R, 3	Critically Endangered
21.	Brown-throated sunbird	*Anthreptes malacensis*	Nectariniidae	R, 5	Common
22.	Paddyfield pipit, Richard's pipit	*Anthus rufulus* (also as: *Anthus novaeseelandiae*)	Motacillidae	R, 5	Common
23.	Asian glossy starling, Philippine glossy starling	*Aplonis panayensis*	Sturnidae	R, 5	Common
24.	House swift	*Apus nipalensis* (also as: *Apus affinis*)	Apodidae	R, 3	Common
25.	Pacific swift, fork-tailed swift	*Apus pacificus*	Apodidae	M, 3	
26.	Great egret	*Ardea alba* (synonym: *Casmerodius albus*)	Ardeidae	M, 4	
27.	Grey heron	*Ardea cinerea*	Ardeidae	R/M?, 4	Vulnerable
28.	Purple heron	*Ardea purpurea*	Ardeidae	R, 3	Endangered
29.	Great-billed heron	*Ardea sumatrana*	Ardeidae	R, 3	Critically Endangered
30.	Chinese pond heron	*Ardeola bacchus*	Ardeidae	M, 5	
31.	Black baza	*Aviceda leuphotes*	Accipitridae	M, 4	
32.	Eastern cattle egret, cattle egret	*Bubulcus coromandus* (also as: *Bubulcus ibis*)	Ardeidae	I/M, 4	
33.	Great hornbill	*Buceros bicornis*	Bucerotidae	Es, NA	
34.	Grey-faced buzzard	*Butastur indicus*	Accipitridae	M, 2	
35.	Common buzzard	*Buteo buteo*	Accipitridae	M, 3	
36.	Striated heron, little heron	*Butorides striata*	Ardeidae	R/M, 5	Common

S/No.	Common Name	Scientific Name	Family	Nativeness and Abundance	National Conservation Status
37.	Tanimbar corella, Goffin's cockatoo	*Cacatua goffiniana* (synonym: *Cacatua goffini*)	Cacatuidae	I, 4	
38.	Yellow-crested cockatoo	*Cacatua sulphurea*	Cacatuidae	I, 3	
39.	Plaintive cuckoo	*Cacomantis merulinus*	Cuculidae	R, 3	Common
40.	Rusty-breasted cuckoo	*Cacomantis sepulcralis*	Cuculidae	R, 3	Vulnerable
41.	Banded bay cuckoo	*Cacomantis sonneratii*	Cuculidae	R, 3	Common
42.	Savanna nightjar	*Caprimulgus affinis*	Caprimulgidae	R, 4	Common
43.	Grey nightjar	*Caprimulgus jotaka* (also as: *Caprimulgus indicus*)	Caprimulgidae	M, 3	
44.	Large-tailed nightjar	*Caprimulgus macrurus*	Caprimulgidae	R, 4	Common
45.	Red-rumped swallow	*Cecropis daurica* (synonym: *Hirundo daurica*)	Hirundinidae	M, 4	
46.	Lesser coucal	*Centropus bengalensis*	Cuculidae	R, 4	Common
47.	Greater coucal	*Centropus sinensis*	Cuculidae	R, 3	Common
48.	Oriental dwarf kingfisher, black-backed kingfisher	*Ceyx erithaca*	Alcedinidae	M, 3	
49.	Common emerald dove	*Chalcophaps indica*	Columbidae	R, 4	Common
50.	Little ringed plover	*Charadrius dubius*	Charadriidae	M, 4	
51.	Lesser sand plover, Mongolian plover	*Charadrius mongolus*	Charadriidae	M, 5	
52.	Golden-fronted leafbird	*Chloropsis aurifrons*	Chloropseidae	Es, NA	
53.	Blue-winged leafbird	*Chloropsis cochinchinensis*	Chloropseidae	R, 4	Common

S/No.	Common Name	Scientific Name	Family	Nativeness and Abundance	National Conservation Status
54.	Little bronze cuckoo	*Chrysococcyx malayanus* (also as: *Chrysococcyx minutillus*)	Cuculidae	R, 4	Common
55.	Banded woodpecker	*Chrysophlegma miniaceum* (synonym: *Picus miniaceus*)	Picidae	R, 4	Common
56.	Olive-backed sunbird	*Cinnyris jugularis* (synonym: *Nectarinia jugularis*)	Nectariniidae	R, 5	Common
57.	Zitting cisticola	*Cisticola juncidis*	Cisticolidae	R, 4	Common
58.	Chestnut-winged cuckoo	*Clamator coromandus*	Cuculidae	M, 3	
59.	Rock dove, feral pigeon	*Columba livia*	Columbidae	I, 5	
60.	White-rumped shama	*Copsychus malabaricus*	Muscicapidae	R, 3	Critically Endangered
61.	Oriental magpie-robin	*Copsychus saularis*	Muscicapidae	R, 4	Endangered
62.	Large-billed crow	*Corvus macrorhynchos*	Corvidae	R, 4	Common
63.	House crow	*Corvus splendens*	Corvidae	I, 5	
64.	Indian cuckoo	*Cuculus micropterus*	Cuculidae	M, 4	
65.	Zappey's flycatcher, blue-and-white flycatcher	*Cyanoptila cumatilis* (also as: *Cyanoptila cyanomelana*)	Muscicapidae	M, ?	
66.	Brown-chested jungle flycatcher	*Cyornis brunneatus* (synonym: *Rhinomyias brunneata*)	Muscicapidae	M, 3	
67.	Asian palm swift	*Cypsiurus balasiensis*	Apodidae	R, 3	Common
68.	Asian house martin	*Delichon dasypus*	Hirundinidae	M, 2	
69.	Sunda pygmy woodpecker, brown-capped woodpecker	*Dendrocopos moluccensis* (synonym: *Picoides moluccensis*)	Picidae	R, 5	Common
70.	Wandering whistling duck	*Dendrocygna arcuata*	Anatidae	I, 3	

S/No.	Common Name	Scientific Name	Family	Nativeness and Abundance	National Conservation Status
71.	Lesser whistling duck	*Dendrocygna javanica*	Anatidae	R, 3	Endangered
72.	Forest wagtail	*Dendronanthus indicus*	Motacillidae	M, 4	
73.	Scarlet-backed flowerpecker	*Dicaeum cruentatum*	Dicaeidae	R, 5	Common
74.	Crow-billed drongo	*Dicrurus annectans*	Dicruridae	M, 3	
75.	Ashy drongo	*Dicrurus leucophaeus*	Dicruridae	M, 2	
76.	Black drongo	*Dicrurus macrocercus*	Dicruridae	M, 2	
77.	Greater racket-tailed drongo	*Dicrurus paradiseus*	Dicruridae	R, 4	Common
78.	Common goldenback	*Dinopium javanense*	Picidae	R, 4	Common
79.	Pied imperial pigeon	*Ducula bicolor*	Columbidae	N/I, 3	
80.	Black bittern	*Dupetor flavicollis*	Ardeidae	M, 3	
81.	Eclectus parrot	*Eclectus roratus*	Psittacidae	Es, NA	
82.	Black-winged kite, black-shouldered kite	*Elanus caeruleus*	Accipitridae	R, 4	Common
83.	Asian koel, common koel	*Eudynamys scolopaceus*	Cuculidae	R/M?, 5	Common
84.	Oriental dollarbird, dollarbird	*Eurystomus orientalis*	Coraciidae	R/M, 4	Common
85.	King quail, blue-breasted quail	*Excalfactoria chinensis* (synonym: *Coturnix chinensis*)	Phasianidae	R, 3	Common
86.	Peregrine falcon	*Falco peregrinus*	Falconidae	M/N, 3	
87.	Common kestrel	*Falco tinnunculus*	Falconidae	M, 2	
88.	Green-backed flycatcher, narcissus flycatcher	*Ficedula elisae* (also as: *Ficedula narcissina*)	Muscicapidae	M, 2	
89.	Mugimaki flycatcher	*Ficedula mugimaki*	Muscicapidae	M, 3	
90.	Yellow-rumped flycatcher	*Ficedula zanthopygia*	Muscicapidae	M, 4	

S/No.	Common Name	Scientific Name	Family	Nativeness and Abundance	National Conservation Status
91.	Watercock	*Gallicrex cinerea*	Rallidae	M, 3	
92.	Pin-tailed snipe	*Gallinago stenura*	Scolopacidae	M, ?	
93.	Slaty-breasted rail	*Gallirallus striatus* (synonym: *Rallus striatus*)	Rallidae	R, 3	Common
94.	Red junglefowl	*Gallus gallus*	Phasianidae	R, 3	Endangered
95.	Chinese hwamei	*Garrulax canorus*	Leiothrichidae	I, 3	
96.	Black-throated laughingthrush	*Garrulax chinensis*	Leiothrichidae	Es, NA	
97.	White-crested laughingthrush	*Garrulax leucolophus diardi*	Leiothrichidae	I, 4	
98.	Greater necklaced laughingthrush	*Garrulax pectoralis*	Leiothrichidae	Es, NA	
99.	Siberian thrush	*Geokichla sibirica* (synonym: *Zoothera sibirica*)	Turdidae	M, 2	
100.	Zebra dove, peaceful dove	*Geopelia striata*	Columbidae	R, 5	Common
101.	Golden-bellied gerygone, flyeater	*Gerygone sulphurea*	Acanthizidae	R, 4	Common
102.	Oriental pratincole	*Glareola maldivarum*	Glareolidae	P, 3	
103.	Malayan night heron	*Gorsachius melanolophus*	Ardeidae	M, 2	
104.	Common hill myna	*Gracula religiosa*	Sturnidae	R, 4	Common
105.	Ruddy kingfisher	*Halcyon coromanda*	Alcedinidae	R/M, 3	Critically Endangered
106.	Black-capped kingfisher	*Halcyon pileata*	Alcedinidae	M, 3	
107.	White-throated kingfisher	*Halcyon smyrnensis*	Alcedinidae	R, 4	Common
108.	Grey-headed fish eagle	*Haliaeetus ichthyaetus* (synonym: *Ichthyophaga ichthyaetus*)	Accipitridae	R, 4	Critically Endangered
109.	White-bellied sea eagle	*Haliaeetus leucogaster*	Accipitridae	R, 4	Common

S/No.	Common Name	Scientific Name	Family	Nativeness and Abundance	National Conservation Status
110.	Brahminy kite	*Haliastur indus*	Accipitridae	R, 4	Common
111.	Grey-rumped treeswift	*Hemiprocne longipennis*	Hemiprocnidae	R, 4	Common
112.	Hodgson's hawk-cuckoo	*Hierococcyx nisicolor* (also as: *Cuculus fugax*)	Cuculidae	M, 3	
113.	Large hawk-cuckoo	*Hierococcyx sparverioides*	Cuculidae	M, 2	
114.	Silver-backed needletail, white-vented needletail	*Hirundapus cochinchinensis*	Apodidae	M, 2	
115.	Brown-backed needletail, brown needletail	*Hirundapus giganteus*	Apodidae	M/N, 3	
116.	Barn swallow	*Hirundo rustica*	Hirundinidae	M, 5	
117.	Pacific swallow	*Hirundo tahitica*	Hirundinidae	R, 5	Common
118.	Cinnamon bittern	*Ixobrychus cinnamomeus*	Ardeidae	R/M, 3	Common
119.	Von Schrenck's bittern	*Ixobrychus eurhythmus*	Ardeidae	M, 3	
120.	Yellow bittern	*Ixobrychus sinensis*	Ardeidae	R/M, 4	Common
121.	Pied triller	*Lalage nigra*	Campephagidae	R, 4	Common
122.	Brown shrike	*Lanius cristatus*	Laniidae	M, 4	
123.	Long-tailed shrike	*Lanius schach*	Laniidae	R, 3	Common
124.	Tiger shrike	*Lanius tigrinus*	Laniidae	M, 4	
125.	Van Hasselt's sunbird, purple-throated sunbird	*Leptocoma brasiliana* (synonym: *Nectarinia sperata*)	Nectariniidae	R, 4	Common
126.	Chestnut munia, black-headed munia	*Lonchura atricapilla* (synonym: *Lonchura malacca*)	Estrildidae	R, 4	Common
127.	Javan munia	*Lonchura leucogastroides*	Estrildidae	I, 3	
128.	White-headed munia	*Lonchura maja*	Estrildidae	R, 3	Common
129.	Scaly-breasted munia	*Lonchura punctulata*	Estrildidae	R, 5	Common

S/No.	Common Name	Scientific Name	Family	Nativeness and Abundance	National Conservation Status
130.	White-rumped munia	*Lonchura striata*	Estrildidae	R, 2	Critically Endangered
131.	Rufous-bellied hawk-eagle	*Lophotriorchis kienerii* (synonym: *Hieraaetus kienerii*)	Accipitridae	M/N?, 3	
132.	Blue-crowned hanging parrot	*Loriculus galgulus*	Psittacidae	R, 4	Endangered
133.	Siberian blue robin	*Luscinia cyane*	Muscicapidae	M, 4	
134.	Bat hawk	*Macheiramphus alcinus*	Accipitridae	N?, 1	
135.	Pin-striped tit-babbler, striped tit-babbler	*Macronus gularis* (synonym: *Mixornis gularis*)	Timaliidae	R, 5	Common
136.	Abbott's babbler	*Malacocincla abbotti* (synonym: *Trichastoma abbotti*)	Pellorneidae	R, 3	Common
137.	Budgerigar	*Melopsittacus undulatus*	Psittacidae	Es, NA	
138.	Blue-tailed bee-eater	*Merops philippinus* (synonym: *Merops superciliosus*)	Meropidae	M, 4	
139.	Blue-throated bee-eater	*Merops viridis*	Meropidae	R/M, 4	Common
140.	Rufous woodpecker	*Micropternus brachyurus* (synonym: *Celeus brachyurus*)	Picidae	R, 3	Common
141.	Grey wagtail	*Motacilla cinerea*	Motacillidae	M, 3	
142.	Western yellow wagtail	*Motacilla flava*	Motacillidae	M, 3	
143.	Asian brown flycatcher	*Muscicapa dauurica* (synonym: *Muscicapa latirostris*)	Muscicapidae	M, 5	
144.	Ferruginous flycatcher	*Muscicapa ferruginea*	Muscicapidae	M, 3	
145.	Brown-streaked flycatcher	*Muscicapa williamsoni*	Muscicapidae	N, 3	
146.	Blyth's hawk-eagle	*Nisaetus alboniger* (synonym: *Spizaetus alboniger*)	Accipitridae	N, 1	

S/No.	Common Name	Scientific Name	Family	Nativeness and Abundance	National Conservation Status
147.	Changeable hawk-eagle	*Nisaetus cirrhatus* (synonym: *Spizaetus cirrhatus*)	Accipitridae	R, 4	Endangered
148.	Black-crowned night heron	*Nycticorax nycticorax*	Ardeidae	R, 3	Critically Endangered
149.	Cockatiel	*Nymphicus hollandicus*	Cacatuidae	Es, NA	
150.	Black-naped oriole	*Oriolus chinensis*	Oriolidae	R/M, 5	Common
151.	Dark-necked tailorbird	*Orthotomus atrogularis*	Cisticolidae	R, 4	Common
152.	Ashy tailorbird	*Orthotomus ruficeps*	Cisticolidae	R, 4	Common
153.	Rufous-tailed tailorbird	*Orthotomus sericeus*	Cisticolidae	R, 3	Common
154.	Common tailorbird	*Orthotomus sutorius*	Cisticolidae	R, 5	Common
155.	Sunda scops owl, collared scops owl	*Otus lempiji* (also as: *Otus bakkamoena*)	Strigidae	R, 4	Common
156.	Oriental scops owl	*Otus sunia*	Strigidae	M, 2	
157.	Eurasian tree sparrow	*Passer montanus*	Passeridae	R, 5	Common
158.	Ashy minivet	*Pericrocotus divaricatus*	Campephagidae	M, 4	
159.	Crested honey buzzard, Oriental honey-buzzard	*Pernis ptilorhynchus*	Accipitridae	M/N, 4	
160.	Arctic warbler	*Phylloscopus borealis*	Phylloscopidae	M, 5	
161.	Eastern crowned warbler	*Phylloscopus coronatus*	Phylloscopidae	M, 3	
162.	Yellow-browed warbler, inornate warbler	*Phylloscopus inornatus*	Phylloscopidae	M, 2	
163.	Laced woodpecker	*Picus vittatus*	Picidae	R, 4	Common
164.	Baya weaver	*Ploceus philippinus*	Ploceidae	R, 4	Common
165.	Pacific golden plover	*Pluvialis fulva*	Charadriidae	M, 5	
166.	Palm cockatoo	*Probosciger aterrimus*	Cacatuidae	Es, NA	

S/No.	Common Name	Scientific Name	Family	Nativeness and Abundance	National Conservation Status
167.	Coppersmith barbet	*Psilopogon haemacephalus* (synonym: *Megalaima haemacephala*)	Megalaimidae	R, 4	Common
168.	Lineated barbet	*Psilopogon lineatus* (synonym: *Megalaima lineata*)	Megalaimidae	I, 4	
169.	Red-breasted parakeet	*Psittacula alexandri*	Psittacidae	I, 4	
170.	Rose-ringed parakeet	*Psittacula krameri*	Psittacidae	I, 3	
171.	Long-tailed parakeet	*Psittacula longicauda*	Psittacidae	R, 4	Common
172.	Grey parrot	*Psittacus erithacus*	Psittacidae	Es, NA	
173.	Jambu fruit dove	*Ptilinopus jambu*	Columbidae	R/N?, 3	Common
174.	Yellow-vented bulbul	*Pycnonotus goiavier*	Pycnonotidae	R, 5	Common
175.	Red-whiskered bulbul	*Pycnonotus jocosus*	Pycnonotidae	I, 3	
176.	Olive-winged bulbul	*Pycnonotus plumosus*	Pycnonotidae	R, 4	Common
177.	Straw-headed bulbul	*Pycnonotus zeylanicus*	Pycnonotidae	R, 4	Endangered
178.	Red-legged crake	*Rallina fasciata*	Rallidae	R/M, 3	Vulnerable
179.	Malaysian pied fantail, pied fantail	*Rhipidura javanica*	Rhipiduridae	R, 4	Common
180.	Sand martin	*Riparia riparia*	Hirundinidae	M, 3	
181.	Crested partridge	*Rollulus rouloul*	Phasianidae	Es, NA	
182.	Coleto	*Sarcops calvus*	Sturnidae	Es, NA	
183.	Crested serpent eagle	*Spilornis cheela*	Accipitridae	R/N, 3	Critically Endangered
184.	Spotted dove	*Streptopelia chinensis*	Columbidae	R, 5	Common
185.	Spotted wood owl	*Strix seloputo*	Strigidae	R, 3	Critically Endangered
186.	White-shouldered starling	*Sturnia sinensis* (synonym: *Sturnus sinensis*)	Sturnidae	M, 3	

S/No.	Common Name	Scientific Name	Family	Nativeness and Abundance	National Conservation Status
187.	Square-tailed drongo-cuckoo, drongo cuckoo	*Surniculus lugubris*	Cuculidae	R/M, 3	Critically Endangered
188.	Great-billed parrot	*Tanygnathus megalorhynchus*	Psittacidae	Es, NA	
189.	Knysna turaco	*Tauraco corythaix*	Musophagidae	Es, NA	
190.	Asian paradise flycatcher	*Terpsiphone paradisi*	Monarchidae	M, 4	
191.	Collared kingfisher	*Todiramphus chloris* (synonym: *Halcyon chloris*)	Alcedinidae	R, 5	Common
192.	Thick-billed green pigeon	*Treron curvirostra*	Columbidae	R, 3	Endangered
193.	Pink-necked green pigeon,	*Treron vernans*	Columbidae	R, 5	Common
194.	Coconut lorikeet, rainbow lorikeet	*Trichoglossus haematodus*	Psittacidae	I, 3	
195.	Common redshank	*Tringa totanus*	Scolopacidae	M, 5	
196.	Eye-browed thrush	*Turdus obscurus*	Turdidae	M, 3	
197.	Barred buttonquail	*Turnix suscitator*	Turnicidae	R, 3	Common
198.	Red-billed blue magpie	Urocissa erythrorhyncha	Corvidae	Es, NA	
199.	Chestnut-flanked white-eye	Zosterops erythropleurus	Zosteropidae	Es, NA	
200.	Japanese white-eye	Zosterops japonicus	Zosteropidae	Es, NA	
201.	Oriental white-eye	Zosterops palpebrosus	Zosteropidae	I?, 4	

Notes to Table 3.9

1. D.L. Yong, K.C. Lim and T.K. Lee, *A Naturalist's Guide to the Birds of Singapore*, 2nd ed. (Oxford: John Beaufoy Publishing, 2016), pp. 1–176.
2. Davison, "The Red List Categories", p. 3; Lim Kim Seng, Alfred Chia, Kenneth Kee, Ho Hua Chew, Lim Kim Chuah, Lim Kim Keang, Alan Owyong, Sunny Yeo, Sutari Supari and Yong

Ding Li, "Birds", in *The Singapore Red Data Book: Threatened Plants and Animals of Singapore*, 2nd ed., ed. Davison et al. (Singapore: Nature Society Singapore, 2008), pp. 266–7.

3. Sodhi and Tan, "Report on the Ecosystem Study of the Proposed Site for the Nature Area at the NUS Kent Ridge Campus", pp. 19–21.

4. Ho Hua Chew and Clive Briffett, *Kent Ridge Environs: A Proposal for Conserving Nature at the National University of Singapore Campus* (Singapore: Malayan Nature Society, 1991), pp. 25–7; Angus Lamont, "The Birds of Kent Ridge Park, Singapore", *Raffles Bulletin of Zoology* 46, 1 (1998): 113–22.

5. David Tan and Zachary Kok, "Checklist of the Birds of the National University of Singapore", https://nusavifauna.wordpress.com/checklist/ [accessed 20 Mar. 2016].

6. Luan Keng Wang and Christopher J. Hails, "An Annotated Checklist of the Birds of Singapore", *Raffles Bulletin of Zoology*, Supplement No. 15 (2007): 1–179; Kim Seng Lim, Alfred Chia, Ding Li Yong and Jimmy Chew, *The Avifauna of Singapore* (Singapore: Nature Society Singapore Bird Group Records Committee, 2009), pp. 1–611; Sylvester J.M. Lim, "A White-Crested Laughing Thrush in a Canteen at Kent Ridge", *Singapore Biodiversity Records* (2015): 74; Tan Heok Hui, "Oriental White-Eye Nesting at Kent Ridge", *Singapore Biodiversity Records* (2014): 2–3; Tan Heok Hui and Li Ling Koh, "Spotted Wood Owls at Kent Ridge", *Singapore Biodiversity Records* (2015): 43–5.

Fish

Of the 14 species of fish found in the two ponds of Kent Ridge Park, only four species are native. One is the crescent fighting fish (*Betta imbellis*) which, although native, is more likely to have been released into the ponds at Kent Ridge as its natural habitat is lowland swamp.[83] Another is the common snakehead (*Channa striata*), which is commercially exploited as a food fish, the flesh of which is thought to be a tonic for wound-healing after operations, like those of the other snakehead found there—the giant snakehead or toman (*Channa micropeltes*). The third native is the Sunda swamp-eel (*Monopterus javanensis*) and the fourth is the soon hock (*Oxyeleotris marmorata*) but the latter species grows in brackish water (for example, mangrove sites).[84] However, owing to the isolation of the ponds in Kent Ridge Park, it is more likely that soon hock were released there rather than migrated from coastal waters. There are such few native fish species because the ponds in Kent Ridge are not natural and do not provide the conditions needed for most native fish species which occur in forest streams[85] that are absent in Kent Ridge.

Kent Ridge has only 10 of the 54 non-native alien fish species recorded in Singapore,[86] and this is likely owed entirely to what people have released into the ponds in Kent Ridge Park. The Midas cichlid (*Amphilophus citrinellus*), koi (*Cyprinus carpio*), red-tailed catfish (*Phractocephalus hemioliopterus*), Sumatran tiger barb (*Puntigrus tetrazona*) and red-tailed rasbora (*Rasbora borapetensis*) are all ornamental aquarium species and are likely to be released into these ponds.[87,88,89] Other fish such as the insectivorous mosquitofish (*Gambusia affinis*) and guppy (*Poecilia reticulata*) were introduced for biological control of mosquitoes[90] and have since become naturalized. Toman is (*Channa micropeltes*), tilapia (*Oreochromis mossambicus*) and red pacu (*Piaractus brachypomus*) are likely to be released into the ponds too as they are food fish species.

Fig. 3.89: Koi (*Cyprinus carpio*) caught in the larger pond of Kent Ridge Park on 29 April 2004. This specimen was most likely released into the pond

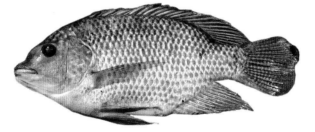

Fig. 3.90: Tilapia (*Oreochromis mossambicus*) caught in the larger pond of Kent Ridge Park on 29 April 2016. This fish was introduced to Singapore for food and has since spread to most water bodies such as reservoirs and ponds

Table 3.10: Fishes of Kent Ridge

The nomenclature and classification largely follows that of Nick Baker and Kelvin K.P. Lim.[1] The national conservation status follows those of the second edition of *The Singapore Red Data Book*.[2] The fish records of the ponds of Kent Ridge Park are courtesy of Tan Heok Hui from surveys he conducted in 2003 and 2004.

S/No.	Common Name	Scientific Name	Family	Native or Exotic	National Conservation Status
1.	Midas cichlid	*Amphilophus citrinellus*	Cichlidae	Exotic	

S/No.	Common Name	Scientific Name	Family	Native or Exotic	National Conservation Status
2.	Crescent fighting-fish	*Betta imbellis*	Osphronemidae	Native	Common
3.	Giant snakehead, toman	*Channa micropeltes*	Channidae	Exotic	
4.	Common snakehead	*Channa striata*	Channidae	Native	Common
5.	Common carp, koi	*Cyprinus carpio*	Cyprinidae	Exotic	
6.	Mosquitofish	*Gambusia affinis*	Poeciliidae	Exotic	
7.	Sunda swamp-eel	*Monopterus javanensis*	Synbranchidae	Native	Common
8.	Mozambique tilapia	*Oreochromis mossambicus*	Cichlidae	Exotic	
9.	Marbled gudgeon, marbled goby, soon hock	*Oxyeleotris marmorata*	Eleotridae	Native	Common
10.	Red-tailed catfish	*Phractocephalus hemiliopterus*	Pimelodidae	Exotic	
11.	Red pacu	*Piaractus brachypomus*	Serrasalmidae	Exotic	
12.	Guppy	*Poecilia reticulata*	Poeciliidae	Exotic	
13.	Sumatran tiger barb	*Puntigrus tetrazona*	Cyprinidae	Exotic	
14.	Red-tailed rasbora	*Rasbora borapetensis*	Cyprinidae	Exotic	

Notes to Table 3.10
1. Baker and Lim, *Wild Animals of Singapore*, pp. 157–8.
2. Davison, "The Red List Categories", p. 3; Lim, "Fishes, Amphibians and Reptiles", pp. 263–4.

Mammals

Of the commensal mammals, the Oriental house rat (*Rattus tanezumi*) is perhaps most despised. This resilient creature is found both in the forest and in buildings. It is an excellent climber and swimmer, and eats just about anything. In buildings, it subsists on scraps of human food, and nibbles on soap bars and books. The occasional rat has been known to make its nest in desk drawers or wall cabinets.

Even though it resembles a rat, the house shrew (*Suncus murinus*) is not even a rodent. Its jaws are lined with a row of sharp teeth. At night, it scurries about on its short limbs on lawns and in drains in search of discarded scraps of food or insects such as cockroaches. Its sense of smell is good, but its eyesight is rather poor. When taken by surprise, a house shrew emits an ear-piercing shriek, which can startle a potential predator.

The diurnally active common treeshrew (*Tupaia glis*) lives in the forest and, except for its long and tapering snout and rows of sharp teeth, acts and looks like a squirrel. Despite it being a good climber, the treeshrew tends to keep to the forest understorey where it travels alone or in pairs, searching for insects and fruits. It appears to be uncommon at Kent Ridge.

On roadside trees, the plantain squirrel (*Callosciurus notatus*) may be seen scurrying along the branches and scaling tree trunks with its tail flicking. Although primarily arboreal, these squirrels do descend to the ground to forage or to access another tree. They often try to cross roads but many of Kent Ridge's less streetsmart individuals have met a grisly end under the wheels of oncoming vehicles.

Resembling little dogs with wings, the common short-nosed fruit bat (*Cynopterus brachyotis*) is common in Kent Ridge campus. Individuals, or groups of individuals, may be seen roosting in buildings, suspended from overhangs in quieter areas. With their large eyes and excellent night vision, they flit among trees at night in search of ripe fruit, such as those of the tiup-tiup. They also obtain nectar from blossoms. They are known to help in forest succession by pollinating flowers, and dispersing seeds far away from the parent trees. However, they are messy, and often dirty buildings with their faeces and uneaten food below their roosting sites.

Another group of bats, though not blind, navigates in the darkness with

Fig. 3.91: Oriental house rat (*Rattus tanezumi*). A familiar and much reviled creature which often frequents urban environments. This adult example was trapped inside a building in Kent Ridge Campus in July 2005

Fig. 3.92: Plantain squirrel (*Callosciurus notatus*). This arboreal rodent is common in Singapore, and can be found in forest, as well as in urban areas. At Kent Ridge, it can occasionally be seen scuttling among the branches of large roadside trees. It has a reddish belly and a black and white stripe on each side of its body

Fig. 3.93: Long-tailed macaque (*Macaca fascicularis*). A mother breastfeeding her child on a road in Kent Ridge Park in August 2009. Macaques usually move about in groups, but lone individuals, perhaps ousted by their troop, are sometimes seen in Kent Ridge

echolocation. These creatures feed mainly on flying insects by taking them on the wing. Of a handful of insectivorous bats recorded from Kent Ridge, the lesser Asiatic house bat (*Scotophilus kuhli*) appears to be the most frequent,[91] being the most common insectivorous bat in Singapore.[92] This species roosts in large numbers in the roof spaces of buildings, as well as in the crowns of palm trees. It takes to the air at dusk, hawking for insects in open areas. The house bat is known to roost in wooden bat boxes installed in trees in Kent Ridge as part of a project to record the bat diversity of Singapore.

The only wild carnivore to frequent Kent Ridge is rarely seen as it is nocturnally active. However, it leaves signs that betrays its presence in the form of faeces, often deposited on exposed concrete surfaces. The Sumatran palm civet (*Paradoxurus musangus*) is about the size of a cat but has a relatively long tail. With its blackish face mask it resembles a raccoon, and has been mistaken for this North American native. This arboreal creature feeds on fruit and seeds, as well as a variety of small animals.

The long-tailed macaque (*Macaca fascicularis*) seems to be the only native wild primate in Kent Ridge. It is gregarious, travelling in groups led by a large male. This omnivorous creature is active both in the trees and on the ground. Individuals that have frequent contact with humans become bold and often resort to begging for human food to supplement their diet. A large alpha male was reported to have attacked three people over three weeks at the Forest Walk in HortPark,[93] which is immediately north of the eastern end of Kent Ridge.

The wild pig (*Sus scrofa*) was once thought to be extinct in Singapore, but it seems to be making a comeback, with animals having swum across the Johor Straits from Malaysia. The wild pig is the only hoofed mammal, and the largest mammal, to be found at Kent Ridge and this is rather surprising considering the fact that it must have crossed unnatural barriers such as expressways[94] to get here. Despite its large size, it can be difficult to see as it is shy and tends to keep to the cover of dense vegetation. The presence of wild pigs in an area is often indicated by patches of turned-over earth, caused by their foraging for grubs, earthworms and roots.

Wild dogs (*Canis familiaris*) roamed Kent Ridge, especially in the forested areas, until the 1990s when the Agri-Food & Veterinary Authority dog shooters eradicated them. They moved in small packs and occasionally harassed and bit a few undergraduate students in Kent Ridge Campus. Hugh T.W. Tan remembers encountering a small pack in the adinandra belukar patch behind the current Institute of Systems Science as well as a small pack in the forest patch behind Block S2 along Kent Ridge Road in the 1990s.

Table 3.11: Mammals of Kent Ridge

The nomenclature and classification largely follows those of Nick Baker and Kelvin K.P. Lim.[1] The national conservation status categories follow those of the second edition of *The Singapore Red Data Book*.[2,3] The checklist of present-day mammals was compiled from various surveys in 1991[4] and publications.[5,6,7,8,9,10,11]

S/No.	Common Name	Scientific Name	Family	Native or Exotic	National Conservation Status
1.	Plantain squirrel	*Callosciurus notatus*	Sciuridae	Native	Common
2.	Wild dog	*Canis familiaris*	Canidae	Exotic	Common
3.	Lesser dog-faced fruit bat	*Cynopterus brachyotis*	Pteropodidae	Native	Common
4.	Smooth-coated otter	*Lutrogale perspicillata*	Mustelidae	Native	Critically Endangered
5.	Long-tailed macaque	*Macaca fascicularis*	Cercopithecidae	Native	Common
6.	Sunda pangolin	*Manis javanica*	Manidae	Native	Critically Endangered
7.	Whiskered myotis	*Myotis muricola*	Vespertilionidae	Native	Common
8.	Sumatran palm civet	*Paradoxurus musangus* (also as: *Paradoxurus hermaphroditus*)	Viverridae	Native	Common
9.	Javan pipistrelle	*Pipistrellus javanicus*	Vespertilionidae	Native	Common
10.	Oriental house rat	*Rattus tanezumi* (also as: *Rattus rattus*)	Muridae	Native	Common
11.	Pouched tomb bat	*Saccolaimus saccolaimus* (synonym: *Taphozous saccolaimus*)	Emballonuridae	Native	Common
12.	Lesser Asiatic yellow house bat	*Scotophilus kuhlii*	Vespertilionidae	Native	Common
13.	House shrew	*Suncus murinus*	Soricidae	Native?	Common
14.	Wild pig	*Sus scrofa*	Suidae	Native	Common
15.	Black-bearded tomb bat	*Taphozous melanopogon*	Emballonuridae	Native	Endangered

S/No.	Common Name	Scientific Name	Family	Native or Exotic	National Conservation Status
16.	Dusky leaf monkey	*Trachypithecus obscurus*	Cercopithecidae	Exotic	
17.	Common treeshrew	*Tupaia glis*	Tupaiidae	Native	Common

Notes to Table 3.11
1. Baker and Lim, *Wild Animals of Singapore*, pp. 162–3.
2. Davison, "The Red List Categories", p. 3.
3. Kelvin K.P. Lim, "Mammals", in *The Singapore Red Data Book: Threatened Plants and Animals of Singapore*, 2nd ed., ed. Davison et al. (Singapore: Nature Society Singapore, 2008), p. 267.
4. Chew and Briffett, *Kent Ridge Environs*, p. 24.
5. Shirley A. Pottie, "Studies of the Ecology and Behaviour of Insectivorous Bat Species in Singapore", MSc thesis (Singapore: National University of Singapore, 1998), pp. 5–7.
6. Ong Say Lin, "Wild Pig (*Sus scrofa*) Distribution in Mainland Singapore and Human-Wildlife Management Challenges", research project (Singapore: National University of Singapore, 2012), pp. 11–3.
7. Baker and Lim, *Wild Animals of Singapore*, pp. 162–3.
8. Tan H.H. and K.K.P. Lim, "Javan pipistrelle at Kent Ridge campus", *Singapore Biodiversity Records* (2017): 49.
9. Derek Wong, "Another lost pangolin this week, found in NUS this time, rescued and released into the wild", *The Straits Times* (*online edition*), 27 Nov. 2016.
10. Diane Leow, "Teacher's pet? Otters spotted at NUS", *Channel News Asia* (*online edition*), 13 Feb. 2017.
11. Hazelina H.T. Yeo, "Dusky langur at Kent Ridge", *Singapore Biodiversity Records* (2013): 125.

Notes

1. John Pitts, "Pre-Quaternary Geology of the Islands", in *The Singapore Story: Physical Adjustments in a Changing Landscape*, ed. Avijit Gupta and John Pitts (Singapore: Singapore University Press, 1992), p. 60.
2. The commemorative plaque at the junction of South Buona Vista Road and Prince George's Park states: "By gracious consent of Her Majesty Queen Elizabeth II this ridge was named Kent Ridge by the Governor of Singapore HE Sir John Nicoll KCMG to commemorate the visit paid to the Army in Singapore by HRH, the Duchess of Kent and HRH, the Duke of Kent, on 3 October 1952."
3. J. Wyatt-Smith, *Manual of Malayan Silviculture for Inland Forest*, Malayan Forest Records No. 23 (Kuala Lumpur: Forest Research Institute Malaysia, 1963), Part III, 7.20–1.

4.   Richard T. Corlett, "Terrestrial Ecosystems", in *Singapore Biodiversity: An Encyclopaedia of the Natural Environment and Sustainable Development,* ed. Peter K.L. Ng, Richard T. Corlett and Hugh T.W. Tan (Singapore: EDM and Raffles Museum of Biodiversity Research, 2011), p. 45.

5.   Ibid.

6.   I.M. Turner and K.S. Chua, *Checklist of the Vascular Plant Species of the Bukit Timah Nature Reserve* (Singapore: Raffles Museum of Biodiversity Research, 2011), p. 4.

7.   Tony O'Dempsey and Chew Ping Ting, "The Freshwater Swamp Forests of Sungei Seletar Catchment: A Status Report", in *Proceedings of Nature Society, Singapore's Conference on 'Nature Conservation for a Sustainable Singapore'—16th October 2011*, ed. Leong Tzi Ming and Ho Hua Chew, pp. 121–66.

8.   E.J.H. Corner, "The Freshwater Swamp-forest of South Johore and Singapore", *Gardens' Bulletin Singapore,* Supplement 1 (1978): 23–4.

9.   H.F. Wong, S.Y. Tan, C.Y. Koh, H.J.M. Siow, T. Li, A. Heyzer, A.H.F. Ang, Mirza Rifqi bin Ismail, A. Strivathsan and Hugh T.W. Tan, *Checklist of the Plant Species of Nee Soon Swamp Forest, Singapore: Bryophytes to Angiosperms* (Singapore: Raffles Museum of Biodiversity Research, 2013), p. 2.

10.   Hugh T.W. Tan, B.C. Soong and T. Morgany, "Plants", in *A Guide to the Mangroves of Singapore Vol. 1*, ed. Peter K.L. Ng and N. Sivasothi (Singapore: Singapore Science Centre, 1999), pp. 151–2.

11.   See Chapter 1 in this volume.

12.   Wong Poh Poh, "The Changing Landscapes of Singapore Island", in *Modern Singapore*, ed. Ooi Jin-Bee and Chiang Hai Ding (Singapore: University of Singapore, 1969), pp. 28–9.

13.   The ridge was apparently occupied by the British army just before World War II. A concrete observation post and two barracks were apparently built in 1936 based on their markings. The barracks were built in two steps below the observation post along northeastern slope of the over 70-metre-tall hill, on the top of which is sited the larger water tank of Kent Ridge Campus. The observation post is just below the base of the tank.

14.   Hugh T.W. Tan et al., *The Natural Heritage of Singapore* (Singapore and New York: Prentice Hall, 2010), p. 297.

15.   J.W.S. Sim, Hugh T.W. Tan and I.M. Turner, "Adinandra Belukar: An Anthropogenic Heath Forest in Singapore", *Vegetatio* 102, 2 (1992): 125.

16.   R.E. Holttum, "Adinandra Belukar: A Succession of Vegetation from Bare Ground on Singapore Island", *Malayan Journal of Tropical Geography* 3 (1954): 27–32.

17.   Alex Thiam Koon Yee, Kwek Yan Chong, Louise Neo and Hugh T.W. Tan, "Updating the Classification System for the Secondary Forests of Singapore", *Raffles Bulletin*

of Zoology, Supplement 32 (May 2016): 13–4, 19, http://lkcnhm.nus.edu.sg/nus/images/data/raffles_bulletin_of_zoology/supplement32/S32rbz011-021.pdf [accessed 7 May 2016].

18. Sim et al., "Adinandra Belukar".

19. See Chapter 1 in this volume.

20. Ibid.

21. Ibid.

22. "Ejected Squatter's Claim: Kim Seng Land Co sued for $3,000", *The Straits Times*, 17 Sept. 1917, p. 10.

23. Richard Corlett, "Vegetation", in *The Biophysical Environment of Singapore*, ed. Chia Lin Sien, Ausafur Rahman and Dorothy Tay B.H. (Singapore: Singapore University Press, 1991), pp. 137–8.

24. Ibid., p. 138.

25. Wee Yeow Chin and Richard Corlett, *The City and the Forest: Plant Life in Urban Singapore* (Singapore: Singapore University Press, 1986), p. 8.

26. Ibid., p. 9.

27. Corlett, "Vegetation", p. 141.

28. Wee and Corlett, *The City and the Forest*, p. 9.

29. Corlett, "Vegetation", p. 142.

30. Ibid., p. 148.

31. The low species richness of adinandra belukar was seen as useful by Timothy Charles Whitmore (1935–2002), renowned tropical plant ecologist and plant biogeographer, when he visited a patch of adinandra belukar with Hugh T.W. Tan in the 1990s. He remarked that this vegetation type would be an excellent introduction to primary tropical rainforest because, if one were to start there, one would be too overwhelmed and awestruck by the sheer number of species in primary forest and give up. The names of the 25 adinandra belukar species can be learnt in a few days or even a day by a hardworking student. Aside from its uniqueness, adinandra belukar should also be conserved for educational reasons.

32. Tan et al., *The Natural Heritage of Singapore*, pp. 55–6.

33. If adinandra belukar is close to forest types further along in succession or primary forest.

34. Teh Joo Lin, "256 Bush Fires Break Out in the First 40 Days of this Year", *The Straits Times*, 12 Feb. 2005.

35. Alexis Hooi, "Smoking Banned in Nature Reserves", *The Straits Times*, 11 May 2005.

36. "Species Profile", Global Invasive Species Database, http://www.iucngisd.org/gisd/species.php?sc=53 [accessed 1 May 2016].

37. "100 of the World's Worst Invasive Alien Species' Global Invasive Species Database", http://www.iucngisd.org/gisd/100_worst.php [accessed 1 May 2016].

38. Julia F. Morton, *Fruits of Warm Climates* (Winterville, NC: Creative Resource Systems, 1987), pp. 331–2.

39. Tan et al., *The Natural Heritage of Singapore*, p. 304.

40. M.F. Choong, P.W. Lucas, J.S.Y. Ong, B. Pereira, Hugh T.W. Tan and I.M. Turner, "Leaf Fracture Toughness and Sclerophylly: Their Correlations and Ecological Implications", *New Phytologist* 121, 4 (1992): 598; see also Alex Thiam Koon Yee, Kwek Yan Chong, Louise Neo and Hugh T.W. Tan, "Updating the Classification System for the Secondary Forests of Singapore", *Raffles Bulletin of Zoology*, Supplement No. 32 (2016): 11–21, 14.

41. Tan et al., *The Natural Heritage of Signgapore*, p. 64.

42. There is a tall specimen in the forest patch at the junction of Vigilante Drive and South Buona Vista Road.

43. Tan et al., *The Natural Heritage of Singapore*, p. 304.

44. Yee et al., "Updating the Classification System for the Secondary Forests of Singapore", pp. 16–7, 19.

45. Wee and Corlett, *The City and the Forest*, pp. 158–61.

46. Richard Corlett, "The Changing Urban Landscape", in *Physical Adjustments in a Changing Landscape: The Singapore Story*, ed. Avijit Gupta and John Pitts (Singapore: Singapore University Press, 1992), pp. 208–9.

47. Carolyn Quek and Michelle Neo, "Crushed to Death on Her Walk to Health", *The Straits Times*, 17 May 2007.

48. Boo Chih Min et al., *Plants in Tropical Cities* (Singapore: Uvaria Tide, 2014), pp. 960–7.

49. "Kent Ridge Park", National Parks Board, https://www.nparks.gov.sg/gardens-parks-and-nature/parks-and-nature-reserves/kent-ridge-park [accessed 5 May 2016].

50. "NParks Flora & Fauna Web", National Parks Board, https://florafaunaweb.nparks.gov.sg/ [accessed 24 Apr. 2016].

51. Boo et al., *Plants in Tropical Cities*, pp. 875–982.

52. An Apple iPhone app to identify the 65 native species that were originally planted at UHall is downloadable at https://itunes.apple.com/us/app/florasg/id707612884?ls=1&mt=8.

53. Alfred Russel Wallace, *The Malay Archipelago: The Land of the Orang-Utan, and the Bird of Paradise. A Narrative of Travel, with Studies of Man and Nature, vol. 1* (London: Macmillan and Co., 1869), p. 37.

54. Marcus Chua and Kelvin K.P. Lim, "Leopard *Panthera pardus*", in *Singapore Biodiversity: An Encyclopaedia of the Natural Environment and Sustainable Development*, ed. Peter K.L. Ng et al. (Singapore: EDM & Raffles Museum of Biodiversity Research, 2011), p. 363.

55. Marcus Chua and Kelvin K.P. Lim, "Wild Pig *Sus scrofa*", in *Singapore Biodiversity: An Encyclopaedia of the Natural Environment and Sustainable Development*, ed. Peter K.L. Ng et al. (Singapore: EDM & Raffles Museum of Biodiversity Research, 2011), p. 506.

56. Marcus Chua and Kelvin K.P. Lim, "Deer Family Cervidae", in *Singapore Biodiversity: An Encyclopaedia of the Natural Environment and Sustainable Development*, ed. Peter K.L. Ng et al. (Singapore: EDM & Raffles Museum of Biodiversity Research, 2011), p. 290.

57. Tony O'Dempsey, "Singapore's Changing Landscape since c. 1800", in *Nature Contained*, ed. Timothy P. Barnard (Singapore: NUS Press, 2014), pp. 26–7.

58. Richard Corlett, "Terrestrial Ecosystems", in *Singapore Biodiversity: An Encyclopaedia of the Natural Environment and Sustainable Development*, ed. Peter K.L. Ng et al. (Singapore: EDM & Raffles Museum of Biodiversity Research, 2011), pp. 47–8.

59. "Ejected Squatter's Claim: Kim Seng Land Co sued for $3,000", *The Straits Times*, 17 Sept. 1917, p. 10.

60. Navjot S. Sodhi and Hugh T.W. Tan, "Report on the Ecosystem Study of the Proposed Site for the Nature Area at the NUS Kent Ridge Campus", internal report (Singapore: National University of Singapore, 2003), pp. 14–6.

61. S.K. Khew and Steven S.H. Neo, "Butterfly Biodiversity in Singapore with Particular Reference to the Central Catchment Nature Reserve", *Gardens' Bulletin Singapore* 49, 1 (1997): 273–96.

62. Ming Kai Tan, R.W.J. Ngiam and M.R.B. Ismail, "A Checklist of Orthoptera in Singapore Parks", *Nature in Singapore* 5 (2012): 66–7, http://lkcnhm.nus.edu.sg/nis/bulletin2012/2012nis061-067.pdf [accessed 20 Apr. 2016].

63. Ming Kai Tan, "Orthoptera in Singapore: Diversity, New Species and Predation", BA (Hons) thesis (Singapore: National University of Singapore, 2015), p. 46.

64. Ming Kai Tan, "Orthoptera in the Bukit Timah and Central Catchment Nature Reserves (Part 1): Suborder Caelifera" (Singapore: Raffles Museum of Biodiversity Research, 2012), pp. 1–40, http://lkcnhm.nus.edu.sg/raffles_museum_pub/z_2013/caelifera_btnr_ccnr.pdf [accessed 17 Apr. 2016].

65. Tan, "Orthoptera in Singapore", p. 46.

66. Ming Kai Tan, "Preliminary Bioacoustics Study of Ensifera (Orthoptera) in and around Bukit Timah Nature Reserve" (Singapore: National University of Singapore, 2011), p. 31.

67. Ibid., p. 15.

68. Ibid., p. 11.

69. Ibid., p. 6.

70. Y. Norma-Rashid, L.F. Cheong, H.K. Lua and D.H. Murphy, *The Dragonflies (Odonata) of Singapore: Current Status Records and Collections of the Raffles Museum of Biodiversity Research* (Singapore: Raffles Museum of Biodiversity Research, National University

of Singapore, 2008), p. 147, http://lkcnhm.nus.edu.sg/nus/pdf/PUBLICATION/
LKCNH%20Museum%20Books/LKCNHM%20Books/Dragonfly_of_Singapore.pdf
[accessed 17 Apr. 2016].

71.   Robin Ngiam, *Dragonflies of Our Parks and Gardens* (Singapore: National Parks Board,
2011), p. 38.

72.   Chen D.X. and N. Sivasothi, *Fauna of Kent Ridge: Spider Diversity and the Identification of
Common Spiders* (Singapore: National University of Singapore, 2010), p. 18.

73.   David Court and Wang Luan Keng, "Golden Orb Weavers Family Nephilidae", in
*Singapore Biodiversity: An Encyclopaedia of the Natural Environment and Sustainable
Development*, ed. Peter K.L. Ng et al. (Singapore: EDM & Raffles Museum of
Biodiversity Research, 2011), p. 328.

74.   David Court and Wang Luan Keng, "Jumping Spiders Family Salticidae", in *Singapore
Biodiversity: An Encyclopaedia of the Natural Environment and Sustainable Development*,
ed. Peter K.L. Ng et al. (Singapore: EDM & Raffles Museum of Biodiversity Research,
2011), p. 353.

75.   Sodhi and Tan, "Report on the Ecosystem Study of the Proposed Site for the Nature
Area at the NUS Kent Ridge Campus", pp. 16–9.

76.   Ho Hua Chew and Clive Briffett, *Kent Ridge Environs: A Proposal for Conserving Nature at
the National University of Singapore Campus* (Singapore: Malayan Nature Society, 1991),
p. 24.

77.   Tan et al., *The Natural Heritage of Singapore*, p. 69.

78.   John Lui, "Former National Athlete Bitten by Snake in Toilet", *The Straits Times*,
4 Aug. 1993.

79.   Jo Oldland et al., *Shorebird Conservation in Australia,* Birds Australia Conservation
Statement No. 14, 2009, http://birdlife.org.au/documents/OTHPUB-shorebirds09.pdf
[accessed 10 May 2016].

80.   Erich D. Jarvis et al., "Whole-Genome Analyses Resolve Early Branches in the Tree of
Life of Modern Birds", *Science* 346, 6215 (2014): 1320–331.

81.   "All About the Peregrine Falcon", US Fish & Wildlife Service Endangered Species
Program, http://web.archive.org/web/20080416195055/http://www.fws.gov/
endangered/recovery/peregrine/QandA.html#fast [accessed 10 May 2016].

82.   "White-Crested Laughingthrush Garrulax leucolophos (Hardwicke, 1816)", Avibase,
http://avibase.bsc-eoc.org/species.jsp?lang=EN&avibaseid=6583F1BCFBBD293B
[accessed 25 Apr. 2016].

83.   Pascualita Sa-a, "*Betta imbellis* Ladiges, 1975", FishBase, http://www.fishbase.org/
summary/12038 [accessed 28 Apr. 2016].

84. Kelvin Kok Peng Lim and Peter Kee Lin Ng, *A Guide to the Freshwater Fishes of Singapore* (Singapore: Singapore Science Centre, 1990), pp. 113, 126, 198.
85. Ibid., pp. 15–20.
86. Heok Hee Ng and Heok Hui Tan, "An Annotated Checklist of the Non-Native Freshwater Fish Species in the Reservoirs of Singapore", *Cosmos* 6, 1 (2010): 113.
87. Lim and Ng, *A Guide to the Freshwater Fishes of Singapore*, pp. 48–9, 92.
88. Ng and Tan, "An Annotated Checklist of the Non-Native Freshwater Fish Species in the Reservoirs of Singapore", p. 105.
89. Nick Baker, "Red Pacu at Catchment Pond, Bukit Timah Nature Reserve", *Singapore Biodiversity Records* (2013): 111.
90. Lim and Ng, *A Guide to the Freshwater Fishes of Singapore*, pp. 74–5, 81.
91. Sodhi and Tan, "Report on the Ecosystem Study of the Proposed Site for the Nature Area at the NUS Kent Ridge Campus", p. 22.
92. R.C.H. Teo and S. Rajathurai, "Mammals, Reptiles and Amphibians in the Nature Reserves of Singapore: Diversity, Abundance and Distribution", *Gardens' Bulletin Singapore* 49, 1 (1997): 353–425.
93. Zengkun Feng, "Attacks Spark Hunt for m=Monkey", *The Straits Times*, 7 Oct. 2011.
94. Grace Chua, "Population of Wild Boars on the Rise", *The Straits Times*, 19 Mar. 2012.

Fig. 4.1: A late 16th-century European rendition of an Asian trading vessel. Reproduced from the first edition of van Linschoten's *Itinerario*, which mentions Singapore's "long beach"

Pasir Panjang, Kent Ridge and the Singapore Story

Ho Chi Tim, Erik Holmberg and Tan Chye Guan

Kent Ridge first enters the historical record where it descends to meet the sea. Pasir Panjang —"long sand" or "long beach" in Malay—is almost certainly a reference to the long sandy beach which graced the shore of this district until it was destroyed by land reclamation in the late 20th century. In the account of the origin of Singapura given in the *Sejarah Melayu* or *Malay Annals*, Sang Nila Utama—who became Sri Tri-buana, the first ruler of Singapura— saw the island's white sandy beach from across the sea, probably from the island of Batam.[1] Is it possible that some of the white sand he saw was on the beach at Pasir Panjang?

It seems that Pasir Panjang has been known by this name for more than 400 years. According to Peter Borschberg, the Flemish writer Jan Huyghen van Linschoten referred to Pasir Panjang in the late 16th century in his *rutter* or book of navigational instructions for sailors.[2] Linschoten referred to Pasir Panjang by the Dutch term *lange strand*, a literal translation of *pasir panjang* into Dutch. The fact that Linschoten mentioned Pasir Panjang suggests that the place and its name may have been known to earlier Portuguese navigators in Southeast Asia, since Borschberg believes Linschoten's work was almost certainly based on one or several older Portuguese *rutters* which no longer survive: "Many Portuguese *rutters* are based on word of mouth from Chinese and Malay pilots, possibly also some written Arab, Persian or Turkish *rutters*." Thus, Linschoten's mention of the *lange strand* over four centuries ago may actually reflect even older knowledge of Pasir Panjang among navigators in the region.[3]

The idyllic palm-fringed beach of old Pasir Panjang must have been a very inviting place for settlers. There may well have been *kampong* or villages of Malay fisherfolk here at various points from the times of Sri Tri-buana through to the 19th century but, if so, they left no imprint on the historical record. Pasir Panjang is not identified on an 1828 map of Singapore drawn by two British officers nor are any villages shown in the area, although the map does show the mouths of the nearby Jurong and Pandan rivers.[4]

Still, less than 20 years later, at the time of the first comprehensive survey of the island, by John Turnbull Thompson, a "Road to Pasir Panjang" was the main access road along the west coast of the island, though the left edge of the 1843 map of Singapore town and environs cuts off the portion of the island west of Telok Belanga.

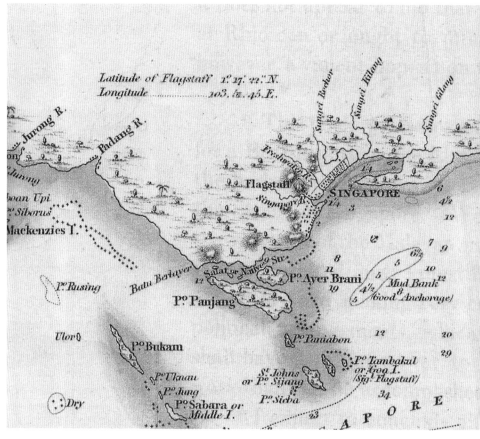

Fig. 4.2: Pasir Panjang does not appear in the earliest maps of Singapore made by the British, though the Jurong and Pandan Rivers are clearly shown. This map was published in 1830

Pasir Panjang On and Off the Map

This first section of the history of the area will give some sense of how Pasir Panjang was incorporated into Singapore's road and property systems, and subsequently integrated into the island's social structure. The earliest mentions in the mid-19th-century *Straits Times* suggest that Pasir Panjang was considered wild and remote, the haunt of tigers and bandits. As far as the written record is concerned, Pasir Panjang often seemed to be both literally and figuratively *off the map*, much as it was also outside municipal limits, and until the end of the 19th century outside the road network. The area gradually comes into sharper focus in the English newspapers around the turn of the 20th century, which gives us a picture of the local society here, its demographic characteristics, its members' occupations and social lives, their class and racial backgrounds, and their criminal activities.

Major Chinese Landowners

Once land in this area was brought into the British cadastral system, parcelled off and sold, the first major landowners in Pasir Panjang were Chinese. Two of the most prominent landowners in the 19th century were Tan Kim Seng and Yeo Hood Ing. While Tan Kim Seng is still commemorated by Kim Seng Road and Kim Seng Bridge, as well as the Kim Seng Fountain at the Padang, the name of Yeo Hood Ing (or Hooding) is less familiar today.

Yeo Hood Ing was already established in Singapore by the late 1820s, and by 1840 "the firm of Hooding & Co. [was] a leading Chinese mercantile house in Boat Quay", according to Sir Ong-Siang Song, who went on to recount that:

This firm continued until 1865, when owing to the death of several of the partners it was dissolved. In 1851 two pieces of land comprised in Grants Nos. 5 and 6 and containing the total area of 128 acres at Telok Blangah (now Pasir Panjang) were granted to Yeo Hooding, Yeo Chi Guan, Yeo Hoot King, Yeo Hoot Seng and Yeo Hoot Hin carrying on business

in co-partnership under the firm of Hooding & Co. Chop Kong Cheang. This property, commonly known as Hooding Estate, was by a trust settlement made the 8th November 1882 ... dedicated as a burial ground called 'Hiap Guan Sun' for the burial, free of any cost or expense, of all persons of the Hokien tribe of the surname 'Yeo,' and was duly licensed as such by the Municipality on the 10th April 1899.[5]

But Yeo Hood Ing's estate was tiny when compared with that of Baba Tan Kim Seng; indeed, a late 19th-century map suggests that the massive Kim Seng Estate encompassed most of the area we now think of as Pasir Panjang and Kent Ridge. Tan Kim Seng was a wealthy Chinese Peranakan businessman from Malacca who settled in Singapore in the early 19th century and became a Justice of the Peace in 1850.[6] He was a Singapore Municipal Commissioner in 1856.[7] According to Lee Kip Lin, Tan Kim Seng owned approximately half of the landed property between Telok Blangah and what is now Clementi Road, amounting to 2,859 acres, likely the most extensive private landholding in the history of Singapore.[8]

Tan Kim Seng's Estate is shown very clearly in the detailed 1898 "Map of the Island of Singapore and Its Dependencies", drawn by John van Cuylenburg in the Surveyor-General's

Fig. 4.3: Portrait of Tan Kim Seng, now in the Asian Civilisations Museum, Singapore

Office.[9] The estate included most of the Pasir Panjang area but at that time anyway did not include the shorelines and the areas along Pasir Panjang Road. The map shows a number of place names along the coast in the Pasir Panjang area, from the mouth of the Sungei Pandan (Pandan River) in the west to Belayer Point in the east; listing them from west to east they are: Kg S. Pandan, Pasir Panjang, Telok Telaga, Sungei Ayer Rajah, Patah Telok, Tanjong Ayer Jembu, Ayer Nipah, Ayer Batu and Belayer Point.

The map indicates there were villages along the shore from the Sungei Pandan to Pasir Panjang, including the areas labelled as "Tanjong Penjuru", "Kg S Pandan" (Kampong Sungei Pandan) and "Pasir Panjang". South Buona Vista Road is shown as a dotted line, indicating it was merely a *proposed* road in 1898, not yet built, while Ayer Rajah Road is not shown at all. Reformatory Road (later Clementi Road) is clearly shown.

Although Tan died in 1864, the estate survived him until at least the mid-1930s, when the landholding was still very large. According to a report in the *Malayan Law Journal* of a case decided in 1935, the Kim Seng Land Company Limited then owned 2,454 acres of land, including property in the areas of Buona Vista Road and Ridout Road.[10]

It seems that Tan Kim Seng encouraged, or at least tolerated, farmers to cultivate parts of his vast estate. At least one account survives, thanks to a report of a court case in 1917. It seems not unreasonable to think that this pattern of cultivation might have held in the 19th century as well. The court case resulted from a lawsuit filed by a Mr Wee against the Kim Seng Land Co. According to *The Straits Times*:

> In the Supreme Court, this morning, Wee Kye Soon, describing himself as a planter, brought action against the Kim Seng Land Co for $3,000 for work done on the company's plantation at Pasir Panjang ... The plaintiff, in consideration of being allowed to reside on the land and use it for the production of crops, paid a monthly rental of $1. The plaintiff stated that he now resided at 5th milestone, Bukit Timah Road, but until recently he had been a squatter for about 12 years on the defendants' estate near the Gap at Ayer Rajah Road. During the first three years he planted vegetables. In the fourth year, a towkay sent a mandore to tell him to plant rubber trees, and he did so. He planted over 2,300 trees on the agreed area of eight acres, and he kept the area weeded, eradicated stumps, etc. ... Later he was offered $65 per acre, but he was to dig up the pineapples.... In his speech for the defence, Mr. Robinson said ... that over 500 squatters had been dealt with, 40

Fig. 4.4: Published by the Singapore Surveyor General's office in 1898, this map is drawn by John van Cuylenburg. The borders of the Tan Kim Seng Estate are clearly delineated in this detail view

of whom had rubber, and there had been no trouble with them.[11]

Tiger-catching and Robbery

Pasir Panjang was apparently still a dangerous frontier area—a place of violence, shady activities, and mysterious deaths—as indicated by the crime reports which found their way into the papers in the 19th century. There was even the risk of being eaten by a tiger. In 1848, *The Straits Times* reported that:

> Yesterday some Malays brought into Town a large male Tiger measuring 8 feet 5 inches from the nose to [the] end of the tail. The animal was taken in a pit at Passier Panjang, but a few miles from the Town, and was killed by throwing some lime into its eyes.[12]

Like other areas outside of town, Pasir Panjang was evidently the haunt of secret societies in the middle of the 19th century. In 1856 *The Straits Times* noted that:

> On Friday morning last a numerously attended Hoey meeting took place at Passir Panjang. Inspector Fish reports that about 1500 persons were assembled: people from Gaylang, Bukit Timah, discharged Police peons, Malays, and others, the

scum of the population, were present. How long is such a state of things to continue?[13]

At least some of the criminality in the area was related to the government's opium monopoly, as indicated by this news report in 1864:

> A case of stabbing and wounding two Malay Chintings [opium monopoly enforcers], arising out of the seizure of contraband Chandoo [prepared opium], took place of [*sic*] Passier Panjang this morning. On three Chinese being arrested who were occupied in the process of preparing chandoo, an attempt was made to rescue them by a great number of Chinese. The prisoners also, who were armed with parangs stabbed a Chinting and hacked the fingers of another in order to effect escape, but the Malays struggled and held them on till further assistance came, and they ultimately brought the prisoners to town.[14]

Pasir Panjang seems to have escaped unscathed the major Chinese faction fights of October 1871, when street battles broke out in the town of Singapore between Hokkiens and Teochews. Much of the fighting and looting occurred in Chinatown, Kampong Glam, Beach Road and Rochor. However, a mention of Pasir Panjang in a newspaper report on the riots suggests fighting was expected in that locality as well: "Mr CJ Irving visited Passir Panjang with some 50 Malays armed with krisses, but found everything quiet."[15]

The following report of a robbery in 1870 suggests not only that criminals were prowling Pasir Panjang, but also that there were local residents who had property valuable enough to tempt gangs of armed robbers:

> A Gang Robbery was committed by a party of armed Chinese on the night of the 19th inst., in the house of a Malay residing at Passir Panjang. The inmates of the house, all females, were assaulted. The thieves took away property valued at $338. The robbers were seen to pull away in a fishing boat in the direction of Pulo Samboo.[16]

However, a word of caution is in order while reading these accounts of an apparently dangerous Pasir Panjang. While these crime reports suggest that Pasir Panjang was still Singapore's Wild West as late as the 1870s, we must remember the majority of the people living in this vicinity could have been enjoying peaceful, idyllic lives beneath the swaying fronds of the coconut palms for all we know; they were not publishing newspapers or books. It seems that ordinary people of Pasir Panjang only interested colonial newspaper reporters and editors when

they became the victims or perpetrators of newsworthy crimes.

Around 1870 we begin to hear accounts of a different sort. In that year an undersea telegraph cable was landed in Pasir Panjang, where a cable house had been built. According to *The Straits Times*:

> The telegraph cable between Singapore and Penang is now being laid down. This morning, at 7 o'clock, the shore end of the cable was landed in the cable house at Passir Panjang, and the health of the cable drunk by a small company assembled there. At 8 o'clock the steamer *William Cory* commenced laying the cable.[17]

On a tragic note, there was a report of an apparent drowning at Pasir Panjang in 1878: "An Inquest was held yesterday, the 23rd instant, on the body of a male Chinese named Lim Eng Hoy at the Sree Passir Panjang beach by AR Ord Esq, HM Coroner of Singapore. Verdict – 'Found Drowned'."[18] This sad news contains an interesting point: by 1878, an accidental death in Pasir Panjang could attract the attention of the authorities quickly enough so that an inquest could be held on the body. Bearing in mind that there was probably no refrigeration in Pasir Panjang at that time, an inquest would have to be performed very soon after death. In this case, Her Majesty's Coroner of Singapore was none other than A.R. Ord, the brother of Governor

Sir Harry St George Ord.[19] This, together with the report regarding the telegraph cable in 1870, suggests that, by the 1870s, Pasir Panjang was being brought more closely into the administrative and communication networks of colonial Singapore.

Roads and Connections

The development of roads in Pasir Panjang begins by the shore. Pasir Panjang Road, the first and most important road, extended all the way west to the Jurong River by 1850. It was built by civil engineer John Turnbull Thomson (1821–84), Government Surveyor in Singapore in the mid-19th century, who also designed and built Horsburgh Lighthouse on Pedra Branca in 1851, and laid out Bukit Timah, Serangoon and Geylang Roads, the main roads in Singapore heading to the northwest, northeast and eastern parts of the island respectively.[20]

The maps based on Thomson's Survey suggest that the construction of Pasir Panjang Road had at least begun before 1846, and that it is possible this road already extended to Pasir Panjang village itself at that time.[21]

The next road to appear on the maps was Alexandra Road, created in 1864, linking Pasir Panjang with River Valley Road.[22] In November 1864, the *Government Gazette* announced that: "The New Road from Passir Panjang via Tanglin, to its junction with Havelock Road, will be called 'Alexandra Road'."[23] The road was named after Princess Alexandra,[24] the Princess of Wales, a Danish princess who married Queen Victoria's eldest son, Prince Albert Edward, the Prince of Wales, in 1863. This royal wedding and the incorporation of this princess into the royal family must have still been fresh in the minds of British people in Singapore (and perhaps many of the Asian residents as well) at the time that Alexandra Road was named in her honour.

In the 1870s, the Alexandra Road area was apparently still far from developed—in fact, at least part of this area was swampland. The writer of a letter to the editor of *The Straits Times* published in 1874 reported that he had watched ducks flying over the swamps along Alexandra Road on several occasions.[25] An article that appeared in the following year indicated that the Alexandra Road area was a place where drunken British soldiers often bothered local inhabitants:

> The River Valley Road is too often made the way of escape from the barracks by soldiers directing their footsteps towards the grog shops in town, and on their return they are frequently not too particular where they visit or how they disturb peaceful residents. We understand the Police authorities themselves are quite alive to the necessity of a station on the

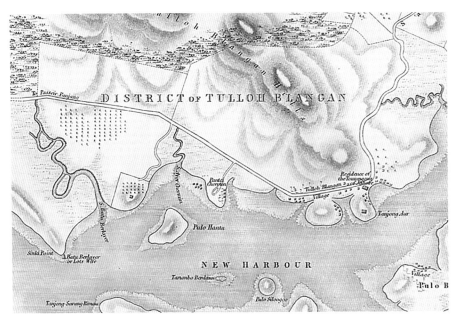

Fig. 4.5: The road to Pasir Panjang visible here was one of the main roads across Singapore island laid out by Government Surveyor John Turnbull Thompson. This map dates to 1848, though we do not know how far the road stretched at this date

Alexandra Road, or on River Valley Road where it joins the Alexandra Road, and we hope the matter will not be allowed to rest too long.[26]

A police station was eventually built at Alexandra, as noted in an article published in 1906; the article, interestingly enough, was also about the criminal activities of British soldiers.[27]

Another notable development in the area was the building of Fort Pasir Panjang at Labrador Park, which was completed in 1878.[28] Fort Pasir Panjang was mentioned in the press in 1889, in connection with the drowning of an artilleryman stationed at Fort Canning.[29]

In July 1903, *The Straits Times* announced that "Heavy gun practice will take place at Fort Pasir Panjang on July 31st and August 1st, 2nd, and 3rd...."[30] In March 1912, there was an announcement that the Singapore Volunteer Artillery Maxim Company was planning to practise with their Maxim Guns at Fort Pasir Panjang.[31]

A bungalow called Labrador Villa was completed near Fort Pasir Panjang by March 1883.[32] In 1896, *The Straits Times* announced that "The Straits Government have bought Labrador Villa."[33] Labrador Villa was the scene of a burglary in December 1906.[34] In 1909, *The Straits Times* reported that "Labrador Villa is now reserved as a convalescent bungalow for the European police and gaol warders. The bungalow was occupied on 42 days during the last six months of the year."[35] It was still being used for this purpose at least as late as 1913, when it was occupied for 78 days.[36] The bungalow may have become somewhat rundown by this time—remember it was described as a "wood and attap bungalow" in 1896. In July 1914, *The Straits Times* reported that the government was "about to rebuild Labrador Villa"[37] and, in June 1915, the newspaper reported that the old Labrador Villa had been demolished and construction of a new building was already underway, at a cost of $10,000.[38] During the global influenza pandemic in 1918, a dozen nurses at Singapore General Hospital who fell ill stayed at Labrador Villa while they were recovering.[39]

At the turn of the century a series of new roads were built in the area, connecting to Pasir Panjang and Alexandra Roads. A report on the proceedings of the Legislative Council which appeared in *The Straits Times* in 1898 indicates that the road which would become known as Reformatory Road was then newly constructed and still nameless. The construction of what would someday become Ayer Rajah Road was still under consideration:

> In the estimates for special services, there appeared a sum of $19,600 for the proposed road from the Municipal limit on the Alexandra Road to the recently-constructed road from Bukit Timah to Pasir Panjang (3½ miles). This sum it was proposed by the committee should be struck out, and the omission was agreed to.[40]

There is evidence in colonial government records that Ayer Rajah Road was constructed between 1900 and 1903. The *Report on the Straits Settlements for the Year 1901* noted: "Under 'roads, streets, bridges and canals,' the following works were completed: ... Construction of a road from the municipal limit on Alexandra Road to near the tenth mile on Reformatory Road."[41] Ayer Rajah Road is mentioned by name in the report for 1902: "Under roads, streets, bridges and canals, progress was made on the Ayer Rajah and the East and West Coast Roads...."[42] Finally, the report for 1903 noted that among the works which had been completed was: "Metalling Ayr [sic] Rajah Road".[43]

The choice of the name "Reformatory Road" may indicate some of the nature of the locality at that time. It requires only a little imagination to read some significance into the choice, and what it suggests about the pace of development and social history of the area. The decision to name the new road after the reformatory located near its northern end (close to Bukit Timah village) suggests that decision makers viewed the road as having no other significant features. This is all the more surprising, considering that Singapore decision makers generally seem to have been eager to name streets and roads after each other.[44] Could it be that no one wanted the road named after himself, because the area was so undeveloped, wild or even disreputable?

Moreover, the decision to site the reformatory along this new road provides quite convincing evidence that no one expected the area to become the upper-class residential neighbourhood it eventually became—King Albert Park was later created almost directly opposite the site of the Reformatory.

These new roads drew Pasir Panjang more firmly into the orbit of urban, or at least suburban, Singapore. The construction of North and South Buona Vista Roads, including the scenic section of road over the height of Kent Ridge, the famous Gap, was underway by 1899. An address delivered to the Legislative Council by Governor Sir Charles Mitchell on 3 October 1899 highlights that: "In Singapore the following new roads are now under construction and should be completed by the end of the year: ... Holland Road to Passir Panjang Road, 3 miles, $16,800."[45] It seems highly likely that this new road became North and South Buona Vista Roads, including

the section over the Gap. Governor Mitchell's speech also suggests Holland Road was already completed and named as such by 1899.

Such development brought a shift in status to Pasir Panjang, from being *beyond* the frontier of civilized Singapore to being *on* the frontier, and then *within* its limits. Civilized, urbanized and suburbanized Singapore was growing ever outwards, especially to the east and west. It could not grow significantly to the south without major land reclamation, and its growth to the north was limited somewhat by the need to set aside catchment areas and reservoirs to provide for a growing population's increasing demands for fresh water. As Singapore grew and developed, extending roads and suburbs outwards, more and more areas of the island were thereby brought into

Year	Population
1849	52,891
1860	81,734
1871	96,087
1881	137,722
1891	181,602
1901	226,842
1911	303,321
1921	418,358
1931	557,745
1947	938,144

Table showing the population of Singapore from 1849 to 1947[46]

the scope of the print media and, thus, the historical record. The development of Pasir Panjang and its incorporation into the growing town of Singapore reflected the steady growth in the island's population, as shown in the table on p. 185.

Still a Frontier Town?

The growth of roads in the area did not entirely change the image of Pasir Panjang as a rather wild place in the pages of *The Straits Times,* as shown in an item under the heading "Lawless Pasir Panjang", of 5 December 1899:

> From various reports to hand, the neighbourhood of Pasir Panjang, – particularly near Plantation House – is badly in need of police supervision, several highway robberies having been committed there during the past few weeks. The robberies generally take place shortly after dusk; the victims have invariably been rather roughly handled. A correspondent residing a little beyond the turn to Alexandra Road complains that his servant was stopped on two or three occasions before 8 p.m. Last evening the man was again waylaid by some Malays, or Buggis, and on nothing valuable

being found in his possession he was assaulted, though not to a very serious extent. Lawlessness of this character should engage the particular attention of the police.[47]

Malay robbers were not the only criminals who prowled this area; in 1898, two Chinese men attacked a Chinese hawker and stole his money. According to *The Straits Times*: "At about half past one, yesterday, at the 4½ mile stone on the Pasir Panjang Road, a Chinese hawker was attacked by two Chinamen. They threw him to the ground and made off with his 'money bag'. The robbers took refuge in a vegetable garden nearly opposite 'Plantation House'."[48]

Where was this "Plantation House" in Pasir Panjang? In 1903, *The Straits Times* reported "a daring gang robbery took place in a Chinese plantation, two miles in from Teluk Blanga Road and nearly opposite Plantation House".[49] Also in 1903, *The Straits Times* described "the site of the forthcoming Volunteer Camp at Plantation House, to the left-hand side of the road, just beyond the Keppel Harbour Dock".[50] In 1909, *The Straits Times* informed its readers that Mrs W.R. Swan had given birth to a son "at Plantation House, Hooding Estate, Keppel Harbour"[51]—this also indicates that Plantation House was located on the property that once belonged to Yeo Hood Ing, mentioned earlier. There is a residence called Plantation House in the Alexandra Park estate. Could this be the same Plantation House?[52] Whether or not it is the same Plantation House, this home is an artefact from the turn of the 20th century that gives us some idea of how well-to-do residents of the Pasir Panjang area lived at that time.

The tragic news of the death of the baby daughter of David and Violet Donaldson at Pasir Panjang in 1894 suggests European families may have started to settle in the area by that time. The record reads simply: "Death. At Passir Panjang, on the 5th inst., aged 4 months and 22 days, Dorothea Violet Sherring, beloved daughter of David and Violet Mabel Donaldson."[53]

Some evidence for residential development in the area can be found in the Singapore National Archives' collection of building plans. In 1897, the New Harbour Dock Company Limited submitted building plans for two blocks of "European Quarters" on Pasir Panjang Road.[54] The Tanjong Pagar Dock Company called for tenders for the construction of a bungalow at Hooding's Estate in 1900.[55] Also in 1900, *The Straits Times* published an advertisement for a furniture sale at Letham House at the Hooding Estate.[56] In 1906, Bea Hock submitted plans for a Buddhist temple on Alexandra Road.[57] Teo Han submitted plans for a dwelling house at the four-and-a-quarter milestone, Alexandra Road, in 1907[58] and, in the same year,

Tan Teng Cheng submitted plans for a bungalow on Alexandra Road,[59] and Lee Yong submitted plans for a house with a tile roof on Alexandra Road.[60]

Another important development around this time was the opening of a railway line that served Pasir Panjang. This event was reported in *The Straits Times* of 21 January 1907:

> The railway extension from Tank Road to Pasir Panjang was opened to the public this morning. The first train steamed out of Tank Road station along the new line at 6.50 exactly.... The line crosses the river in two places at Pulau Saigon and runs through a cutting near Neil Road.... With the exception of a run along the sea beach near Keppel Harbour, the scenery consists mainly of cuttings, black swamps, and the backs of native huts.... In twenty-five minutes exactly after leaving Tank Road, the engine drew up at Pasir Panjang station.... The tickets refer to this station as 'Alexandra Road'.... The extension to Pasir Panjang will enable many residents to live at this pleasant little seaside resort.[61]

It seems likely that this prediction proved quite accurate and the railway line did contribute to the development and settlement of Pasir Panjang, especially in the remaining years before cars and buses displaced it.

Bricks and Drugs

Pasir Panjang's gradual evolution into a residential area was matched—if, perhaps on a smaller scale—by its development as a manufacturing area; to be precise, a centre for the manufacture of bricks. The most famous brick-making factory in the history of Pasir Panjang was probably the Alexandra Brickworks, founded by the Borneo Company in 1899.[62] However, it should be noted that Alexandra Brickworks was not the only brickworks in Pasir Panjang.[63] In fact, Alexandra Brickworks succeeded earlier brick factories run by Chinese brick makers.

In his history of the Borneo Company Limited (BCL), Henry Longhurst explained that:

> In 1899 BCL bought some Chinese brickworks in the Pasir Panjang district, four or five miles from the centre of Singapore, where they installed new machinery and laid the foundations of what was to be, after a certain number of ups and downs, a profitable venture. ... in 1928 the original venture was floated as a public company registered in Singapore with a capital of 1,400,000 Straits dollars and the name of Alexandra Brickworks. Today [in 1956] the works can produce a million and a half bricks a month and countless millions of their bricks have gone towards the building of modern Singapore.[64]

The Borneo Company also entered the automobile retailing business, and this branch of the company's operations eventually became Borneo Motors.

Alexandra Brickworks is shown in Dol Ramli's 1942 map as having been along Pasir Panjang Road, just west of the junction with Alexandra Road and southeast of the Opium Factory; thus Alexandra Brickworks was southeast of the eastern end of Pasir Panjang Ridge,[65] at the site where the PSA Building is today.[66] The Alexandra Brickworks factory was closed early in the 1970s, according to Victor R. Savage and Brenda S.A. Yeoh.[67] Alexandra Brickworks was the original site of the Sri Ruthra Kaliamman Temple (now along Depot Road in Bukit Merah), founded in a small wooden building in 1913. This building was replaced by a brick structure in 1923. According to the temple's website, this temple was formerly located "... in the Alexandra Brickworks precincts at 20, Pasir Panjang Road (4½ ms), Singapore. ... The old demolished Temple at Alexandra Brickworks, where PSA's Multi-Storey Warehousing Complex now is, was a brick building with a tiled roof."[68]

Opium Hill, or Bukit Chandu in Malay, is another historic feature of

Fig. 4.6: The old government opium factory and warehouse buildings survived in Pasir Panjang until at least 1984

the area's landscape. This location was the site of the Singapore Opium Factory. Dol Ramli's 1942 map shows the opium factory at the eastern end of Pasir Panjang Ridge (now Kent Ridge). The opium factory and a warehouse were located along Pepys Road prior to World War II.[69] During much of the 19th century and into the early 20th, the colonial government rented or "farmed" out to Chinese merchants exclusive rights to sell opium here, for specified periods of time. These Chinese opium merchants were known as opium farmers. This opium revenue-farming system provided income for both the Chinese merchants and the colonial government. Large amounts of money were involved in the opium and spirit revenue farms. For example, the *Report on the Straits Settlements for the Year 1904* noted that: "The Singapore Opium and Spirit Farms had been relet for a term of three years from the 1st January, 1904, at a rental of $465,000 a month...."[70]

In 1905, the colonial government purchased the Excise Farm Buildings in Singapore, as mentioned in the annual reports of 1905 and 1906.[71] Perhaps these buildings included an opium factory at Bukit Chandu?[72] By 1940, there was both an "Opium Packing Plant" at Pasir Panjang and an "Opium Factory" at Telok Blangah.[73] According to the *Annual Report on the Straits Settlements for the Year 1907*, "An opium factory was constructed at Telok Blangah which is rented by the farmers."[74] Could this passage actually refer to an opium factory at Bukit Chandu in Pasir Panjang, or to a different opium factory located in Telok Blangah? There is reason to believe there was some overlap between the terms *pasir panjang* and *telok blangah*.[75]

The colonial government took over the opium business on 1 January 1910, after abolishing the excise farming system.[76] A "new Opium Packing Factory at Pasir Panjang" was completed in 1929.[77] By 1940, there was both an "Opium Packing Plant" at Pasir Panjang and an "Opium Factory" at Telok Blangah.[78] British authorities decided, during World War II, that opium would be prohibited after the war. In 1946, Major-General H.R. Hone reported that "His Majesty's Government declared in the course of 1944 that its future policy would be directed to the total prohibition of opium smoking in British and British-protected territories in the Far East."[79]

Barracks and Soldiers

From the foothold at Labrador, the British army's presence grew to become a defining factor of the area for nearly a century. Alexandra Barracks became one of the major landmarks along Alexandra Road. In July 1902, *The Straits Times* reported: "It is understood that no white battalion will be brought to Singapore until new barracks have been erected for the troops.... We understand that a suitable site has been obtained and that building operations will be commenced as soon as possible."[80] In February 1903, *The Straits Times* reported that barracks were being built along Alexandra Road for the Madras Native Infantry.[81]

Apparently the original name for the new barracks was Alexandra Camp. In July 1903, Captain S. Mildred announced that troops of the Singapore Volunteer Corps (SVC) would parade at Alexandra Camp: "6.15 am Field Day. Parade at Alexandra Camp, dress drill order with sun hats, putties, haversacks and water bottles, (20 rounds of blank ammunition per man to be issued on Saturday)."[82]

In August 1903, *The Straits Times* referred to "the newly erected temporary barracks at Alexandra Camp".[83] A report of a rifle shooting match in November 1903 suggests that regular troops were already stationed at Alexandra Camp.[84] The 73rd Carnatic Infantry was a British Indian Army regiment, one in a long line of Indian regiments that garrisoned colonial Singapore. Finally, what was possibly the first mention of Alexandra Barracks by that name in *The Straits Times* appeared on 19 November 1904, in an advertisement for a "small pony and trap" put up for sale by Lieutenant J. Mansfield of the Royal Engineers, who was about to leave the Colony. The advertisement indicates that Lieutenant Mansfield was stationed at "Alexandra Barracks". A report of a musical performance in the Botanical Gardens in 1905 indicates Russell's Infantry was then stationed at Alexandra Barracks.[85]

Russell's Infantry was another Indian Army regiment. In October 1905, the Subadar Major of the 95th Russell's Infantry hosted a lavish Indian festival at Alexandra Barracks. Normanton Barracks also began to feature in the news around this time.

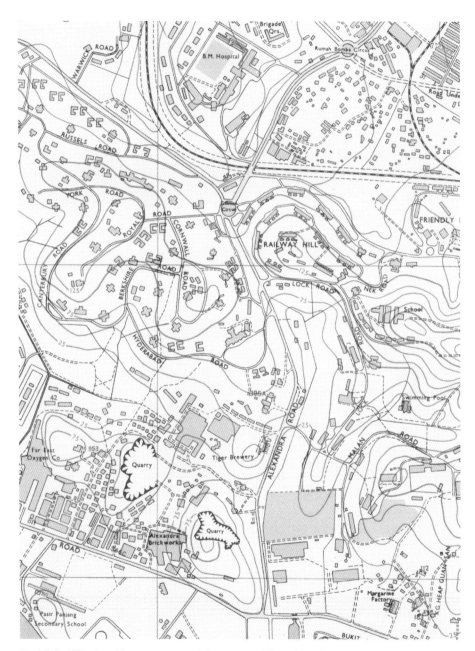

Fig. 4.7: By 1957, when this map was created, the area near Gillman Circus linking Ayer Rajah and Alexandra Roads was dominated by buildings—including what is now Alexandra Hospital—put up by the British military

The newspaper gives us a story that begins with three soldiers going for a stroll in the countryside on 20 May 1906. This report, like other reports of crimes, tells us something about the types of people who lived in the Pasir Panjang area, and how they interacted with each other:

> Privates J Oscroft and W Hartshorne and Drummer J Christie, of the Sherwood Foresters, left Tanglin Barracks for a walk to Alexandra Road. They took a cut across country and in Buona Vista Road they met a Chinaman named Tua Poi. He had a pineapple in one hand, an umbrella in the other and a bag containing $8.20 over his shoulder. The place where they met was more a pathway than a road and it connected Buona Vista Road with Alexandra Road. The three men attacked the Chinaman at this place. Two of them seized him by the arms while the third snatched his bag and made off. The two who held him took him to a swamp nearby and threw him in. He called for help and a Chinese grass-cutter came along. When he came in sight, the two men plunged into the bushes, but one of them, Hartshorne, dropped his helmet. This led to the arrest of the three. The grass-cutter helped Tua Poi out of the swamp, and the latter went to Alexandra Police Station and made a report. He took the helmet with him. There was no mistaking the regiment to which it belonged. Having taken the report, the corporal went to the scene of the robbery, and also to the swamp. Tua Poi's trousers were evidence of his having been in the water. The helmet was placed in the hands of Sergeant Tredgold and he at once commenced to investigate the matter. He went to Tanglin Barracks and, as a matter of course, found Hartshorne who had no helmet.... The three men were arrested.... After a short deliberation, the Court sentenced each of the defendants to six months' rigorous imprisonment.[86]

General Sir John French inspected the Deccan Infantry at Alexandra Barracks in 1910, and was reported to have been pleased with them.[87] On 15 October 1910, the 99th Deccan Infantry staged a festival at Alexandra Barracks; as *The Straits Times* explained:

> A whimsical facsimile of the Dusserah, the great battle in which Rawan came to grief, is reproduced year by year to remind good Hindus, and yesterday afternoon it was

reproduced on the parade ground of Alexandra Barracks, by men of the 99th Deccan Infantry. Round the square were grouped the spectators, Deccans, casual Hindus, an occasional curious Chinaman, and the flower of Singapore society. His Excellency the Governor was present.... The pageant was stage-managed by the Indian officers of the regiment....[88]

Meanwhile, a report of the murder of an Indian shopkeeper in 1910 near Alexandra Barracks suggests that Indian merchants settled in the neighbourhood of the barracks, to serve the population of Indian soldiers there. According to *The Straits Times*:

A Bengali petty shop-keeper whose place of business is near the Alexandra Barracks, was found dead at 4:30 p.m. to-day. His head had been nearly chopped off by some heavy instrument, the blow having been struck on or near the mouth. The police ... have not yet come to any conclusion as to the cause or the perpetrators of the crime.[89]

In January 1911, the 99th Deccan Infantry was replaced by the 3rd Brahmans, who marched from the docks to Alexandra Barracks with their brass band playing.[90] Local soldiers in the SVC also continued to use Alexandra

Barracks. As *The Straits Times* reported in December 1911:

The Chinese and Malay companies of the Singapore Volunteer Infantry, with the SVC Band and the Cadets and Bearer Company, held their annual inspection yesterday. They left the SVC Drill Hall, headed by the Band, for Tank Road Station, where they entrained for Pasir Panjang. Thence they marched to Alexandra Barracks and after being inspected and put through various evolutions they engaged in field exercises.[91] In October 1912, local medical students planned a 'cross-country race from the Alexandra Barracks through Mount Washington to the Medical School'.[92]

There was a mosque inside Alexandra Barracks by 1913, as described in a report of stolen goods hidden on the roof of the mosque by Amanat Ali, a drummer in the band of the 3rd Brahmans. A much more serious crime occurred in February 1914, when one of the soldiers of the 3rd Brahmans, Rampadarath Misr, was murdered near Alexandra Barracks. The report on this crime, under the headline "Mutilated Body Found in the Jungle", noted that the body was discovered "in the jungle behind the Alexandra Barracks and close to the neighbouring kampong.... The body had been hacked about in a terrible manner, although a gaping gash at the back of the neck was sufficient to cause death".[93] The reports of the murder show that there was a *kampong* near the barracks; one of the reports mentioned "huts near where the body was found",[94] another article mentioned a "Malay kampong" neighbouring Alexandra Barracks,[95] still another mentioned "Malay houses that stood not very far away from the barracks on the way to Pasir Panjang Village"; this last article also indicated that at least some of the people who lived in this *kampong* were Javanese.[96] Thus the reports of the grisly crime tell us something about the residential patterns and ethnic composition of the local population. The Indian soldiers stationed at Alexandra Barracks were in close contact with the people outside the barracks, who apparently included Chinese, Indians, Javanese and Malays. The fact that at least some of the Indian soldiers were Muslim (as indicated by the presence of the mosque inside Alexandra Barracks) suggests that a shared religion might have facilitated interactions between Muslim soldiers and Muslim local residents.

In April 1914, the 3rd Brahmans were replaced by the 5th Light Infantry.[97] This regiment included soldiers who perpetrated a deadly mutiny in February 1915, which resulted in them being sentenced to death and publicly executed by firing squad. Chiang Ming Shun presents an account of this mutiny

in Chapter 5 of the book *Between Two Oceans*. His account describes the start of the mutiny at Alexandra Barracks on 15 February 1915, the mutineers' attack on Tanglin Barracks and their shooting of a number of civilians, before a multinational force crushed the uprising. Scattered fighting also took place in the officers' quarters next to the barracks, on what is now the site of the AIA building, and along Pasir Panjang Road. Fifty-six mutineers were killed during the military operations, and 41 were subsequently sentenced to death and executed.[98]

Not all the men executed following the mutiny were soldiers in the 5th Light Infantry. Among the men convicted and put to death was Kassim Ismail Mansoor, a local trader described as "a native of Rander, a suburb of Surat, in the Bombay Presidency".[99] Kassim reportedly "allowed soldiers of the 5th Light Infantry to frequent his plantation at Pasir Panjang…." A field general court martial convicted Kassim of high treason and sentenced him to death. He was executed by hanging in the Singapore Criminal Prison on 31 May 1915, a fact reported that same day by *The Straits Times* under the headline "Fitting End for an Infamous Traitor".

The Alexandra area continued to see military-related developments in the years between the world wars, with the opening of Gillman Barracks in 1936,[100] the construction of coastal defences along Pasir Panjang Road and atop the ridge, and the opening of Alexandra Hospital in 1940.[101] These developments may be seen as the steady expansion of the major military presence in the area—a history that began with the Volunteer manoeuvres there in the late 19th century, expanded with the construction of Alexandra Camp in the early 20th century, and evolved into the Alexandra and Gillman facilities.

Becoming a Suburb

The early 20th century also saw the development of Pasir Panjang as a seaside suburb. *The Straits Times* reported in 1915 that:

> Many improvements are being effected between the fifth and sixth milestones on the Pasir Panjang road where the new bungalows erected on the hillside near the site of the ruined brickworks are practically completed and the estate, with

its new roads and neatly laid out lawns, is in an advanced state.[102]

By 1919, Pasir Panjang was home to well-to-do Singaporeans as well as fishermen and labourers in the Alexandra Brickworks. A photograph almost certainly taken just off the shore of Pasir Panjang in December 1928 showing an outboard motorboat race also shows a row of substantial houses along the shore. We might wonder: how did the inhabitants who lived in these types of homes in Pasir Panjang interact or get along with the *kampong* people who were their neighbours? We might get some idea of the situation by reading *Amber Sands: A Boyhood Memoir* by Lee Kip Lee.[103]

Although Lee Kip Lee describes his childhood in Amber Road along Singapore's East Coast rather than Pasir Panjang, it is reasonable to assume conditions in these two areas were similar. Lee Kip Lee was born in 1922 into a prosperous Chinese Peranakan family. In 1935, when Lee Kip Lee was

Fig. 4.8: According to the 1929 article in *British Malaya*, this was the first speed boat race organized in Asia. Note the fine seaside bungalows

13, he moved to his family's seaside house near the Chinese Swimming Club. He recalled that:

> Until the 1950s there were seaside bungalows dotting the east, west and north coasts of Singapore – in Tanjong Rhu, Katong, Marine Parade, Siglap, Bedok, Changi, Pasir Panjang and Ponggol. Some families even extended their houses into the water by means of a pier which led to a sea pavilion where there were bedrooms. Others had a swimming enclosure, called a *pagar*, on the beach in front of the house. This was a protective measure to prevent marauding sharks from attacking them.[104]

Close by the seaside homes of the well-to-do residents of Lee Kip Lee's neighbourhood was a *kampong* inhabited by fishermen. He enjoyed playing football with the *kampong* boys, and listening to the anecdotes told by a fisherman named Ghani.[105] It is easy to imagine that the children of Pasir Panjang interacted in much the same way, whether they lived in thatched *kampong* huts or shorefront bungalows. But now they lived in an area that connected barracks to brick factories to bungalows, cheek by jowl with traditional *kampongs*.

Spectacular vs Serene: Pasir Panjang and the Wider World

This more diverse and mature Pasir Panjang area was both marked by, and made a mark on, Singapore and the wider world in the years after the end of the Great War. Big events gave the area an exciting public profile, but the seemingly mundane maintained its essential character. Indeed, the period from the late 1920s to the 1970s saw the consolidation of an "old Pasir Panjang" despite the influx of outside influence and considerable alterations to land use. Industry, sports and well-known personalities boosted its connections to the world beyond but had little effect on the rhythm of daily existence. War dramatically affected life here and made the name of the area resonate still in other contexts, but its effects quickly dissipated in the area itself, which to a large extent reverted to pre-war patterns after the Japanese Occupation ended. Pasir Panjang's serenity was jarred but not terminated; not, at least, until the changes of the 1980s.

War and Military Occupation in Pasir Panjang

The battle of Pasir Panjang, like the 1915 mutiny, was a short but dramatic episode which left deep impressions on those who experienced it and those who came to know what happened here. While preparations for war greatly increased the British Army's domination of land use from the mid-1930s, the civilians who lived beyond camp compounds were little affected until combat ravaged the entire Pasir Panjang district, and occupation completely eclipsed whatever idyllic resonance nature provided. The main characters involved in this episode were not from Pasir Panjang and most did not stay afterwards, but they certainly shaped its history in significant ways.

The sharp end of a world war pointed straight at Pasir Panjang as the Lunar New Year approached in February 1942. By this time, it was obvious the Japanese would capture Singapore within days. However, "much depended on how hostilities ended".[106] General Yamashita's forces were facing poorly coordinated but intense resistance along much of General Percival's final perimeter around Singapore Town. The British could no longer deny them victory, but could still draw the invaders into mutually

Fig. 4.9: The pillboxes along Pasir Panjang Road allowed the 1st Malays to put up a short resistance along the coastal road

costly street-fighting. Singapore was only the first of many objectives these Japanese units were tasked to take. They were going to win fast, but it was up to the defenders whether they would win cheap enough not to jeopardize the success of follow-on missions. Yamashita airdropped an appeal to surrender on 11 February. To his consternation, British resistance seemed to stiffen in the face of certain defeat. No reply was received by 13 February when the battle for Pasir Panjang began.

Percival's principal subordinates urged him to surrender "while Japanese soldiery could [still] be controlled by their commander".[107] But his distant superiors continued to emphasize the need to fight to the death, even if only some units had the means to do so.[108] Japanese atrocities committed in Pasir Panjang graphically showed what would have happened had Percival gone along with higher command's expressed intentions. He also had to finish destroying key military assets and drain large stocks of alcohol to prevent post-fighting drunken pillaging, while organizing a final evacuation of selected personnel by sea. The eastern flank of the final perimeter was stable, but fighting in the north was intense. However, only in the west did the Japanese succeed in advancing into the municipal area in strength. The defenders of Pasir Panjang bought Percival two days, just enough time to carry out his final tasks. Crucially, this time also allowed higher authority to rescind orders to fight on regardless of consequences to soldiers or civilians.[109]

Second Lieutenant Adnan Saidi was only the most well-known of many heroes to emerge from the 1st Battalion of the Malay Regiment (1st Malay). This famous unit bore the brunt of the fighting in Pasir Panjang but was not the only one to offer fierce resistance. However, the Japanese 18th Division fought as a cohesive formation in this action, while its adversaries failed to coordinate their efforts. The under-strength Australian 8th Division pulled itself together around Tanglin Barracks, repulsing heavy Japanese attacks and forcing them to divert their main effort against Pasir Panjang. But despite having fought loyally and well alongside other contingents in Johor, the Australians were sadly no longer part of Percival's team. In what one Australian historian called "a selfish act of no small consequence", General Gordon Bennet ordered his men into an all-round perimeter and to save ammunition for their own fight.[110] The Japanese exposed their flanks to the Australians as they advanced through Pasir Panjang along the Ayer Rajah roadway (now the AYE), but were not fired upon.

Japanese artillery pounded the north-western corner of Pasir Panjang, killing most of A Company 1st Malay's officers and forcing it to withdraw. Battalion headquarters at "the Gap" in South Buona Vista Road was also severely

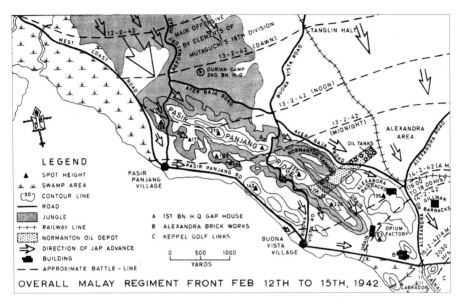

Fig. 4.10: The Japanese advance along Kent Ridge was aimed at capturing Keppel Harbour

hit, greatly impairing communication with individual companies. Nevertheless, initial Japanese probes along the coast were roughly handled. The defenders were dug in on high ground with support from the 6-inch guns of Labrador and concrete pillboxes covering Pasir Panjang Road. The Japanese set fire to the grass and moved a mortar team forward under cover of smoke to pound the defenders, but Private Yacob bin Bidin of C Company sallied forth with his Bren gun and knocked this team out of action. The attackers had more success along Ayer Rajah Road as the lack of coordination between different brigades on either side of it allowed a Japanese column to storm and occupy parts of Pasir Panjang Ridge (now Kent Ridge). This allowed them

to fire down into defensive positions on either side and forced a general withdrawal to Buona Vista Road that night. Meanwhile, another Japanese column approached a small hill on which Masjid Tentera Diraja now stands on Clementi Road, and was initially repulsed by another C Company detachment. But heavy shelling soon forced the latter to retreat through what is now the National University of Singapore (NUS) campus. B Company occupied Buona Vista village at the junction of Pasir Panjang and South Buona Vista Roads.[111]

Uncharacteristically, the Japanese did not launch any night attacks during the entire battle of Pasir Panjang as supply problems and fatigue started to take their toll, but they did continue to move forward through the forest astride the ridge. On 14 February neighbouring Indian troops retreated back to Delta Road; one British unit, 2nd Battalion the Loyal Regiment (2nd Loyals) returned to Gillman Barracks, its own home station, for a last stand. C Company 1st Malaya, left behind atop the ridge on a blocking position above Bukit Chandu, fired into the flanks of pursuing Japanese and soon drew unwelcome attention. A tank-led, artillery-supported Japanese attack drove B Company from Buona Vista Village, though Lieutenant Khalid's cut-off platoon held on along the beach and fired on straggling Japanese soldiers. Further shelling badly damaged Normanton Depot and caused a river of burning oil to flow continuously down a wide drain behind Bukit Chandu. C Company was trapped but, inspired by commanding officer Captain H.R. Rix, fought on with determination.

Adnan and Abbas bin Abdul Manan saw through a feeble Japanese attempt to pass themselves off as Punjabi soldiers and waited for the column to approach before shredding them with machine gun fire. The attackers returned in strength, and overran and scattered what remained of the company. They tortured Adnan to death, probably in retaliation for taking heavy losses. Lieutenant Stephens died leading his platoon in a bayonet charge. Abbas fought his way through the enemy and got three men across the burning river. Only two others made it out alive.[112]

Having retreated to Gillman Barracks, the Loyals absorbed costly Japanese assaults before retreating to the east end of their camp. Another British detachment helped D Company 1st Malay ambush and decimate a Japanese company as it advanced towards Alexandra Brickworks. Two tanks were disabled, ending the final Japanese attempt to reach Keppel Harbour. The Japanese held Pasir Panjang and parts of Alexandra Road. They shelled Alexandra Depot, denying the British access to their last major ammunition store. Having completed his last duties, Percival called for another conference and decided it was time to surrender, just as he received permission to capitulate at his discretion.

This cut matters a little too close. The bravery of individual units defending Pasir Panjang could not make up for the confusion of poor coordination. British and Indian units gave up the Alexandra Hospital area on 14 February, but no one ordered any evacuation. Retreating Indian troops fired from hospital grounds, which provoked the already angry Japanese to perpetrate a gross atrocity. Some patients were bayoneted on operating tables; others, plus some medical staff, were shot in the corridors. Hospital staff elected to stay behind to look after the patients. They were crammed into small quarters across Ayer Rajah Road overnight; next morning, they were pulled out in pairs to be shot by Japanese soldiers embittered by fierce British resistance and shelling. Such atrocities would have been multiplied many times had 18th Division broken clear into the city before Percival could effect surrender.

The Malay Regiment left little impression on the landscape with its makeshift tents and huts at Normanton Barracks. But its effect on Pasir Panjang's history runs a lot deeper than this. Both Malaysia and Singapore see the battle as an important event on the road to nationhood. While nothing suggests that 1st Malaya fought so stubbornly for nationalistic reasons, their dedication to duty and soldierly valour are undoubtedly worthy of praise and emulation. In an era when the colonial authorities were uneasy about arming Malaya's Asian population, the regiment won the respect of comrades and countrymen and proved popular stereotypes wrong.[113] This was sadly not the case for all locally raised forces.

Militia training for the large pool of Chinese Malayans eager to take up arms against Japan was carried out far too late and haphazardly to be effective. Teo Choon Hong related how his company was given drill instruction in English and armed mostly with air rifles.[114] He was issued a proper rifle because he did well on the range, having learned how to use a gun in China. While air-rifle ammunition was more plentiful, Teo was issued only three rounds and ordered not to fire without permission. Earlier batches of recruits had interpreters who translated the instructions of

English-educated Chinese officers. His section did not, rather unfortunate as recruits came from a variety of linguistic backgrounds. Teo's section did not receive grenade training. His company was sent to guard a makeshift camp in the swamps of Pasir Panjang. His unit was disbanded well before the fighting spread to Pasir Panjang. This ironically made some modern rifles available. The militiamen prepared these for storage, harbouring hopes of a guerrilla campaign. Unfortunately, the arms were transported to an unknown location. Teo and his comrades were sorely disappointed with the response of the authorities to their enthusiasm. To be sure, few resources, qualified trainers and weapons were available by the time training began. The experience with the Malay Regiment ought to have opened up possibilities of increasing Chinese recruitment—a number already served in the Straits Settlement Volunteers Force. This was, however, thought to be politically difficult.

Occupation cast a long shadow on Singapore and Pasir Panjang was not spared. The trials and tribulations of the Malay Regiment continued throughout the three-and-a-half years of Japanese rule. Several officers who refused either to collaborate or discard their uniforms were taken to Pasir Panjang beach and executed, according to a Chinese survivor. Others were killed after they boarded trains for Malaya. Most survivors subsequently walked to

Johor before making their way home. Their identity as British loyalists kept them under suspicion throughout the occupation. Some kept moving around while others took on new identities and passed information to guerrilla units. One even attempted to make contact with the British by driving his fishing boat far out to sea. Their loyalty to the Allied cause did not go unnoticed. The Malay Regiment was greatly expanded upon the return of British rule. It played a vital role in fighting both the communist Emergency and resisting *Konfrontasi*.[115]

Artisan Teoh Veoh Seng recalls how a Japanese soldier shot his grandfather in their *attap*-hut quarters in Haw Par Villa after they had inflated his flat bicycle tire as instructed.[116] The Japanese subsequently took over the villa and closed it off completely for the duration of the war. By the war's end, the buildings stood largely intact but empty, with the exception of two antique water vessels. The swimming pool dried up and the Aw family had to rebuild the villa's former splendour from scratch. Pasir Panjang photographer Chew Kong got on rather congenially with Japanese customers, soldiers and prostitutes included.[117] He remembers one exceptional incident in which a soldier slapped and kicked him because he did not like the fact that Chew was short-sighted. The soldier even reached for his sword but Chew wisely offered no resistance and survived. The photographer found Japanese "military

prostitutes" rather mean as well. They would tip him with cigarettes if they liked his work but would refuse payment and hit him otherwise. These "military prostitutes" wore monograms with the Chinese character (家), denoting which "house" they belonged to.[118] A pre-war cinema housed many prostitutes. He thought many were probably Taiwanese and Korean. Pasir Panjang had never been a red-light district before the war.

There was at least one Prisoner of War (POW) camp, a work camp, in Pasir Panjang. Mary Turnbull briefly mentioned the daring escape of 17 prisoners under former RAF man C.E. McCormac, which occurred with the connivance of a Portuguese Eurasian guard at a Pasir Panjang camp (Turnbull 1989). Sir John Leslie Carrick, an Australian lieutenant just returned from Burma's Death Railway, recounted how a POW camp was set up for Dutch, British and Australian prisoners from Sime Road Camp.[119] It is unclear whether the two referred to the same camp. The latter was a cluster of bombed-out Chinese homes along the coast surrounded by barbwire. Carrick obtained permission to build a latrine on a platform out to sea and was glad not to have to worry about toilet facilities for once, even though the excrement was exposed at low tide!

This new camp was reasonably sheltered from the elements. Work was light enough to not require officers to participate in manual labour and the Japanese generally let Allied officers run the camp. Carrick spoke to them through his Russian interpreter. The visits by the *Kempeitai* were not as congenial, especially since the prisoners were hiding a radio. A disgruntled sergeant accused of stealing a 100-kilogram sack of rice threatened to tell on his comrades and was forced to fake appendicitis to get transferred to a hospital. Carrick believed he was eventually "pushed off the cliffs of Dover". Prisoners at Pasir Panjang Camp were sometimes detailed for dock repair. Apart from getting out of their quarters, this entailed contact with often sympathetic Chinese locals and a chance to scavenge valuables for barter. The Japanese used Vaseline by the barrel for unknown aviation purposes. Local Chinese apparently valued this for making Tiger Balm. They promised handsome payment for barrels that might roll off during transportation.

According to Carrick, the average Japanese soldier was paid $70 a month in banana currency. Wartime inflation saw rice go from 3 cents to $1,600 a *kati*, incidentally, the price of a brothel visit. The Japanese Army never increased pay to keep pace so the common soldier was rather cash-strapped. Carrick and his men chatted up a Japanese sentry and told him some Chinese they did not trust promised ¥40,000 per barrel of Vaseline. The sentry got the picture and started aiding the scheme for ¥30,000 per barrel. The Chinese offer was actually ¥100,000 per barrel. Having corrupted their custodian, they started to squeeze

him for extra "rice polishings" by telling him that "weakness" might cause them to break during nightly *Kempeitai* visits. While Carrick thought Changi was more comfortable, one could understand why the POWs found Pasir Panjang a haven!

Life as a prisoner in Pasir Panjang was of course not always pleasant. Lack of medical supplies caused less-than-qualified doctors to resort to fermented coconut juice and hypnosis for anaesthesia. Six ounces of rice was the usual daily diet. Malnutrition and insanitary conditions led to cholera, dysentery, malaria and beri-beri. Catching a combination of two diseases usually led to death. The orderlies braved infection and held many such patients in their arms until they passed away.

Footprints of War

Pasir Panjang recovered quickly from war. Factories resumed full production, sporting events were organized and new housing appeared. But, for many, the emotional scars of war lingered painfully on. Monuments were built or gazetted to commemorate the stoic resistance of the victims. One such victim, however, endeavoured to build a monument to reconciliation. In 1954, Chinese philanthropist Lee Choon Seng built Poh Ern Shih Temple, the Temple of Thanksgiving, at Chwee Chian Hill, "to remember the ultimate sacrifice of the soldiers (both Malays and Japanese) as well as all the Kampong folks who perished in the killing fields of Pasir Panjang". He also hoped to "dedicate merits to them in the hope that they will be able to eradicate any thoughts of revenge and hate and rest in peace".[120] Though the temple was Buddhist, Lee instituted the tradition of donating 80 percent of all proceeds to charities run by any religion, a practice "scrupulously followed till this day".

Life for millionaire Aw Boon Haw was never the same again, even though his wealth continued to grow throughout his remaining years. He lost two young sons and his brother Boon Par during the war. The last hit him particularly hard because Tiger insisted on visiting Hong Kong as war approached, ignoring Leopard's premonition that they would never meet again. Boon Par's family never moved back into Haw Par Villa, relocating to a former residence along West Coast Road. This was close to the pre-war Haw Par Lodge, where Tiger housed his favourite second wife Kyi Kyi while conceiving a son with her attendant, Siew Eng, who eventually became his fourth and last wife.[121]

The famous Haw Par Villa monuments visitors remember were mostly constructed from scratch after the war. The remains of the original western-styled residence were levelled and two teams of artisans responsible for previous sculptures returned from Swatow to craft the Ten Courts of Hell.[122] These were constructed without blueprints, largely from descriptions in authoritative Chinese texts combined with a healthy dose of imagination and Aw Boon Haw's personal inputs. His nephew and successor to the helm of the Tiger Balm Empire, Aw Cheng Chye, added several "national corners" to commemorate his own overseas visits. These seemingly out-of-place statues were built by contractors instead of in-house staff.[123] The orchid collection at Aw Cheng Chye's residence and the Jade Collection at Nassim Road were both wonders in their own right, but neither could match the draw of Haw Par Villa, Pasir Panjang's top attraction of all time.

Confined to Barracks

While World War II ravaged Pasir Panjang, Cold War conflict increased the military's presence in the area without affecting the civilian sector to any great degree. While Pasir Panjang would never again host an army as large and as diverse as it had during World War II, the military facilities here were expanded and upgraded as Singapore became an important support base for the Malayan Emergency, *Konfrontasi* and SEATO. Violence did not come to the district this time. And unlike Sembawang and Changi, military expansion was not the primary cause of development in Pasir Panjang.

Before the war, the sudden influx of infantry in preparation for hostilities meant that buildings were often makeshift or hastily erected. A major building programme in the late 1950s changed this, transforming camps into self-contained communities with bakeries, shops, cinemas, air-conditioned messes, a full range of sporting facilities including a golf course, and even a church and cemetery. Many of the colonial-style bungalows found outside present-day camps were originally inside the fence. Post-war barrack-building did leave noticeable effects on the landscape after the British pullout. The large number of surviving colonial bungalows at the corner of Alexandra Road and the AYE, Gillman Village, the Colbar and the camps around the Portsdown area are all legacies of this age.

Senior officers stayed in bungalows with gardens and servants' quarters while junior officers and other ranks stayed in block apartments. Two or three junior officers shared a local batman who took care of uniforms, boots and barracks cleanliness. These soldiers lived in single rooms in two-storeyed blocks in Gillman Barracks but showers and bathrooms were shared between two. The enlisted men and junior NCOs stayed in large shared rooms of up to 30. "Ah Mahs" took care of laundry and other minor tasks but the rank and file were expected to do their own spit and polish, which as Corporal Richard England explained in an interview with Singapore's Oral History Unit, was a low priority unless they were chosen as guard-of-honour for a visiting dignitary.

Life inside and outside the barracks was markedly different and servicemen tended not to seek recreation in the area. Asian civilians growing up in the barracks had a more varied experience. This section explores post-war barracks life in Pasir Panjang through the memories of those who lived it.

Former Second Lieutenant Robin Eccles remembers barracks life being

Fig. 4.11: Now the site of Tony art galleries, today's Gillman Barracks were built for British forces post-war

Fig. 4.12: Siva Choy's home at the corner of Pasir Panjang and Pepys Roads

very comfortable at Alexandra Park, Gillman Barracks in the 1960s. He quickly saved enough to buy a car but rarely ventured to other parts of Pasir Panjang except Haw Par Villa. As with Corporal England in the 1950s, he spent most of his leisure time in camp and preferred Singapore town or Malaya for an outing. They also took army launches out to the southern islands to scuba dive instead of hanging around the beach and waters of Pasir Panjang. Eccles enjoyed field exercises with the Gurkhas in Malaya but still regretted his work transfer from Alexandra Park, with its modern facilities, to Ayer Rajah Camp which had corrugated iron and *attap* huts for offices. His workday in Singapore was from 8 am to 5 pm, unusually long compared to the Gurkhas at Nee Soon and his colleagues

in Malaya and Hong Kong who only worked from 7 am to 1.30 pm! Even then, one afternoon a week was set aside for sports.[124]

Eccles was posted here only in 1967, towards the end of the troubles. Corporal England, a logistician here since the 1950s, had a somewhat tougher life. His unit would rotate in three shifts (7–11 am, 1–5 pm and 11 pm–7 am) when movement was heavy, but would get extra days off in compensation. Singapore was more roughhouse during his tour of duty. Rival gangs, the "08s and 24s", as he called them, frequently got into gun fights at Keppel Harbour where he worked—he saw dead bodies on the day he arrived. While he did not experience strikes, he did remember that dock workers moved a lot quicker if they found cash attached to the cargo nets they unloaded. All servicemen, regardless of vocation, were also periodically deployed in battle order at checkpoints around the island because of *Konfrontasi* and communist agitation. They brought arms and live ammunition with them to Malaya, even for pleasure trips.[125]

Corporal England remembered relations with camp servants and the children of Asian civilians staying in the barracks as being generally very good. He recalled a somewhat macabre episode when an *ah mah* "so-soh" came to him calmly with her finger, which had just been severed because her hand got caught in a door hinge as it slammed shut. She asked Ah Eng (his nickname with the *ah mah*s) to put it back again and he told his interviewers he re-attached it with superglue.[126] Celebrity Siva Choy spent his earliest years in the Depot Road Quarters inside Gillman Barracks, where his father worked for the British Army as a foreman.[127] He remembers how the camp baker often declined to charge them for bread purchases. The children could borrow game equipment and use the fields and obstacle courses in camp. British officers sometimes shamed their men by pointing out how easily the older kids were clearing these. The drum major also took a liking to Siva and his brothers. He saw them drumming with improvised sticks and surfaces and got them to demonstrate their prowess to his underperforming percussionists.

Choy remembered how different life was between the wells and huts just beyond the railway line at Alexandra Village and the stone quarters and amenities on his side of the fence. Asian locals living on either side did not necessarily share a lot in common. Barracks life had its own rhythm and culture which rivalled and transcended the influence of ethnicity and creed at times. Not all soldiers lived in the camps, though. Siva's father moved the family out to a corner shophouse at the junction of Pasir Panjang and Pepys Roads where British soldiers, presumably lower-ranking, occupied rooms in the second and third storeys with their families. Out here in the civilian area, the boy ended up spending a lot of time with the other neighbourhood kids and little if any with soldiers. This is despite the fact that Siva's father kept his job with the British Army.

Abdul Latiff bin Zainal was perhaps the classic "army brat". As his father was an officer in a British Army unit—the Singapore Guard Regiment, a unit staffed largely by Malays—Latiff stayed in a bungalow along Island View Road until the withdrawal of the British military began in 1969. He recalls rather ruefully that, as a boy, he was teased to the point of tears by schoolmates, as he spoke with a British accent. Latiff remembers cutting classes to go fishing and play with his friends who were children from the nearby West Coast villages or the small businesses supporting Pasir Panjang.[128]

Old Pasir Panjang

The civilian sector of Pasir Panjang before and after World War II exuded a quiet, idyllic atmosphere, though light industry dominated the eastern end of the area. Sporting extravaganzas and popular entertainment spots added a bit of spice to the area. This section describes the rhythm of life in "old Pasir Panjang". It presents, via the memories and reminiscences of former residents and newspaper articles, a social snapshot of the areas surrounding Pasir Panjang Road, moving along the road from the junction of Reformatory and Pasir Panjang Roads to the southern end of Alexandra Road.

For former residents, "old Pasir Panjang" was larger, starting from the Telok Blangah area (one milestone) in the east, moving along Pasir Panjang Road and then west along West Coast Road until the tenth milestone near the Pandan River.

This area encompasses the southern reaches of Henderson Road, Alexandra Road, South Buona Vista Road and Reformatory Road (present-day Clementi Road). The area north of Ayer Rajah Road was generally reserved for pre-war and post-war military encampments and installations. The ridges formed a natural division between the military installations and residential zones of Pasir Panjang area. Before World War II, the land area along and above the next set of ridges towards Holland Road to the north was known as Pasir Panjang Rubber Estate.

Moving westwards from Pepys Road along the coast, we reach the beginning of the Pasir Panjang residential zone, which includes the area between Pepys Road and Reformatory Road on both sides of Pasir Panjang Road. The area was sparsely populated and relatively undeveloped, not as built up as is today's mass of condominiums and private residential developments. The residential area of Pasir Panjang was often described as dark and quiet by former residents, so quiet the joke was that if someone dropped a coin at Batu 6 (sixth milestone), the sound could be heard at Batu 7 (seventh milestone).[129] The quietness and openness of the area did not immediately change after the Japanese Occupation. Myra Isabelle Cresson, a pre-World War II resident, remembers that there was no fear of thievery or robbery and that windows and doors of bungalows in the area could be left open without any problems.[130]

The bungalows and mansions built along the waterfront were the most characteristic features of old Pasir Panjang. There were no barriers surrounding the seaside bungalows to prevent people from getting to the beach. Madam Kok Oi Yee remembers being able to cross Pasir Panjang Road, walk past the houses of the "big shots" and head straight into the inviting waters of the sea. The road could be seen as a man-made class division of sorts, separating the sea-front bungalows from the smaller *kampong*s and communities on the other side. The ridges and their down slopes included rubber and fruit plantations and small farms where chickens and pigs were reared.[131]

The major landmark within this residential zone was, and still is, Haw Par Villa, known then in English as the Tiger Balm Gardens. It was located around the sixth milestone, between the junctions of South Buona Vista Road and Reformatory Road. Michael John Sweet, who worked on the land reclamation of Pasir Panjang, recalled that before such activities began in earnest around the 1970s, there was a canal in front of Haw Par Villa which led to what he called the Harbour Master's House. According to Sweet, the reclamation project at Pasir Panjang called for the building of five harbours, and he remembers digging up parts of West Coast Road to fill up the sea.[132]

Haw Par Villa neatly divides the Pasir Panjang residential zone into two areas: from Pepys Road to Haw Par Villa, and from Haw Par Villa to the seventh milestone on Reformatory Road. Both areas were more or less similar with seaside bungalows and villages opposite along the road and below the ridge, but the latter area also accommodated senior officers and civil servants working for the British Army in bungalows built atop the ridge, on what is now the site of the NUS campus.

Staying in Island View Estate, Latiff remembers an area before university students and condominiums. He recalls that, as a child, he and his partners-in-crime would raid a farm formerly located at the site of the present-day Kent Ridge bus terminal for chickens or fruits. Moving south along Reformatory Road towards the junction of Pasir Panjang Road, there were sundry stores that delivered groceries (ranging from daily necessities like butter or sugar to luxuries like whiskey). Their successors are present in the same location today, serving NUS students as well as the residents of Pasir Panjang. Latiff also recalls a *penghulu* jetty once located near the junction at a site long reclaimed by steel and concrete, where the headman of the southern islands would sometimes take him and his friends out for boat rides.[133] Grace Taylor stayed in Pasir Panjang during the 1950s in the vicinity of the seventh milestone and remembers she enjoyed beautiful views of the sea and fishermen returning with their catch. Although ebbing tides would at times give out a stench, the sea was generally clean. The entire area was "cool, quiet and peaceful".[134]

Moving eastwards along Pasir Panjang Road on the left, after the junction with Reformatory Road, there were sundry shops, a coffeeshop, a bus stop for the one bus which plied the entire Pasir

Fig. 4.13a: Haw Par Villa mixed Art Deco styling with fantasies of Chinese tradition

Fig. 4.13b: Haw Par Villa remained an important attraction through the 1980s. This image is later in date than the other three on these pages

Fig. 4.13c: This postcard view shows the lovely view of the sea from Haw Par Villa, before the land reclamation in the 1970s

Fig. 4.13d: The Signature Pond at Haw Par Villa takes the shape of the seal character for Aw, the family name of Aw Boon Haw, the builder of the gardens

Panjang area, a rattan factory, a post office and a salvage company located at 392 Pasir Panjang Road called Singapore Salvage Engineers. As his sister worked for the company as a secretary, Latiff would follow the divers out on the company's barges. He remembers dive "training", when he was mercilessly repeatedly dropped overboard. By the third or fourth time, the non-swimmer had learnt how to tread water.

On the right of Pasir Panjang Road were, as Latiff recalls, houses on stilts or mansions built right next to the sea. Some of the mansions even had outhouses connected to shore by gangplanks, called "sea pavilions". The home of the "Tiger Balm boss" was one such structure. It was located in a site currently occupied by a condominium called The Village. Latiff recalls waiting patiently by the house gates, after spending the night at his friend's house nearby, so that he could receive red packets on Chinese New Year from the *ah mah* serving the Aw family.

Latiff attended Clementi School, which was along Pasir Panjang Road after Heng Mui Keng Terrace. The school no longer exists and its structures and buildings were taken over by the Jamiyah Halfway House (Darul Islah), next to the Salvation Army facility. Clementi School is just one of several that disappeared from the Pasir Panjang area. There was another Malay school or a madrasah on the other side of the road, near Heng Mui Keng Terrace. The father of Othman

Wok, once cabinet minister and MP for Pasir Panjang Constituency during the 1960s and 1970s, was the head of the school.[135] Other schools which no longer exist include Pasir Panjang Secondary, Pasir Panjang Primary—located at the present-day premises of Breakthrough Mission—Batu Berlayer School (a Tamil school) and a Chinese school close to the sea opposite South Buona Vista Road.

Other institutions which have disappeared over time include a home for boys called Perak House.[136] It was located within the vicinity of the Jamiyah Halfway House and the Salvation Army Headquarters. Dopps. Inc, a blogger who grew up in Pasir Panjang, recalls that Perak House was run by a Mr Foo Kia Pang, "a typical English-speaking local gentleman". As the Scout District Commissioner, Foo initiated the 34th Sea Scouts and opened the troop's participation to non-residents of Perak House. Their scout den along Pasir Panjang Road, with walls full of inscriptions and paintings was demolished some years later, while a totem pole replicated from the Jamboree in Canada was removed from the front of Perak House.

Pre-war structures and buildings still stand at various points along Pasir Panjang Road, Clementi Road, South Buona Vista Road and Pepys Road. Old coastal bungalows, now marooned by land reclamation, stand amidst rampant private and public development as poignant reminders of days long past.

Fig. 4.14: Perak House was once a familiar landmark along Pasir Panjang Road

Just as there are provision shops and restaurants in today's Pasir Panjang Village at the South Buona Vista Road junction, there were similar shops and markets catering to a slightly different clientele in the same area not too long ago. Madam Kok remembers smallholders congregating regularly around the coffeeshop's radio to listen to the day's rubber prices. Farmers would bring their fresh fruit and freshly slaughtered meat to the markets to sell. Further up the road, opposite Pasir Panjang Secondary School, there was an open-air cinema called Starlight. At the food stalls nearby, an ice *kachang* ball could be procured for a mere 10 cents (with an option to "upsize" for 20 cents). The foodstalls mainly catered to cinema-goers, workers from the brickworks and the Chandu factory, and other light industry factories located in the vicinity, selling food such as 20-cent plates of *wanton mee*, *mee rebus*, satay and *nasi lemak*.[137]

Working

Moving westwards along Pasir Panjang Road towards Alexandra Road, we approach what could be seen as the industrial zone of Pasir Panjang, roughly starting from the fourth milestone, or just after Pepys Road. The imposing PSA (Port of Singapore Authority) Building and other modern-day structures found at the junction of Pasir Panjang and Alexandra Roads are the successors of earlier industries long past.

In the early 1930s, Malayan Breweries at Pasir Panjang and the Archipelago Brewery Company (ABC), a short distance up Alexandra Road, brought cutting-edge technology into the area, producing world-class products at local prices. Despite the Great Depression and the destruction of war, they achieved their goals in the decades ahead, becoming as Singaporean as the neighbourhood coffeeshop in the process. No other factory or plant in Pasir Panjang ever

Fig. 4.15a: Lee Kip Lin photographed the villas of Pasir Panjang in 1984. The handsome house at 190 Pasir Panjang Road was owned by Lee Choon Seng

Fig. 4.15b: The bungalow at 375 Pasir Panjang Road belonged to Tan Kay Guan

Fig. 4.15c: This is the seafacing south side of the house at 485 Pasir Panjang Road, built in 1918 according to the inscription on the gable

Fig. 4.15d: According to building plans available from the National Archives, Mr E.C. Woon's house at 241 Pasir Panjang Road was built in the mid-1930s

had this kind of reach. The two rivals actually agreed on collaboration in 1930 but the German founders of ABC decided to incorporate in Batavia, setting up plants in the Dutch East Indies.[138] Malayan Breweries' founders Fraser and Neave (F&N), Heineken and their Swiss partner Finanzgesellschaft fur Brauerreiunternehmungen of Zurich built their state-of-the-art brewery, Singapore's first,[139] at "478, Pasir Panjang (Off Alexandra Road)" (*Singapore Malayan Directory 1933*).[140] The seven-storeyed structure, tall for that period, was an impressive sight to behold. What is more, Malayan Breweries opened up its premises to private citizens to showcase its technology and hygiene,[141] a practice Asia-Pacific Breweries (name changed in 1990) continues at its Tuas plant till this day.

Rimau Beer rolled off the conveyor belts in 1932 and a Singapore icon was born.[142] ABC decided to give Malayan Breweries serious competition, despite some issues over their freedom of action arising from the 1930 agreement. The newcomers offered free beer for a day (they brewed Anchor Beer, Diamond Beer and Malta Tonic Stout in addition to Lionhead, forerunner of ABC Stout) while "Tiger's proud proprietors" countered by offering to sponsor a Malayan footballer to England "to study the game".[143] Beer and sports were bosom buddies even then.

Apart from advertising "Asian prices", Malayan Breweries managed to

sell the beer-drinking culture to non-expatriates in other ways. F&N extended its door-to-door delivery service to cover its subsidiary's products.[144] Malayan Breweries and ABC became popular and commonplace enough to become frequent targets of counterfeiting and dilution scams by the outbreak of war in Europe.[145] The rivalry between the two firms ended when the British government confiscated ABC, an enemy-owned asset, and sold it to Malayan Breweries in 1941,[146] whose directors wisely set up a separate management to continue ABC's business. Despite the cost of acquisition, the directors announced record profits, paying out 25 percent in annual dividends in 1940, as compared to 15 percent the year before. Well aware of the vulnerabilities of the colony to external aggression, they also donated $100,000 that year to its defence, 20 percent of their net profits.[147]

The breweries survived the war and were soon paying out record dividends again, 30 percent in 1949.[148] ABC was doing so well that it invested in an overhead "beer arch" across Alexandra Road, which transported its products directly to the railway for export upcountry.[149] Anchor also joined Tiger as an award-winning brew in 1950, much to the elation of its management, staff and workers, beating 600 other entries to become the best beer in the British Empire. The winners thought their trophy worthy of a town-to-town tour in Malaya, "just like the Thomas

Fig. 4.16: The Singapore Rubber Works, photographed in 1930 by an RAF serviceman, employed around 750 people in the years before WWII

Cup"![150] The breweries might no longer be in Pasir Panjang but they certainly left their imprint on Singapore life when they were here.

Other industries in the area which existed since before World War II included long-gone factories such as the Opium Packing Plant, Singapore Rubber Works and Alexandra Brickworks. George Kennedy, a one-time employee of the Department of Customs and Excise, recalled the process of manufacturing chandu in the opium plant by cooking opium packed into bamboo tubes.[151] Badron bin Sainullah worked in the Singapore Rubber Works in 1938 manufacturing products such as tyres. He remembered that the rubber works was owned by a Dutch company and employed 700–800 people, most of whom resided in Pasir Panjang.[152] Such small or light industries were arguably the forerunners of the present-day industrial and office zone marking the area between Pepys Road and Alexandra Road.

Opposite this industrial area (Boon Leat Terrace) and across Pasir Panjang Road, around the present-day vicinity of the Centre for Animal Welfare and Control of the Agri-Food and Veterinary Authority of Singapore (AVA), the famed Tiger Swimming Pool and former Pasir Panjang Secondary School were once located. The swimming pool no longer exists.[153] The structure of the school still stands but is now occupied by the MOE (Ministry of Education) Labrador Adventure Club. Rudy William

Mosbergen, a former principal of the school in the late 1960s, remembers that:

> the Pasir Panjang School was
> built as a secondary school ...
> [and had] two storeys, two levels.
> Ground floor and it had a hall and
> beneath that hall were the Science
> Labs and it was immediately
> next to the swimming pool. The
> hall plus swimming pool, the
> public swimming pool in Pasir
> Panjang. So as you may expect
> a number of the students in the
> school were quite good swimmers.
> It had a nice field. Nice in the
> sense that it was a full sized
> field. It was low lying and so it
> flooded every now and then.[154]

There were over a thousand students attending Pasir Panjang Secondary, and "a lot of their parents were working in the Harbour Board, as clerks, labourers and other things. But the profile of the school would be more the profile of the population of Singapore. 70 percent Chinese, 20 percent Malays and 10 percent Indians".[155]

Mosebergen remembers having to patrol Alexandra Brickworks, situated on:

> [a] huge piece of land and laterite....
> And this was the place where ...
> students played truants, skipped
> school and would go and gamble,
> smoke and do things like that. I
> remember, on at least three or

four occasions when I would go with my teachers in my car. We would get into the Alexandra Brickworks and spread out, [to] try to catch these students who would be playing hide and seek with us. So that was it.

The Pasir Panjang Power Station was located next to the school and was visible from the ridges overlooking Pasir Panjang Road. The station had its origins in the urgings of J.M. Jumabhoy, a city councillor from 1950 to 1955. He saw the project as one of several achievements during his political tenure. In his own words:

> You see, it used to have a lot of
> blackouts in those days. There
> was a power shortage. And
> the City Council had set up a
> sub-committee for rationing of
> electricity. Rationing means we
> used to have zones where power
> was shut down every third day
> or fourth day for certain hours.
> But beyond that, when new
> applicants came in, new buildings
> or industries, they had to apply
> to this committee for power
> ratio. Now, this was going on.
>
> The City Council had in hand a
> project to set up a power station.
> But that had been dogged by lot
> of delays in supply of steel, supply
> of building materials and so on.
> Labour of course was available

Fig. 4.17: The view from Alan Cottrell's bedroom window at Prince George's Park—looking across Pasir Panjang Power Station and the islands in the Straits of Singapore beyond

in those days. And then we set up this Pasir Panjang. So we said that it cannot be handled by the normal committees. And the City Council set up a five-man committee especially for this, with full delegated authority to act. Sir George Oehlers was on it. A P Rajah, Chan Kum Chee, myself. And who was the other ... I think it was a European if I'm not mistaken. Anyhow, five of us. And we had full delegated authority. And we went all out to try and get it.

So one day when the new Governor came, Sir John Nicoll – he wanted a tour of the Pasir Panjang site to see how the progress was going on. And we all were together with him. And he said, 'Why is it not progressing?' He was a little impatient. 'Why is no progress being made?'

So I told him point-blank. I said, 'Sir, we can't get the steel.

If you can shake your colonial government, your British Government to get us the steel....' Steel was coming from Belgium, but steel was in short supply in those days. Every country used to have a quota from the manufacturing countries. And then you have to wait your turn for your order. So I said, 'If you can shake your Colonial Office and get us the steel, we can go ahead. Otherwise there is no way we can....' So he promised he would do it, and he did it, and we got the steel. And we got the power station going almost within the project time.[156]

Living

The post-war demographics of Pasir Panjang remained generally more Malay, intermingling with wealthy Chinese who lived in the mansions and seaside bungalows, particularly after the resettlement of Malay communities from the Kallang River Basin area during the 1930s as a consequence of the construction of Kallang Airport. Indeed, the Malay settlement became known as the West Coast Malay Settlement in 1957.[157] The image of Pasir Panjang as a predominantly Malay area is given more credence by Baidon's vivid descriptions of a Kampong Pasir Panjang which was once located between Haw Par Villa and Reformatory Road. He noted that the 40–50 houses located at Batu 6¾ ms were occupied mostly by Malays. He also noted a Kampong Bawean (or Boyan) but did not give a specific location. Latiff noted that there was a clear distinction in living standards between those living along Pasir Panjang Road and those staying along West Coast Road.[158] Facing swampy land, the inhabitants of the houses on stilts along West Coast Road were decidedly less well-off than the wealthy Chinese and other smallholders living along Pasir Panjang Road.

The residential area between South Buona Vista Road and Pepys Road can boast of several other well-known post-war Singaporean personalities. Siva Choy once resided in one of the shophouses on Pepys Road; Goh Chok Tong lived in a building which still stands on Chwee Chian Road, after South Buona Visa Road; and Tan Eng Liang, a former water-polo player and one-time Minister of State, grew up in a two-storeyed bungalow, which is also

still standing between Yew Siang Road and Jalan Pasar Ria. Chia Boon Leong, a Singaporean footballer before, during and after the Japanese Occupation, grew up in a compound house around the 5½ milestone, in between Pasir Panjang Park and Pasir Panjang Primary. Yew Siang Road was named after his father, who bought land in that particular area of Pasir Panjang.

Chia remembers going to watch football matches played between the employees of the Opium Packing Plant and the Excise (or Customs) Department at a field near the plant. He recalls that the employees were mostly locals, and the matches could be watched by a couple of hundred spectators at times. He was part of the Pasir Panjang Rovers football team which played during and immediately after the Japanese Occupation. The team comprised, in his words, "real 'kampong' boys in Pasir Panjang", and was cosmopolitan in outlook as it included "Malays, Indians, Sikhs, Chinese, Eurasians, [and] Bengalis". Formed in 1936, the team stood out in stark contrast with the other communal football teams plying their trade in the pre- and post-war football league.[159]

The multiethnic aspect of Pasir Panjang is something former residents— albeit Chinese—are quick to emphasize. Chia remembers a mixed *kampong* area from his home to Jalan Mat Jambol, where about 10–20 Malay and Chinese families lived together. Madam Kok also observes that, unlike other known racial enclaves elsewhere in Singapore, for instance Geylang or Chinatown, the *kampong*s or villages in Pasir Panjang were not identified as purely Malay or Chinese. According to Madam Kok, Chinese and Malay families lived side by side. Even in *kampong*s identified as predominantly Malay, there would be Chinese and other ethnic groups residing within the village itself. For instance, Mr Tan Mok Lee was born in a compound house within a village called Kampong Abu Kassim (a *kampong* might be named after the person who owned the land, or after the person who resided longest in the village). His home—and Kampong Abu Kassim—was located at "Fifth Mile" or the fifth milestone, roughly around South Buona Vista Road. In contrast, a former Malay resident, who was initially relocated from Kallang in 1937 to Kampong Pasir Panjang (located at "Batu 5½" or five-and-a-half milestone), remembers Pasir Panjang as mostly a Malay enclave, which gradually began to include more Chinese, Eurasians and Indians.

The acid test for many was how the various ethnic groups in Pasir Panjang reacted to two major racial incidents in Singapore's history—the Maria Hertogh riots of 1950 and the racial riots of 1964. When queried about the impact of the first incident, Dr Tan Eng Liang recalls:

Well, the good thing was that actually my father was more or

less like a headman of the district. In fact, so his relationship with the 'penghulu' (Malay: headman) because we have kampong all behind our house. In fact, we had … there were two houses that were, I think, mansions in those days. And I think because of his personality and his PR, we had extremely good relationships with the kampong. And the other good about the kampong were not 100 per cent Malays. Although it is kampong, it may be 60, 70 per cent Malays, then you have Chinese 30, 40 per cent. So I think we had no problem actually in what you called 'Goh Goh Jiok', 'Lark Goh Jiok' (Hokkien: Fifth, Sixth milestone) in Pasir Panjang. So relationship was good and in fact because of those relationship, we did not see any ugly scenes at all.[160]

On the impact of the 1964 disturbances on Pasir Panjang, Dr Tan also did not recall any untoward incident, observing that:

No, Pasir Panjang, no. Comparatively or relatively. Although there were Malay kampongs behind and so on. No problem at all. In fact the Pasir Panjang area hardly … Goh Chok Tong's place is only four doors away from our house. And behind his place, in fact directly behind,

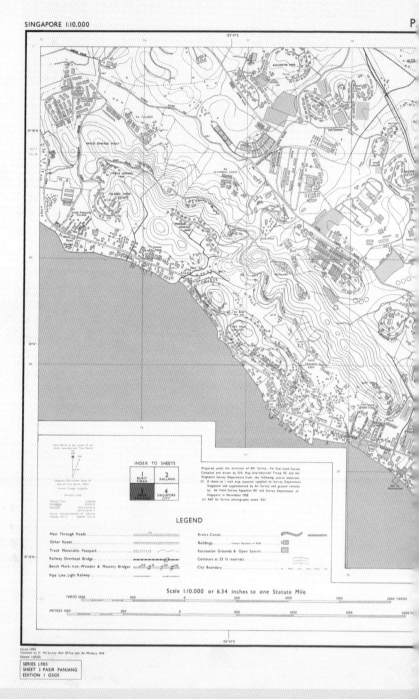

Fig. 4.18: This 1957 1:10,000 scale typographical map of the Pasir Panjang area is in treasure trove of historical information

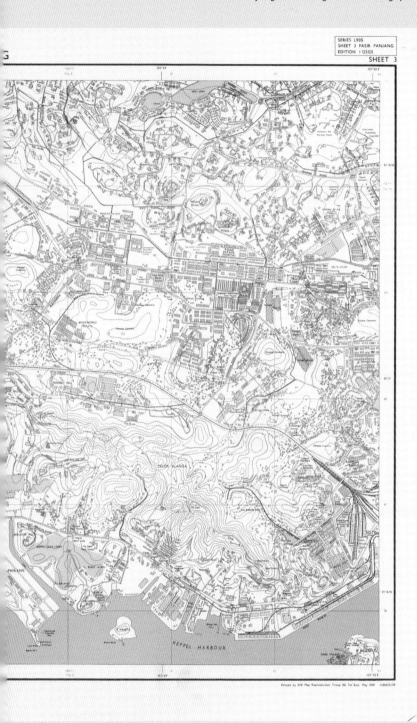

SERIES L905
SHEET 3 PASIR PANJANG
EDITION 1 GSGS
SHEET 3

on the right hand side of Chok Tong's place is Mat Jambol.

Now that is mainly Malay kampong and no problem. Now the kampong directly behind us, of course, we had a fairly good relationship in the sense that most of the kids, we played around there, we go to the provision store, we … and in fact the relationship is extremely good in those days. And I think maybe it's partly also it's a mixed kampong – it's not entirely Malay. But I think Mat Jambol side also, I don't recall any problem at all I think suppose like all kampong, it's really the penghulu or whoever instigate or whoever hates. So the headman, if the headman has a very good relationship with the neighbours who are all Chinese, there should be no problem. I think Othman Wok was staying also on Pasir Panjang, you know, during that period I think further up. His is six mile [near Haw Par Villa].

So Pasir Panjang, I think all along has been a fairly good community as far as inter-racial mixing is concerned. And I think that is partly maybe because although the middle class and the wealthy are all by the seaside. But I think somehow, the Chinese and the Malays, they are all staying together in … even in Buona Vista. Buona Vista actually has a lot of big villages or kampongs. But I think they are all mixed up – Chinese and Malay, so there's no fairly exclusive like Geylang Serai, I suppose. So perhaps I think because of that mix, things do not blow up.[161]

The racial harmony of Pasir Panjang was also acknowledged by politicians such as Lee Kuan Yew and the former Member of Parliament for the Pasir Panjang constituency, Othman Wok (Lee 1965). They would know better than anyone else as during the height of politicking during Singapore's difficult stint in Malaysia from 1963 to 1965, the Singapore branch of the political party UMNO (the United Malays National Organisation) had a strong presence in the area. Indeed, even when Othman Wok won the seat in 1963, he acknowledged that the majority of the Malay vote went to the UMNO candidate.[162] That there were no conflicts between the communities living in Pasir Panjang, even during the 1964 racial riots, remains an interesting and strong testament to peaceful and mutual understanding of differences.

The social life of the village residents remained centred on Pasir Panjang's eponymous "long sands". The beach started before the junction of South Buona Vista Road and Pasir Panjang Road, and stretched all the way to the seventh milestone, that is, the junction of Reformatory Road and Pasir Panjang Road. Beyond that point (going along today's West Coast), the coast became more swampy and was generally populated by houses on stilts and prawn ponds. Along the sandy beach, however, residents living in the area during the 1950s and 1960s vividly remember the large bungalows, where families hosted evening or weekend parties.

For children living in post-war Pasir Panjang, the nearness to the sea provided plenty of possibilities for fishing and sea sports. The ridges at the back offered open spaces and slopes to run around. The various plantations also suffered from young thieving hands. Madam Kok and Mr Latiff recall the little streams or drains running in between houses and other structures, flowing down from the foot of the ridge into the sea; the children would follow the streams down to the sea with glee after (or even during) school. In Dr Tan Eng Liang's words:

As I was saying that I think if you can imagine every afternoon, after school I came back, … I did do my homework, and normally, you do it within the hour; we came back lunch, do your arithmetic or whatever it is. Then every afternoon, it's playing field and weekend, we were swimming by the open sea. And then later on, at the Haw Par or Tiger Swimming Pool. So it was a very contented period [immediate post-war period] and the fact that we were able to … with a

little bit of luck, or as you said, effort plus luck, we managed to get into RI (Raffles Institution).

… [W]e played marbles … after schools, weekends I think, of course we went 'sampan' (Malay: canoe); we catch crabs, we catch prawns, all outdoor, by the open sea. Then we go and dig mussel or 'ham.' Then of course, by the roadside, we catch spiders. Now most of our games are out door. The only indoor is table-tennis and even badminton was played outdoor. Every other game is outdoor and that means in other words, if you don't like the sun, then you are finished; you can't enjoy, I think, you know … like fishing, because as I said our house, the sea was actually two hundred metres in front. So swimming, fishing, catching crab with the iron stick; we walked down during shallow tide and then we literally poked. Then to do fishing, we used to 'liah' (Hokkien: catch) the worm; you put your hand on the water as the tide flows in, and then you throw some rice water. And then the worms will bite bite your … and then you pull it out and use that as bait to fish.[163]

Singaporean artist Ong Kim Seng, who grew up in neighbouring Telok Blangah near Mount Faber, gives a succinct description of *kampong* life:

Kampong life [this was in Silat Road] is very simple, we don't get what the kids today used. It was more or less running about, going up the hill, catching spiders, catching frogs, chasing pigs and so on. I remember in those days, we used to play in the graveyard, and you know soil erosion, I can still very clearly remember there was a coffin that was projected out of the ground. And we used to sit down there and talked and we jumped, but when it comes to night, we quickly run away. Because a lot of imagination starts coming so it is very funny when you think of it in those days. One of the things we liked to stay is, there are little huts that we built in the hills there. When it rains, we just hide together in that little hut there. Those are very simple kampong life. We really played most of the time, no electronic, no television, not even radio. The nearest thing we can get to radio was Rediffusion. So that was the only entertainment those days. Movies yes, movies but movies were quite cheap. But even so cheap also we can't afford it. Movies were about 10 cents. And it is open air movie. They just erect a piece of cloth and they just show…. All were fenced up by cloth. They covered up by cloth. Sometimes we try to steal a show by tearing some holes in the canvas and peeped through and looked at it, but we couldn't. Very soon, we caught and were chased away. They don't really hammer us, but they tell us, 'Kids, you are not supposed to see', because soon the hole becomes bigger and bigger because more people like to peep through (Ong 2002).

For adults or soon-to-be adults, Pasir Panjang was a mixture of idyllic as well as serious entertainment. There were open-air cinemas located at South Buona Vista Road, in nearby West Coast Road, further up in Telok Blangah, and in O'Carrol Scot [within the present-day vicinity of the National University Hospital (NUH)]. Latiff remembers making the trek from his Island View Estate home with his siblings—along Hog's Back (what could be the present-day road starting from the Central Library of NUS, heading along the Ridge towards South Buona Vista Road)—to catch a movie in the evenings. This was, of course, a predominantly British area, occupied from the ridge and then to the north by the lodgings of British senior officers. The most senior were housed in private bungalows atop the ridge in the middle of what is now NUS campus, enjoying green space and an unobstructed view of the sea.

Playing

Pasir Panjang was a great area for playing and hosting outdoor sports and other activities. These activities disappeared over time—with land reclamation and as the roads became more regulated. The entire Pasir Panjang area was a cycling circuit for several major competitions. Motorcycle races were very popular in Singapore between the late 1920s and the 1970s. Old Pasir Panjang regularly hosted big events on the "99 bends" of South Buona Vista Road. The Gap Hill Climb attracted car- and motorcycle-racing enthusiasts and well-known overseas motor-sports competitors, who were often bested by home boys on the wildly swerving circuit. Though traditionally western sports, such activities quickly acquired Asian stars and a local following, even before the Japanese invasion. This premier motor-racing competition goes back to the 1920s, making the Pasir Panjang circuit the oldest and longest-lasting arena for motor sports in Singapore. Many stars of the better-known Thomson-Mile circuit cut their teeth here.[164] Anyone who has whizzed along the snake-like Gap can understand its attraction to sportsmen and dare devils.

The earliest photographic and newspaper record of an official race at the Gap goes back to 1927. The SVC motorcycle platoon ran the Malayan Gap Hill Climb annually from 1927 to 1929, a sprint event of only 1,660 yards involving motorcycles and cars. Pictures and the winners' list suggest

Fig. 4.19a: The twists and turns of the curves of South Buona Vista Road made the ascent of motorcylists in the Gap Hill Climb particularly thrilling

Fig. 4.19b: The Gap Hill Climb was an important event in the Asian motorsports calendar from the 1930s to the 1970s

this was largely an expatriate affair. The highlight of the course was a hairpin turn at the top of the hill. The thrill of swerving one way and then the other in quick succession at speed on this snaky road was apparent from comments that a nimble passenger provided substantial ballast for the sprint.[165]

No further competitions were held until 1939, when locally built cars were included in a shortened half-mile race. The Automobile Association of Malaya (AAM) revived and scaled up the hill climb. A grandstand overlooking the course was accessible to the public from the Ayer Rajah end, and AAM officials loaned out film footage and encouraged amateur recording. Seats were booked at John Little's and ticket sales were donated to the War Fund. Air Vice-Marshal Babington's wife officiated. The 1939 event also saw Lim Peng Han, "Possibly Malaya's foremost competition motorist", returning the fastest time for a car, 44.8 seconds in an LA special, a model he built in his local garage for himself and other participants.[166] Lady driver Eunice Lee, a prize-winning speed trial competitor, unfortunately failed to win here. This event was clearly a highlight in what was then a busy Malayan racing calendar.

The Gap Hill Climb became even more popular in post-war Singapore, alongside races at Bukit Batok, Lim Chu Kang, Seletar, Sembawang and, of course, Thomson Road. Local speed demons often won overseas regional

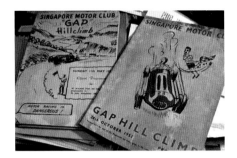

Fig. 4.20: Souvenir programmes for the Gap Hill Climb event in the 1950s testify to the popularity of the event, which was held annually until the early 1970s

events and some foreign racing veterans found the sharp turns of the Hill Climb too much of a challenge, skidding off the road and even causing fatalities.[167] It is unclear when or why motor-racing in Pasir Panjang stopped. The last mention of the Dunlop Gap Hill Climb in the newspapers was in 1973, the same year the Grand Prix event at Thomson ended because of safety concerns and the growing difficulty of closing roads for sporting events.[168] This, of course, did not put an end to the course's appeal. Latter-day hell-riders found the poorly lit Gap circuit, comprising "Ayer Rajah Road ... the whole of South Buona Vista Road ... Lorong Sahad and Lorong Sari" the most dangerous and thus the most thrilling of nine challenging circuits in Singapore.[169]

While challenging enough for motor sports, the Pasir Panjang circuit proved especially punishing for cyclists. Only 11 out of 31 riders finished the Alfred Montor Memorial Trophy in 1955.[170] As with the Hill Gap Climb, pre-war competitions here were speed trials,[171] but the 100-mile long McGregor Watt Trophy Challenge of the 1950s was a mass-start endurance race which flagged off at 6.30 am. The circuit started at Pasir Panjang Post Office, continued up and down South and North Buona Vista Roads into Dover then turning left down Clementi Road and back onto Pasir Panjang.[172] Pasir Panjang was the season opener for the Singapore-Malacca Race, hosting time trials for the 1961 SEAP Games and a variety of other regular competitions,[173] most of which appeared to be serious events of 50 miles or more.[174]

This 100-kilometre race cut left at Ayer Rajah instead of Dover Road. Major competitions usually drew 40–70 participants, many from organized clubs, but these numbers could swell to 300 for shorter events. Cycling was a serious sport in Singapore at the time, with the winner of the Tour of Singapour in 1975 going on to the Tour de France.[175]

There was also entertainment available in the form of restaurants and music bars. Mary Turnbull recorded a recreation place called Coconut Grove located in Pasir Panjang. Although Kok and Latiff did not have any recollection of the place, they do remember West Point Gardens, an open-air bar-cum-dance hall, which over time featured some of the more prominent bands in 1960s Singapore, including the Quests. West Point was located at the seventh milestone, near the junction of Reformatory Road (perhaps in the present-day site of the car-park opposite the shop-houses). It was more popular among the English-speaking dating crowd as the bands played the top English pop songs of the time. Latiff recalls that his brother mentioned that it was too expensive after going one time. Daniel Teo, a local entre-preneur, remembers:

[Tea parties were] rotated. We go to different places. Oh, that time West Point was very popular. We go all the way to West Coast. And it is open air, of course they play bands. We go there to dance.

Interviewer: It was open air performance?

Teo: With a band. And then a nice concrete floor where people can dance.

Interviewer: What do you call that, is a dance hall?

Teo: It is not covered; it is an open air thing. West Point was very popular among teenagers because it is open air, it is reasonably charged. You just pay an entrance then you are entitled to two drinks. They played mainly sort of … Then it was Rock and Roll, Cha-Cha, Foxtrot and Waltz type of music. It's quite an attraction with nice colour bulbs and all the tress and green…. So it is real tropical kind of atmosphere.

Fig. 4.21a and 4.21b: Cycling at Pasir Panjang, 13 December 1964

Interviewer: Was it fenced up?

Teo: Of course! It is a big building with proper dining. But every Saturday and Sunday they have weekend special and they have live bands. It is a complex. Where will it be now? West Point, it's after Haw Par Villa on the left, also facing the sea.

Interviewer: Palace 88? Seafood?

Teo: Further up, further up, almost towards the NUS. But on the left hand side is a big chunk of land, with a building. Maybe again, like Grange Hotel type of set up, where they have some rooms also to rent out.

Interviewer: Do you have any idea about the background of this place?

Teo: Well, from my memory serves me correct, I think it was towards the end of Pasir Panjang Road, almost corner of Pasir Panjang and Clementi Road. Maybe at least two acres land, on the other side is facing the sea. Weekends a lot of powerboats [were] parked so it is very popular among the locals as well as expatriates. Weekends [are] always full of activities. I only remember because we were still young and cannot drive, so we sometimes have to carpool or have chance, sometimes borrow some friend's driver to drop us there. And it is an open air concept, lots of coloured bulbs and concrete floors for dancing. A lot of tables around it and there's a little sort of band stand. Weekends, they have live bands. It is very popular for the teenagers as well as the expatriate community.

Interviewer: Because it is open air, it depends on the weather?

Teo: Oh yes, again weather has a lot to do with it. But they have also similar to Grange Hotel they have some terraces with counters for bars and proper restaurants also. So, if it rains then they move inside, under cover.

Interviewer: And you mentioned that they charged quite reasonably, how much was it, can you remember?

Teo: You were allowed two soft drinks for something like four, five dollars.

Interviewer: That was in the sixties?

Teo: Or maybe even less. I can't remember. Maybe two, three dollars then. I know we don't drink beer, don't drink hard liquor so just Greenspot or fruit punch.

Interviewer: That would be the period, 1960s? About that?

Teo: Yeah, before I went overseas, even late '50s.[176]

Old Pasir Panjang Passes into History?

When speaking to former residents of Pasir Panjang, the author(s) were struck by persistent remarks such as: "You can never imagine how it was before" or "It has completely changed." The Pasir Panjang of today is thoroughly different from the "old" Pasir Panjang that survived into the 1970s. The physical landscape where former residents once lived, worked and played has completely altered. The sea and the long sandy beaches, once upon a time within touching distance after a quick dash across Pasir Panjang Road, are today replaced by wharves, an overhead highway and other concrete structures. Whole institutions have relocated or completely disappeared.

The story the former residents try to tell when they share their memories of a Pasir Panjang of which only footprints now remain is a story of change, change so drastic it physically erased their former haunts. While they accept change as part of Singapore's overall development, there remains the nagging regret and pull of nostalgia, the fear their memories if not recorded will be forever lost—and the old neighbourhood with them.

The drastic change to Pasir Panjang's physical landscape is due in no small part to the economic and industrial development since 1965. Universities, wharves, container terminals and concrete roads not only replaced the

long sandy beach Pasir Panjang took its name from, but also erased institutions such as schools, entertainment and recreational spots. The once sparsely developed landscape, with plenty of open spaces, hilly ridges and streams where children could play, has been replaced by claustrophobic private residential development. The sea, the common playground for all, is also no longer within touching distance. Driving along the new Pasir Panjang Viaduct, the urban landscape seems so different very few people would see any trace of the old Pasir Panjang area.

On the other hand, it could be argued that while the landscape of Pasir Panjang has fundamentally and dramatically changed over a short period of time (considering that land reclamation only took place some 40 years ago), and while some institutions have disappeared completely, the overall nature and function of some of Pasir Panjang's localities remains somewhat similar. Amenities still remain and grow in support of a growing student, upper middle-class and expatriate population, some in the very spots where sundry stores and small- to medium-size businesses once plied their trade, serving the British military and the local elite of Singapore.

This duality of development versus heritage does beg the question of the price of development. Most Singaporeans and other observers would agree with the necessity of industrialization and economic development, particularly during the early years after independence. But they may not always agree with the seemingly destructive outcome, and, judging by some of their actions, have not been passive in voicing their concerns. As seen above, there are substantial local and international websites dedicated to remembering aspects of Singapore's past, of which Pasir Panjang is included. Madam Kok herself is a walking guide with a civil-society group dedicated to increasing public awareness of Pasir Panjang's heritage. There is a nostalgic impetus to collect memories before they vanish completely without the opportunity to be recorded. Do old neighbourhoods, like old soldiers, also just "fade away"?

No outsider could have known "old" Pasir Panjang as well as its own residents. Nonetheless, history is never solely about what happens in a place. The district was and remains important to many because events here touched the lives of multitudes beyond. The big dramatic episodes of mutiny and war are part of the story of old Pasir Panjang, but they are not what changed the area beyond all recognition in the 1980s. The great change in the human geography of the area comes from the less dramatic but more fundamental social and economic change that took place in Singapore as a whole.

Notes

1. John Leyden, *Malay Annals*, translated from Malay by the late Dr John Leyden, with an Introduction by Sir Thomas Stamford Raffles (London: Longman, Hur, Rees, Orme and Brown, 1821). The text of this book has been reproduced in Virginia Matheson Hooker and M.B. Hooker, *John Leyden's Malay Annals* (Kuala Lumpur: Malaysian Branch of the Royal Asiatic Society, 2001), p. 42.

2. Jan Huygen van Linschoten, *Itinerario: Voyage Ofte Schipvaert Van Jan Huygen Van Linschoten Naer oost ofte Portugaels Indien 1579–1592* [Itinerario: Voyage Ofte Schipvaert By Jan Huygen Van Linschoten Naer East of Portugaels from 1579–1592] (The Hague: Martinus Nijhoff, 1939), p. 95. Special thanks to Peter Borschberg for providing this information. See his *The Singapore and Melaka Straits: Violence, Security and Diplomacy in the 17th Century* (Singapore: NUS Press, 2010), Ch. 1.

3. E-mail from Peter Borschberg, 20 May 2009: "a *rutter* is more than just a set of navigational instructions. It also contains market intelligence: buy this product here and sell it when you reach xyz."

4. Victor R. Savage and Brenda S.A. Yeoh, *Toponymics: A Study of Singapore Street Names* (Singapore: Eastern Universities Press, 2003), Fig. 4.

5. Song Ong Siang wrote: "Telok Blangah (now Pasir Panjang)". See Song Ong Siang, *One Hundred Years' History of the Chinese in Singapore* (London: John Murray, 1923), p. 95.

6. Ibid., p. 46.

7. "Municipal Commissioner", *Singapore Free Press*, 18 Dec. 1856, p. 3.

8. Lee Kip Lin, *The Singapore House, 1819–1942* (Singapore: Times Editions, 1988), p. 55.

9. 1898 Map of the Island of Singapore and its Dependencies, Source: Survey Department, Courtesy of National Archives of Singapore, Ref: TM000012.

10. Kim Seng Land Company Limited v The Rural Board [1935] 1 *Malayan Law Journal*, 1 (Singapore, 1935), p. 153. See also *The Straits Times*, 7 Mar. 1935, p. 12.

11. "Squatter's Rubber Trees", *Singapore Free Press*, 20 Sept. 1917, p. 186.

12. *The Straits Times*, 24 June 1848, p. 2.

13. *The Straits Times*, 29 July 1856, p. 5.

14. *The Straits Times*, 19 Nov. 1864, p. 4.

15. See a newspaper clipping dated 23 Oct. 1871, enclosed in CO273/50/11545, p. 171.

16. *The Straits Times*, 24 Dec. 1870, p. 4.

17. *The Straits Times*, 3 Dec. 1870, p. 4.

18. *The Straits Times*, 26 Oct. 1878, p. 3.

19. P.L. Burns and C.D. Cowan (eds.), *Sir Frank Swettenham's Malayan Journals 1874–1876* (Kuala Lumpur: Oxford University Press, 1975), p. 260n2.

20. Charles Burton Buckley, *An Anecdotal History of Old Times in Singapore* (Singapore: Fraser & Neave, 1902), pp. 410–11, 510–9.

21. Savage and Yeoh, *Toponymics*.

22. Buckley, *An Anecdotal History of Old Times in Singapore*, p. 714.

23. "News of the Week", *The Straits Times*, 19 Nov. 1864; see "Government Gazette", *The Straits Times*, 14 Nov. 1864.

24. Savage and Yeoh, *Toponymics*, p. 33.

25. "Game Preserver", *The Straits Times*, 5 Dec. 1874.

26. *The Straits Times*, 20 Mar. 1875, p. 3.

27. "Betrayed by a Helmet", *The Straits Times*, 30 May 1906, p. 5.

28. Chiang Ming Shun, "Britannia Rules the Waves? Singapore and Imperial Defence 1867–1891", in *Between Two Oceans: A Military History of Singapore From First Settlement to Final British Withdrawal*, Malcolm H. Murfett et al. (Singapore: Oxford University Press, 1999), p. 102.

29. *The Straits Times*, 15 Oct. 1889, p. 2.

30. *The Straits Times*, 29 July 1903, p. 4.

31. "SVC Orders", *The Straits Times,* 7 Mar. 1912, p. 2.

32. "Notices", *The Straits Times*, 21 Mar. 1883, p. 4.

33. "Lands for Military Purposes", *The Straits Times*, 8 June 1896, p. 2.

34. "Burglary at 'Labrador Villa'", *The Straits Times*, 3 Dec. 1906, p. 7.

35. "Singapore Government Bungalows", *The Straits Times*, 14 Aug. 1909, p. 6.

36. *The Straits Times*, 9 May 1914, p. 8.

37. *The Straits Times*, 29 July 1914, p. 8.

38. *The Straits Times*, 15 June 1915, p. 6.

39. *The Straits Times*, 28 Oct. 1918, p. 8.

40. "Legislative Council", *The Straits Times*, 8 Nov. 1898, p. 3.

41. "Report on the Straits Settlements for the Year 1901", in *Annual Reports of the Straits Settlements 1855–1941,* ed. R.L. Jarman (London: Archives Editions Ltd, 1998), vol. 5, p. 89.

42. "Report on the Straits Settlements for the Year 1902", in ibid., p. 190.

43. "Report on the Straits Settlements for the Year 1903", in ibid., p. 273.

44. Rajpal Singh s/o Santokh Singh, "Street Naming and the Construction of the Colonial Narrative in Singapore: 1819–1942", Academic Exercise (Singapore: Department of History, Faculty of Arts & Social Sciences, National University of Singapore, 2002).

45. Address of Governor Sir Charles Bullen Hugh Mitchell, at a Meeting of the Legislative Council, 3 Oct. 1899, in Jarman, *Annual Reports of the Straits Settlements 1855–1941*, vol. 4, p. 462.

46. Saw Swee Hock, *The Population of Singapore*, 2nd ed. (Singapore: Institute of Southeast Asian Studies, 2007), p. 10, Table 2.1.
47. "Lawless Pasir Panjang", *The Straits Times*, 5 Dec. 1899, p. 3.
48. "Highway Robbery", *The Straits Times*, 25 May 1898, p. 2.
49. "Daring Gang Robbery", *The Straits Times*, 15 Aug. 1903, p. 5.
50. "The Volunteer Camp", *The Straits Times*, 27 Jan. 1903, p. 5.
51. *The Straits Times*, 6 Jan. 1909, p. 6.
52. This home is one of the houses featured in Julian Davison, *Black and White: The Singapore House 1898–1941* (Singapore: Talisman, 2006), p. 30.
53. "Death", *The Straits Times*, 6 Aug. 1894, p. 2.
54. "2 Blocks of European Quarters, Pasir Panjang Rd", Building Plan No 217, Owner: New Harbour Dock Co Ltd (Singapore: National Archives of Singapore).
55. "To Contractors", *The Straits Times*, 14 May 1900, p. 2.
56. *The Straits Times*, 25 July 1900, p. 2.
57. "Buddhist Temple, Alexandra Rd", Building Plan No. 8167 (Singapore: National Archives of Singapore).
58. "Dwelling House, Alexandra Rd, 4.25 Milestone", Building Plan No. 9070 (Singapore: National Archives of Singapore).
59. "Bungalow, Alexandra Rd", Building Plan No. 8692 (Singapore: National Archives of Singapore).
60. "Tile Roof House, Alexandra Rd", Building Plan No. 8891 (Singapore: National Archives of Singapore).
61. "Extension of the Railway", *The Straits Times*, 21 Jan. 1907, p. 8.
62. Alexandra Brickworks was registered in 1899. See "Registered Companies", *The Straits Times*, 24 Apr. 1900, p. 2.
63. Another brickworks located in Pasir Panjang was Kim Wan Brickworks Co. See *The Straits Times*, 11 July 1902, p. 5.
64. Henry Longhurst, *Straits Times, the Borneo Story: The History of the First 100 Years of Trading in the Far East by the Borneo Company, Limited* (Newman Neame, 1956), pp. 85–6.
65. This map of the Pasir Panjang area as it was in 1942 is found in Dol Ramli, "History of the Malay Regiment 1933–1942", *Journal of the Malaysian Branch of the Royal Asiatic Society* 38, 1 (1965): 234.
66. This information was found in 2004 at the following website which is no longer in operation: http://www.pasirpanjang.org.sg/history.htm.
67. Savage and Yeoh, *Toponymics*, p. 62.
68. See http://www.ruthrakali.org.sg/htmlfiles/history.htm.

69. This information was found in 2004 at the following website which is no longer in operation: http://www.pasirpanjang.org.sg/history.htm.

70. "Report on the Straits Settlements for the Year 1904", in *Annual Reports of the Straits Settlements 1855–1941*, ed. R.L. Jarman (London: Archives Editions Ltd, 1998), vol. 5, p. 386. The next page of this report notes that, after the farmers "found themselves in difficulties", the government reduced the rents in the second half of 1904.

71. This map is from Dol Ramli, "History of the Malay Regiment 1933–1942", *Journal of the Malaysian Branch of the Royal Asiatic Society* 38, 1 (1965): 234.

72. "Annual Report on the Straits Settlements for the Year 1905", in *Annual Reports of the Straits Settlements 1855–1941*, ed. Jarman, vol. 5, pp. 471, 561.

73. *The Singapore and Malayan Directory for 1940* (Singapore: Printers Limited, 1940), p. 985.

74. "Annual Report on the Straits Settlements for the Year 1907", in *Annual Reports of the Straits Settlements 1855–1941*, ed. Jarman, vol. 5, p. 673.

75. Song Ong Siang wrote: "Telok Blangah (now Pasir Panjang)". See Song, *One Hundred Years' History of the Chinese in Singapore*, p. 95.

76. "Annual Report on the Straits Settlements for the Year 1909", in *Annual Reports of the Straits Settlements 1855–1941*, ed. Jarman, vol. 6, pp. 185–6.

77. "Annual Report on the Colony of the Straits Settlements for the Year 1929", in *Annual Reports of the Straits Settlements 1855–1941*, ed. Jarman, vol. 9, p. 407.

78. *The Singapore and Malayan Directory for 1940*, p. 985.

79. H.R. Hone, *Report on the British Military Administration of Malaya September 1945, to March 1946* (Kuala Lumpur: Malayan Union Government Press, 1946), p. 9, para. 50.

80. *The Straits Times*, 29 July 1902.

81. *The Straits Times*, 21 Feb. 1903.

82. *The Straits Times*, 30 July 1903.

83. *The Straits Times*, 17 Aug. 1903.

84. *The Straits Times*, 12 Nov. 1903.

85. *The Straits Times*, 2 May 1905.

86. *The Straits Times*, 30 May 1906.

87. *The Straits Times*, 3 Jan. 1910, p. 6.

88. "The Ramlila", *The Straits Times*, 15 Oct. 1910, p. 7.

89. *The Straits Times*, 19 Jan. 1910, p. 6.

90. "The Third Brahmans", *The Straits Times*, 11 Jan. 1911, p. 8.

91. "Volunteer Inspection", *The Straits Times*, 11 Dec. 1911, p. 6.

92. "Notes in General", *The Straits Times*, 31 Oct. 1912, p. 10.

93. "Brahman Murdered", *The Straits Times*, 23 Feb. 1914, p. 11.

94. "Pasir Panjang Murder Trial Opened", *The Straits Times*, 9 June 1914, p. 9.

95. "The Murdered Brahman", *The Straits Times*, 24 Feb. 1914, p. 8.

96. "Brahman Murder", *The Straits Times*, 2 Apr. 1914, p. 9.

97. "The Relief of the 3rd Brahmans", *The Straits Times,* 24 Mar. 1914, p. 8.

98. Chiang Ming Shun, "The Weakest Go to the Wall: From Money to Mutiny 1892–1918", in *Between Two Oceans*, Malcolm Murfett et al., pp. 128–31, 135.

99. Ibid., p.127.

100. "Second Infantry Regiment in Their New Home", *The Straits Times*, 1 Apr. 1936, p. 1.

101. "New Military Hospital Now Open", *The Straits Times*, 28 July 1940, p. 6.

102. *The Straits Times*, 20 Dec. 1915, p. 8.

103. Lee Kip Lee, *Amber Sands: A Boyhood Memoir* (Singapore: Federal Publications, 1999).

104. Ibid., p. 42. Lee Choon Guan is mentioned on pp. 48, 50.

105. Ibid., pp. 47–52.

106. Brian P. Farrell, *The Defence and Fall of Singapore 1940–42* (Stroud: Tempus, 2005), p. 367.

107. Ibid., p. 375.

108. Upon being informed that water supply to the town was about to collapse, Percival's immediate superior General Wavell insisted that "fighting must go on wherever there is sufficient water, house to house if necessary".

109. S. Woodburn Kirby, *The War Against Japan*, vol. 1 (London: HMSO, 1957), p. 416, Map 25.

110. Alan Warren, *Singapore 1942: Britain's Greatest Defeat* (London: Hambledon Continuum, 2002), p. 260.

111. Mubin C. Sheppard, *The Malay Regiment 1933–47* (Kuala Lumpur: Department of Public Relations, 1947), pp. 15–7; see also Farrell, *The Defence and Fall of Singapore 1940–42*, pp. 372–3.

112. Ibid., p. 18.

113. Mubin C. Sheppard, "The Malay Soldier from a District Officers' Point of View", in *Straits Times Annual 1939* (Singapore: Straits Times Press, 1940), pp. 26–35. Even officers who practised racial profiling understood how well rural Malays could soldier if properly led and trained. The enthusiasm of Malay recruits for police positions and volunteer military units also convinced experienced British officers of good prospects for setting up a regular unit.

114. Teo Choon Hong, Oral History Interview, National Archives of Singapore, Accession No. 000328, Reel 6.

115. Mubin C. Sheppard, *The Malay Regiment 1933–47* (Kuala Lumpur: Department of Public Relations, 1947).

116. Teoh Veoh Seng, Oral History Interview, National Archives of Singapore, Accession No. 004647, Reels 7–9.

117. Chew Kong, Oral History Interview, National Archives of Singapore, Accession No. 000056, Reel 8.

118. These "military prostitutes" were, in all probability, comfort women brought in by the Japanese military.

119. John Leslie Carrick, Oral History Interview, National Archives of Singapore, Accession No. 002791, Reel 4.

120. Poh Ern Shih, "Temple of Thanksgiving", http://www.pohernshih.org/History(E).htm [accessed 5 May 2009]. Current website at https://pohernshih.org.sg/pes/history/ is less detailed but contains gist of information found in this account.

121. Sam King, *Tiger Balm King: The Life and Times of Aw Boon Haw* (Singapore: Times Book International, 1992), pp. 7, 314–36.

122. Judith Brandell and Tina Turbeville, *Tiger Balm Gardens: A Chinese Billionaire's Fantasy Environments* (Hong Kong: Aw Boon Haw Foundations, 1998).

123. Teoh Veoh Seng, Oral History Interview.

124. Robin Eccles, Oral History Interview, National Archives of Singapore, Accession No. 001135, Reel 1.

125. Richard England, Oral History Interview, National Archives of Singapore, Accession No. 002700, Reel 1.

126. Ibid.

127. Siva Choy, Oral History Interview, National Archives of Singapore, Accession No. 002821, Reel 8. Siva's father stayed at his post manning the generator in Gillman Barracks even as the Japanese charged in and took over. They were spared and kept on the job because the Japanese needed their technical expertise.

128. Abdul Latiff bin Zainal, personal communication with Ho Chi Tim, 2009.

129. Badron bin Sainullah, Oral History Interview, National Archives of Singapore, Accession No. 000614, Reels 11 and 12.

130. Myra Isabelle Cresson, Oral History Interview, National Archives of Singapore, Accession No. 000594, Reel 4.

131. Kok Oi Yee, personal communication to Ho Chi Tim, 2009. Madam Kok stayed in three different places along Pasir Panjang Road from the late 1940s to the late 1950s. The site of her family's first home no longer exists. Her mother had rented two rooms in a mansion which was located across Pasir Panjang Road, just after South Buona Vista Road (heading eastwards). The mansion was next to Hua Chiao Secondary School and faced the sea. She then moved to South Buona Vista Road (near the duck rice stall) and finally ended up in Balmeg Hill, just after Haw Par Villa.

132. Michael John Sweet, Oral History Interview, National Archives of Singapore, Accession No. 001716, Reel 4.

133. Latiff, personal communication with Ho Chi Tim.

134. Grace Taylor, Oral History Interview, National Archives of Singapore, Accession No. 000511, Reel 16.

135. Othman Wok, Oral History Interview, National Archives of Singapore, Accession No. 000133, Reel 13.

136. Information taken from *Dopps. Inc: Pasir Panjang - 34th Sea Scouts*, http://doppsinc. blogspot.com/2008/09/pasis-panjang-34th-sea-scouts.html [accessed 14 June 2009].

137. Kok Oi Yee, personal communication with Ho Chi Tim, 2009.

138. "Malayan Breweries Limited", *The Straits Times*, 21 Mar. 1932, p. 14.

139. "Modern Brewery for Singapore – Nearing Completion", *The Straits Times*, 5 Apr. 1932, p. 7.

140. 478 probably referred to an Alexandra Road address as the numbering of Pasir Panjang Road addresses starts (present day) from this junction and progressed towards the 400s only close to the junction with Clementi Road. Construction began in 1931 and brewing started the following year.

141. *The Straits Times*, 16 Dec. 1933, p. 16.

142. The plant also produced Heineken and other brands but Rimau or Tiger, as it became known, was its flagship product.

143. "Notes of the Day", *The Straits Times*, 3 Nov. 1933, p. 10.

144. "A New Industry for Malaya", *The Straits Times*, 5 Apr. 1932, p. 7.

145. See, for example, "Diluted Beer: Two Chinese Convicted", *The Straits Times*, 18 Mar. 1939, p. 13 and "Beer Taken to Court", *The Straits Times*, 17 Feb. 1940, p. 10.

146. "New Company to Run Brewery: Former German Concern has been Sold", *The Straits Times*, 27 Jan. 1941, p. 9.

147. "Malayan Breweries Profit almost Doubled", *The Straits Times*, 14 Mar. 1941, p. 4.

148. "Breweries Make a Profit", *The Straits Times*, 2 Oct. 1949, p. 3.

149. "Brewery's $750,000 Scheme", *The Straits Times*, 27 May 1949, p. 5.

150. "Brewers' Tails were 'in the air'", *The Straits Times*, 6 Oct. 1950, p. 7.

151. George Kennedy, Oral History Interview, National Archives of Singapore, Accession No. 000591, Reel 7.

152. Badron bin Sainullah, Oral History Interview.

153. See ygblog4's blog posting for more information on the Tiger Swimming Pool, http:// ivyidaong4.blogspot.com/2009/05/haw-par-swimming-pool-site-of-former.html [accessed 14 June 2009].

154. Rudy William Mosbergen, Oral History Interview, National Archives of Singapore, Accession No. 000510, Reel 32.

155. Ibid.

156. J.M. Jumabhoy, Oral History Interview, National Archives of Singapore, Accession No. 000112, Reel 4.

157. Savage and Yeoh, *Toponymics*, 2003.
158. Latiff, personal communication with Ho Chi Tim.
159. Chia 1997.
160. Tan Eng Liang, Oral History Interview, National Archives of Singapore, Accession No. 001951, Reel 13.
161. Ibid.
162. Othman Wok, Oral History Interview.
163. Tan Eng Liang, Oral History Interview.
164. "Leading Drivers, Rider for this Year's Grand Prix", *The Straits Times*, 23 June 1961, p. 11.
165. "Hill Climb Attracts Good Entry", *The Straits Times*, 31 July 1940, p. 15.
166. Incidentally, Lim Peng Han was the son of Chinese community leader Lim Boon Keng. See "Peng Han Builds 4 Cars for Hill Climb", *The Straits Times*, 23 Oct. 1948, p. 12.
167. See, for example, "Report is Wanted on Race Crash", *The Straits Times*, 28 May 1952, p. 7.
168. "Gerry Wins Fastest Time of the Day Award", *The Straits Times*, 24 Sept. 1973, p. 23.
169. "Roads that Make Some Riders Go Round the Bend", *The Straits Times*, 18 Apr. 1982, p. 11. The others were the Bonza at Dhoby Ghaut, Daytona at Mountbatten, Corner Seven, Garden Gap, Jervois, Shangri-La, Cargo Complex and Holland circuits. SBS Bus service 137 drivers were also popularly known as Mandai Hellriders in the 1980s.
170. "Jaffa First in Gap Race", *The Straits Times*, 31 Oct. 1955, p. 11.
171. "Cycling Speed Trial Postponed", *The Straits Times*, 14 Apr. 1939, p. 19 and "Gurdial Singh Wins Gap Hill Climb", *The Straits Times*, 15 May 1939, p. 19.
172. "100-M Cycle Race Today", *The Straits Times*, 23 Oct. 1955, p. 19.
173. "Singapore-Malacca Cycle Race Shortly", *The Straits Times*, 18 May 1958, p. 18.
174. "Salleh First", *The Straits Times*, 22 July 1963, p. 16 and "Choon Kiat Wins Gap", *The Straits Times*, 17 June 1974, p. 26.
175. "Rahman Fails By a Wheel to Win Tour of Singapore", *The Straits Times*, 17 Mar. 1975, p. 23.
176. Teo Choon Hong, Oral History Interview, National Archives of Singapore, Accession No. 000326, Reel 6.

The Building of the National University of Singapore

Kevin Y.L. Tan, Peck Thian Guan and Lee Fook Ngian

Introduction: Campuses of NUS[1]

Today, the siting and building of any university is a major exercise and expense, and inevitably draws huge public attention. However, this has not always been the case. When the first college, the Straits Settlement and Federated Malay States Government Medical School was established in Singapore in 1905, it occupied a number of small refurbished buildings that had previously been part of the Female Lunatic Asylum in the Sepoy Lines.[2] This institution was renamed the King Edward VII Medical School in 1913 after it received a donation of some $125,000 from the King Edward VII Memorial Fund and, in 1921, it was again renamed the King Edward VII College of Medicine. It was only in 1926 that the College moved into its own purpose-built neoclassical College of Medicine Building—which, together with the adjacent Tan Teck Guan Building, became home to what was to become the NUS Faculty of Medicine in 1982.

Fig. 5.1: College of Medicine Building, Sepoy Lines

When it was proposed to establish Raffles College as a first step towards a university in Singapore (and the Straits Settlements), two sites were considered for its buildings. The first was a 40-acre site at Mount Rosie which the Straits Government had purchased in 1919;[3] the second was the Economic Gardens section of the Botanical Gardens bounded by Cluny Road and Bukit Timah Road.[4] The second site was chosen on account of its accessibility and the practical lay of the land. Construction began in 1927 and Raffles College opened its doors in 1929. Despite agitation and protests to create a full-fledged university[5] in Singapore rather than a university college,[6] the University of Malaya would not be established until 1949, some 20 years later.

Fig. 5.2: Raffles College in 1938

The Carr-Saunders Commission reviewed the state of tertiary education in Singapore and recommended the immediate establishment of a university with full degree-granting powers. It also recommended that the land and buildings of Raffles College at Bukit Timah be sold and a new campus be built in "a large expanse of ground a few miles outside Johore Bahru".[7] Prominent lawyer and community leader Roland Braddell proposed that the new university be located in Penang rather than in Johor "because of her long history and the splendid quality of her schools and training colleges".[8] Kuala Lumpur was yet another site proposed for the new university.[9] The

Carr-Saunders Commission rejected two sites at Bukit Timah near Raffles College, opining that the sites had "the characteristics of an area in process of unplanned development" and were situated in unattractive suburbs:

> A university ought to dominate its environment but, on this site, it is likely to shut in by a mixed residential and industrial development. Even if the development were better controlled than it is now, it would still leave the University on an unimpressive site in the middle of a region which is lacking in character.[10]

On the other hand, the Commission deemed the Johor Bahru site to be:

> near enough to Singapore to
> share fully in its cultural life
> and yet at the same time have
> the great advantage, for a
> residential university, of being
> in surroundings of great natural
> beauty, near enough to Singapore
> for effective contacts and yet in
> a place where it would not be
> dominated by that great city.[11]

Fig. 5.3: The Eusoff College building still stands along Evans Road, across from the Bukit Timah complex

This proposal was taken seriously and, by June 1948, the government started the process of acquiring 1,500 acres of land in Johor Bahru for the new university.[12] The process of land acquisition would take a further four years. It was estimated that the cost of building the new campus would be between $25 million and $30 million, and it would take five years to complete.[13] Sir Patrick Abercrombie, an expert in town planning, was expected to be consulted on the layout of the new campus but this did not happen as the necessary legislative framework for the new university had not yet been put in place when Abercrombie arrived in Singapore in November 1948.[14] Formal legislation to establish the university— the University of Malaya Bill—was only introduced in the Singapore Legislative Council on 15 March 1949[15] and passed on 29 March 1949.[16]

When the University of Malaya granted its first degrees in July 1950,

nothing had yet been done about the proposed new site in Johor and the whole matter came "under general consideration".[17] It would appear that the university authorities were in no particular hurry to move campuses. Indeed, as if to cement its tenure at Bukit Timah, the university took out a lease on 16 acres of state land off Dunearn Road in December 1950. On this site were built 60 modern two-storeyed terraced bungalows to be leased to staff and students for accommodation.[18] Completed in 1952, this "estate" was initially simply known as Dunearn Road Hostel, and is today called College Green.

In the meantime, John Murray Easton and Sidney Edward Thomas Cusdin of the firm Easton & Robertson[19] were appointed architects to design the new buildings in Johor.[20] Developments within the university put a brake on the Johor plan. By early 1954, in preparation for the impending independence of

Fig. 5.4: Raffles Hall was one of the residential hostels at the Bukit Timah campus of the University of Singapore. This postcard view was taken from the top of the hill across the Raffles Valley in the 1960s

the Federation of Malaya from Great Britain, the university's Government Council began discussions on splitting the University of Malaya between Singapore and Kuala Lumpur, thus putting paid to the short-lived Johor campus idea.[21] The final nail in the coffin came from the Joint Committee appointed by the governments of Singapore and Federation of Malaya to look into the future of the University of Malaya, which recommended a total abandonment of the plan.[22] The site was subsequently developed as an industrial and residential satellite town.[23]

On 15 January 1959, the University of Malaya was split into two autonomous divisions with two campuses in Singapore and another in Pantai Valley, Kuala Lumpur. They were known respectively as the University of Malaya in Singapore and the University of Malaya in Kuala Lumpur. This split was to become permanent as the governments of the Federation and Singapore moved to transform their respective branches of the University of Malaya into national universities. On 1 January 1962, the University of Malaya in Singapore became the University of Singapore while the University of Malaya in Kuala Lumpur became the sole campus of the University of Malaya. In the process of this split, Singapore lost its Faculty of Engineering which was located in Kuala Lumpur. At this time, the university's various faculties and departments were physically scattered at two separate locations: law, science, arts and social sciences at Bukit Timah;[24] and medicine and dentistry at Sepoy Lines.

The faculties of accountancy, engineering and architecture had not been traditionally part of Raffles College nor

Fig. 5.5: The Singapore Polytechnic building at Prince Edward Road housed the Engineering Faculty and the Engineering Library of the University of Singapore in November 1971

Time to Move Again: Choosing Kent Ridge

In 1962, the student population on Bukit Timah campus was 2,400, even as plans were to expand to 3,000 by 1965.[25] Capacity at Bukit Timah campus was further expanded with the building of a ten-storey Science Tower. When the plan was announced in March 1964, it was stated that the building would "have the most modern laboratories and equipment to be built" and would "provide teaching and laboratory facilities for 800 students" as well as "three rooms for professors and 20 staff rooms for lecturers and other members of the teaching staff".[26] The architect was Ho Kok Hoe who went to Britain in 1963 "for research into the chemistry buildings at Cambridge, Nottingham, Swansea and London universities with the help of the Inter-University Council for higher education overseas".[27]

of the University of Malaya. They began as schools in the Singapore Polytechnic at Prince Edward Road which opened in 1959. These schools, which eventually awarded degrees, were transferred to and absorbed by the University of Singapore in 1964 (engineering) and 1969 (architecture and accountancy). As a result, they were housed in buildings at Prince Edward Road. In 1970, to make room for the growth of the Faculty of Engineering, the Faculty of Architecture and Building moved to No. 3 Ladyhill Road, off Orange Grove Road. The building, known as Kinloss House, had previously been the officers' mess of the British Forces. When the School of Accountancy merged with the Department of Business Administration at the University of Singapore in 1969, it moved to the Bukit Timah campus.

Just before Christmas in 1967, the Singapore government announced plans to build a $3 million cultural and sports centre at the Bukit Timah Campus. The project would include a multipurpose hall, swimming pool, sports oval and VIP room, and was to have been sited at the "field adjacent to Bukit Timah Road bordered by the approach road to the University from Bukit Timah Road, Cluny Road and the road running to the Students' Union House and the Administrative Building".[28] The field was then "being filled with 200,000 cubic yards of earth from the Singapore Turf Club up to the level of 3 feet" and building was to have been implemented in phases. The largest building was the $1.8 million multipurpose hall which would have a seating capacity for 3,106 with provision for further extension, and which would be used for university convocations and other programmes. This hall would be "constructed in a manner which allows it to be divided into lecture theatres with folding partitions". Also included in the plan was an Olympic-size swimming pool that was estimated to cost $500,000; a changing room and canteen; an alumni house and a large carpark that could double as a parade ground for the People's Defence Force units in the university.[29] Reading this news, one would never imagine that the university was soon slated to be relocated to a new campus.

About a year later, the government announced a $150 million plan to move the university to a totally new campus. Quite naturally, the plan for the cultural and sports complex was jettisoned. The spokesman at the Ministry of Science and Technology stated that the new plan, which had been outlined by UNESCO experts, was a step towards "restructuring the university to meet the needs of the republic's economy in the 1970s".[30] Unknown to the public, the government had already requested assistance from UNESCO for the planning of the new campus. In November 1968, UNESCO sent a team

of three experts—Thorleif H. Barlag (Project Officer, UNESCO); K.A. Elerend (UNESCO Adviser on Postgraduate Studies); and J. Learmonth (Architectural and Planning Consultant)—to study the state of the polytechnics and technical education in Singapore.[31] Among other things, the team recommended a new site for the expanding university, arguing that it would not be possible for the university to remain at Bukit Timah.[32]

The Straits Times report stated that the UNESCO Report, with its list of recommendations, had been submitted to Toh Chin Chye, who was concurrently Minister for Science and Technology and Vice-Chancellor of the university. If the cabinet approved of the plan, it was expected that the first new building would be ready as early as mid-1971.[33] Earlier that year, Toh outlined plans to expand the facilities for engineering education to divert student enrolment in pure science to engineering and the setting up of an institute for higher education and development to be sponsored by UNESCO, although UNESCO would not be expected to be responsible for the financing of this institute.[34]

In an editorial on 6 December 1968, *The Straits Times* noted that these expansion plans would mean the abandoning of Bukit Timah campus, and speculated that either the Tanglin Barracks complex or the RAF Changi would be possible sites for the new campus, given the impending departure of British forces from Singapore by the end of 1971.[35] As the report made reference to the cost of land acquisition, *The Straits Times* speculated that the experts had in mind a third locality "where some purchase of private land may be necessary".[36] The advantage of a new campus was obvious as it would be much easier "to build a new university to fit the new concepts than to juggle around with the inadequate facilities at Bukit Timah", especially with plans to offer degree courses in engineering through a full-fledged Faculty of Engineering.[37]

At the convocation ceremony of the University of Singapore on 7 June 1969, Vice-Chancellor Toh Chin Chye publicly stated:

> The advisory services of an expert campus planner have been applied for under the United Nations Development Programme technical assistance. It will be the task of the campus planner to present a Master Plan for the university which will serve not only this present generation but also other generations of students who will study in the university 15 to 20 years from now.[38]

Toh further stated that, due to a shortage of physical facilities, the university's Faculty of Engineering and School of Architecture and Building were "stranded" at the Singapore Polytechnic campus on Prince Edward Road. It was also necessary to expand the polytechnic and engineering faculties simultaneously and this "made it urgent to seek a new site for the faculty and the School of Architecture".[39] Toh noted that the Bukit Timah campus was never originally intended to house a university and that a third of its grounds was not usable as it would be flooded during a thunderstorm. In 1969, there were some 4,350 students distributed between 12 courses as compared to 645 students in five courses in 1949 when the University of Malaya was started.

> Bukit Timah has become cramped and the absence of a Master Plan has prevented orderly development of the campus. It is difficult to conceive how all these additional buildings can be contained in the Bukit Timah campus.[40]

The space crunch was exacerbated by the fact that the Singapore Polytechnic was also bursting at its seams. On its Graduation Day a few days later, on 13 July 1969, its principal, A. Robert Edis, told the students that the polytechnic, with an enrolment of 3,850, was facing major space problems and that, in addition to the 1,534 freshmen enrolled, it also housed 590 degree students of the University of Singapore on its campus. "It is clear," he said, "that with the present enrolment, the Polytechnic is now close to the maximum utilisation possible for its accommodation."[41]

By this time, it was clear that the government had determined to move the university to a new site, but where? On the same day as the polytechnic's graduation day, Finance Minister Goh Keng Swee announced that an engineering college would be built at Kent Ridge,[42] which was part of the British army's 2,400-acre holding at Pasir Panjang, and *The Straits Times* speculated that since "it is most unlikely that planners have in mind a fragmented university dotted throughout the Republic, it is a fair guess that Dr Goh has indicated the site of the new campus".[43] The editorial surmised that this plan made "complete sense" since the workshops and houses as well as the "schools within the complex, for instance, that could be readily converted to university work, especially the air-conditioned St John's School with its various laboratories, a big library and dormitories".[44] Francis Rozario, writing for *The Straits Times*, described the proposed site:

> Kent Ridge itself is about three miles in length, stretching from Clementi Road at one end to the National Youth Leadership Institute at the other. It is about half a mile in width, bounded by Ayer Rajah Road and Pasir Panjang–West Coast roads. On the ridge, there are the Princess Marina and Kent officers' messes, bungalows and one-storey terrace houses occupied by officers. Taking the complex as a whole – bounded by Dover, North Buona Vista, Portsdown, Ayer Rajah, Kent Ridge and Clementi roads – there are in all 311 bungalows and houses. There are also seven Army schools within the complex, which with minor renovations could be utilised as faculty buildings. Topping this list is the St John's School, completely air-conditioned.[45]

To help with the expansion of the university, the United Nations Technical Assistance Scheme provided $4.5 million—channelled through UNESCO—to fund professorships, scholarships for training, local academic personnel and technical equipment.[46] Malcolm Adiseshiah, then Deputy Director-General of UNESCO, pledged his organization's support to help Singapore achieve "a higher standard of living and development" over a three-year period through funding for the expansion and improvement of the university, including its move to a new and bigger campus; establishing a natural science museum; setting up a science and technology documentation centre; and expanding technical teacher training programmes.[47] Following Adiseshiah's visit to Singapore, the government announced that it had revised the UNESCO recommendations and would submit the plans to a "high-level university-campus planning expert" from the United Nations Development Programme (UNDP).[48] Adiseshiah also revealed that both Toh Chin Chye and Goh Keng Swee (finance minister) told him that the Singapore government would request an interest-free loan from the World Bank if plans for the new campus would proceed.[49]

In the meantime, the campus at Bukit Timah would simply have to continue adapting and reorganizing its spaces for the projected increase in student intake. It made no sense for the existing buildings to be further renovated since it was unclear as to what would become of the buildings once the university moved out,[50] so temporary structures had to be put up to house the increased enrolment. In January 1972, the university announced the erection of seven "low-cost" Nissan huts "to relieve the inadequate accommodation facilities".[51] Of these, two would be used to house books which the main library could no longer contain while the remaining five huts—with a seating capacity of 200 each—would be used "as lecture hall and tutorial rooms". By this time, student enrolment at the university had risen to 4,700. Each Nissan hut cost $15,000, was fully air-conditioned and could be easily dismantled when no longer needed.[52]

The Kent Ridge Masterplan

Van Embden Comes On Board

In 1969, following the submission of the UNESCO report, Toh established the University Development Committee (UDC) with himself as chairman. The other early members of the UDC were K.R. Chandra, Tan Jake Hooi, Teh Cheang Wan and Hiew Siew Nam, all of whom were seconded to the university from various government departments like the Housing and Development Board (HDB), Urban Redevelopment Authority (URA), Public Utilities Board (PUB) and Public Works Department (PWD). The team was housed in a former officers' mess up on the Ridge. This committee was the predecessor of what became the University of Singapore Development Unit (USDU).

The committee was charged with studying the UNESCO report and establishing a local project team to work with the foreign consultants to prepare a project paper for the government and to also appoint a master planner. UNESCO's assistance was once again requested and Samuel Josua van Embden (1904–2000)[53] was engaged as consultant. Van Embden was a well-known Dutch architect and urban planner who had a distinguished career in his native Netherlands and featured prominently in the post-war reconstruction and planning of Rotterdam. Prior to his appointment in Singapore, he worked on the design of the campuses of the University of Bandung in Indonesia, and the Eindhoven University of Technology and the University of Twente, both in the Netherlands. In 1964, at the age of 60, he was appointed Distinguished Professor at the Department of Architecture at the Technical University of Delft. Beyond his obvious eminence and competence, Van Embden had come highly recommended by Singapore's economic advisor, Albert Winsemius (a Dutch economist)[54] and Education Minister Ong Pang Boon.[55] Funding for Van Embden's appointment came through the Singapore Science Council—a statutory body under Toh Chin Chye's ministry—as the university did not have the funds to pay for him.[56]

After leading missions to Singapore between 1969 and 1970, Van Embden worked on a master plan for the development of the University in Singapore, which he completed in June 1970.[57] This master plan was subsequently accepted by the Singapore Government "as the basis for the design of the new campus".[58] As the nature of campus planning "demanded a conti-nuing involvement of the planners during its implementation, the project was extended to comprise the continuing services of the consultant [Van Embden], including regular visits to Singapore, and the establishment of the post of specialist in campus planning".[59] The specialist was expected

to act as liaison between Van Embden and the Singapore counterparts on all technical matters and to also advise and assist the Singapore team on the planning of the new campus.[60]

Van Embden did not intend to stay beyond the master-planning stage to actually work on the architectural design of the university, as he was confident that local architects could implement his masterplan competently.[61] However, Toh Chin Chye managed to persuade him to continue on the project and he agreed to provide advice from the Netherlands while appointing one of his staff, Meng Ta Cheang (b. 1937), a China-born architect and urban planner[62] as chief designer and coordinator for the project. Meng arrived in Singapore in December 1970, worked for a month and left, and then returned to Singapore in June 1971 to continue work on the project.[63] So while it was Van Embden who "set out the broad aspects of the masterplan, it was Meng who, despite his young age, ensured that the project stayed on course true to the masterplan's vision and fleshed out the abstract planning guidelines".[64]

The "closely-guarded long-awaited" master plan for the new university campus was unveiled on 23 July 1970.[65] All faculties of the university were to be brought together "under one roof" on the 173-acre site. The horseshoe-shaped layout of the buildings, linked by a covered walkway, "provides for one continuous structure ... with all the allied disciplines housed next to each other".[66] The new campus would also include a teaching hospital allied to the university, something which had not hitherto existed.[67] Speaking at a public lecture, the campus' architectural advisor and master planner Van Embden said:

> The site will provide sufficient space not only for the university's academic programme now elaborated for 1980 – arriving at a total of about 10,800 students – but also for further extension afterwards. When the time comes to meet changes in the university's needs, the unified character of the continuous structure will facilitate internal re-arrangements. At the same time, as the present programme for 1980 requires occupation of only half the site, ample space remains available for future expansion. ... But the buildings on the top should not be too high – in order not to dwarf the appearance of ridge and hills, which are relatively modest in height although they look impressive. The university will be a characteristic city of learning perched on a crest, with the flanks mainly untouched except at the western end where low laboratory structures will descend the slopes.[68]

Ultimately, the university campus would take up all 473 acres of the Kent Ridge and adjoining hilltop sites—bounded by Clementi Road, Pasir Panjang Road, South Buona Vista Road and Ayer Rajah Road. Van Embden stated that the campus would remain open to the public in line with the concept of integration of and interaction between "Town and Gown". Hostels on the campus would house only one-sixth of the student population while another sixth would be provided with hostel facilities outside the campus.[69]

Preparing the Site

The first transfer of British army land in Kent Ridge took place in February 1971 when a piece of land, which was a car park, was handed over to Singapore for a "specific purpose".[70] In March 1971, Finance Minister Hon Sui Sen told Parliament that $1.25 million was being provided for "preliminary expenses connected with the new campus".[71] As of March 1971, the land needed for the campus had yet to be acquired and still needed to be settled between the Bases Economic Conversion Unit (for the Singapore government) and the British Services.[72] The government was also waiting for the World Bank to decide on how much financial support it would give to the project.[73] Toh Chin Chye told parliament that, of the 95 houses in Kent Ridge that were occupied by British army officers, 55 would be demolished to make way for the first phase of the university's development while the remaining 40 would be used to house staff of the university.

Planning priority was accorded to the buildings for the "homeless" engineering and architecture faculties, as well as for the newly-created Faculty of Accountancy and Business Administration. Furthermore, the Faculty of Engineering was expanding rapidly and was expected to be the largest faculty of the university.[74] However, work could only begin after Kent Ridge was completely vacated by the British military authorities at the end of 1971. Work on the campus was targeted for completion by 1977–78, and enrolment at the university was expected to reach 8,000 students, up from 4,700 students in 1971.[75] Simultaneously, Singapore Polytechnic's new campus was being built on a 40-acre site on Dover Road and was expected to be completed by 1974,[76] while the Ngee Ann Technical College was in the midst of expanding its 40-acre campus on Clementi Road at the cost of $11 million.[77]

The University of Singapore Development Unit (USDU) was established on 15 September 1970 as the Project Implementation Unit for an integrated University of Singapore at Kent Ridge. It started with a modest staff of 14 members headed first by Ho Pak Toe (1970–74) and then by See Chay Tuan as Director. At its peak it employed 85 members, consisting of officers seconded from the university, government bodies such as the HDB, PWD and PUB, and others employed by the university on contract.

The unit was responsible for the financial and administrative control of the project and its scope of work in implementing the project included: (1) liaison and coordination with the master planner; (2) designing the buildings in accordance with the master plan, including the preparation of construction drawings and documents; (3) engagement, briefing and coordination of the specialists to be employed under the technical assistance provision of the project; (4) preparing master lists of equipment and furniture; (5) obtaining and evaluating international bids for construction, equipment and furniture; (6) supervision of construction and procurement; (7) coordination with ministries and government agencies; and (8) liaison with the World Bank. At its inception, the unit was supervised by the Ministry of Science & Technology. On 16 June 1975, the supervision of the unit was transferred to the Ministry of National Development.

In May 1971, Ho Pak Toe, Director of the USDU, said that soil-boring tests had already commenced but that development would only commence in 1972 with a soil-breaking ceremony on 2 January. Work would be in three phases, with Phase I—which included the engineering and architecture complexes, Computer Centre, nine lecture theatres

Fig. 5.6: Dr Toh Chin Chye (far right) and President Benjamin Sheares (to his right) view the architectural models of the new Kent Ridge campus at the ground-breaking ceremony on 25 March 1972. Among the guests looking on are Minister for Communication Mr Yong Nyuk Lin (far left) and Mr Ho Pak Toe from the University Development Unit (to his left)

and two canteens, the students' union and students' health centre and halls of residence for between 2,000–3,000 students, the science and technology and humanities libraries, the faculties of accountancy and business adminis-tration and the administrative buildings—ending around 1975.[78] The task of designing the Computer Centre was assigned to Conrad A. Wogrin, a computer scientist and director of the computing centre at the University of Massachusetts who arrived in Singapore on 1 July 1971 and spent 28 days deve-loping his design which would include "drawing up the administrative structure

of the centre, estimating the number and types of staffing required, recommending the types and amount of computers, to buy or rent, and suggesting alternatives for various aspects of the plan".[79]

The World Bank's team of experts, comprising A. Cespedes, R. Johanson, D. Lewis and J. McNown, arrived in Singapore on 27 June 1971 to appraise the Singapore government's application for a loan towards constructing the new campus.[80] The proposal to take a loan for this project was first mooted by Finance Minister Goh Keng Swee back in October 1968 when he visited Washington, DC. Following his visit, a team of experts

Fig. 5.7: President BH Sheares watering the juniper he planted at the ground-breaking ceremony on 25 March 1972

led by Lester Pearson, former prime minister of Canada and chairman of the World Bank, visited Singapore in April 1969 under the sponsorship of the Commission on International Development.[81] In November 1971, during his visit to Singapore, World Bank President Robert McNamara announced that the World Bank would offer Singapore $300 million in loans, $24.5 million[82] of which would go towards Phase I of the building of the Kent Ridge campus.[83] The Singapore government subsequently secured a further $48.75 million loan from the World Bank, part of which was to finance Phase II of the campus development.[84]

President Sheares (Fig. 5.7) planted a juniper tree during the university's ground-breaking ceremony on Saturday, 25 March 1972.[85] The ground was "broken" by Dr Toh using a changkul (Fig. 5.8) and, thereafter, he and President Sheares each planted a juniper tree. They then inspected the models and construction plans of the campus.[86] Tenders for the construction of the new campus were announced in September 1972[87] and construction began in November 1973.[88]

Speaking about the design of the campus at a lecture organized by the Singapore Institute of Planners entitled "University Planning", Meng Ta Cheang, the architect behind the master plan, explained that the Faculty of Engineering would be sited at the east end of the campus next to the sciences while the humanities faculty would occupy a hillock linked by the Ridge by an extensive system of pedestrian malls both covered and uncovered, and the Computer Centre would be situated near the library which was designed as the "core" of the university. Meng, who had been involved in the design and planning of two universities in Rotterdam and Brussels explained:

> The most significant part of the entire plan is the accent on the humanistic approach. The new university has been designed with an eye to the social and cultural needs of students, who need to interact. Provision has been made for big open spaces, including a green heart, which will link the university together. The ridge will remain a sight-seeing feature both for the students and the public. It will also be part of the green recreational chain stretching from Mt Faber, Telok Blangah and Marina Hill.[89]

Fig. 5.8: Dr Toh Chin Chye wields a changkul at the 1972 ground-breaking ceremony

Toh Chin Chye's Fingerprints

As vice-chancellor and minister in charge of the university, Toh Chin Chye took an active part in the planning of the campus. He set himself up at the vice-chancellor's lodge, an old bungalow at No. 14 Kent Ridge Road, which sat at the top of the Ridge, from which he would oversee and supervise the development of the campus with an iron fist. It was no accident that the USDU offices were just next door to his lodge.

In the early days, Toh was keen on creating "some sort of distinctive campus" and threw out all kinds of ideas during his long rambling meetings.[90] However, Van Embden persuaded him otherwise, arguing that during the 1970s, changes in university education would be fast and furious and it was necessary to have a campus that could readily respond to such changes. To do this, the buildings would need to look similar so that any alteration or additions will not only easily fit the floor plate but would be aesthetically consonant as well.[91] Members of the USDU dreaded Toh's long meetings which he held after finishing his duties at the ministry:

> He used to come after his office
> hours, as Minister of Science
> and Technology, and he will hold
> meetings with us, and … he will
> ramble, just ramble on and give
> us his visions and his views,
> and then at about 6.30, 7.00, he
> will call it quits but instead of
> going off, he would say, 'Come,
> let's go down and walk the
> site!', and so we will obediently
> follow him to walk the site so he
> could see more for himself.[92]

As building progressed, Toh became increasingly concerned about student activism and its potentially disruptive possibilities on campus. During one meeting, when he saw the design of the Yusof Ishak House, he became ballistic and lambasted the USDU team:

> He will review the plans with
> us, and during one of those
> sessions, he was very critical.

That concerned the Yusof Ishak House architecture. He called us 'a bunch of nincompoops' because we designed the kind of big open spaces for the students. He said, 'They are going to gather down there!' That was a time of 'student power', when Ungku Aziz in the University of Malaya was held hostage by students who invaded his office. So in the end, we had to do post-damage control and we put in grills so that the students could be locked out so they could not go into the building and occupy the place.… And he also said, 'Never, never call it a Students' Union building (which was the initial plan) because you are giving them a proprietary sense, as if the building belonged to them and they have a right to be there.'[93]

This preoccupation with large gathering spaces translated into the campus' linear design as well. Toh was anxious that there should not be large quadrangles for students, which was why all the buildings are all linear. As Lim Tuan Seng, who was on the USDU recalled: "at that time, they were saying that there shouldn't be a lot of these wide open spaces, where it's easy for the students to congregate, that's how it influenced the design process".[94] Toh was also concerned with the proximity of the central library to the main administration building as students could get up to the roof of the library and throw rocks at the administration building.[95]

As the university was being built, the world experienced a major energy crisis when, in 1973, the Organisation of Petroleum Exporting Countries (OPEC) proclaimed an oil embargo. Toh became concerned about energy consumption and began browbeating the various deans and heads of departments into agreeing with him that they did not need air-conditioning. Lim Tuan Seng, who was a member of the USDU, recalled:

> Dr Toh went and asked all the deans point blank: 'Why do you need air-con?' He scolded them. Everyone kept quiet and nobody dared to say that they wanted air-conditioning.[96]

This was, of course, impractical. As Meng Ta Cheang noted:

> Toh Chin Chye actually did not want more than 22% of the rooms air-conditioned because of the energy crisis.... But it never happened that way. Most of the facilities require air-conditioning, so we specified a central air-con system.[97]

Toh's frugality also led him to demand that academics share telephones, resulting in a hole cut between two staff offices and rotating panel inserted, on which a shared telephone was hung. The materials chosen for the finish of the buildings were also to be as affordable and maintenance-free as possible. This resulted in a lot of Shanghai plaster being used in the engineering, architecture and arts and social sciences blocks. This austerity led Toh to reject plans to build a private toilet in the vice-chancellor's office. "You people never use your brains," he bellowed. "I have the same bladder as everyone else."[98]

Van Embden's Masterplan

Van Embden adopted a "tartan grid" development pattern as a planning guide for the Kent Ridge site (Fig. 5.11). The "grid" consisted of six bays of 4 foot x 4 foot grids in both directions with 2-foot intermediate grids to house column and services. Physically, this translated to a low-rise development of three to four-storeyed buildings that integrated harmoniously with the undulating contours of Kent Ridge. Meng Ta Cheang, who was responsible for the final architecture, explains the grid system:

> We used the 26 feet grid because it was an extension of the Industrial module – 300mm, 600mm and 1200mm. The smallest module is of course the brick dimension, which is made to fit into a person's hand easily. In the grid system, there's always a service grid for

Van Embden's Masterplan

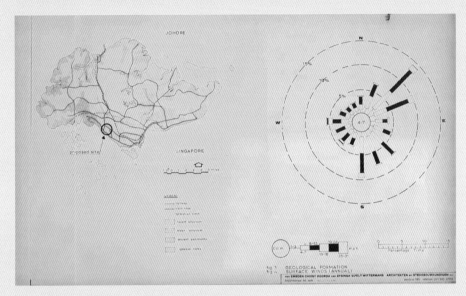

Fig. 5.9: Qualities of the site: geology and prevailing winds

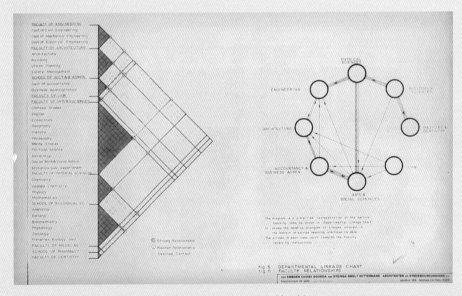

Fig. 5.10: Planning for the relationships between departments and faculties

Van Embden's Masterplan

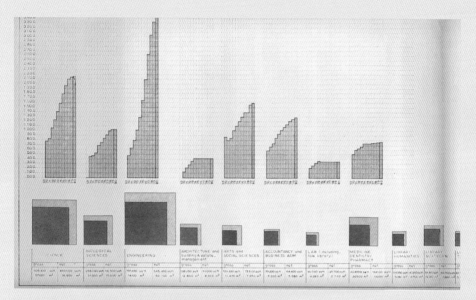

Fig. 5.11: Estimated student enrolments for the different faculties

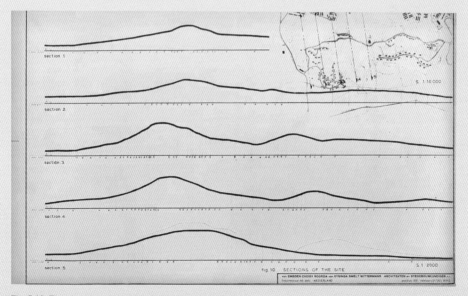

Fig. 5.12: The elevation of the Kent Ridge site, in sections

Van Embden's Masterplan

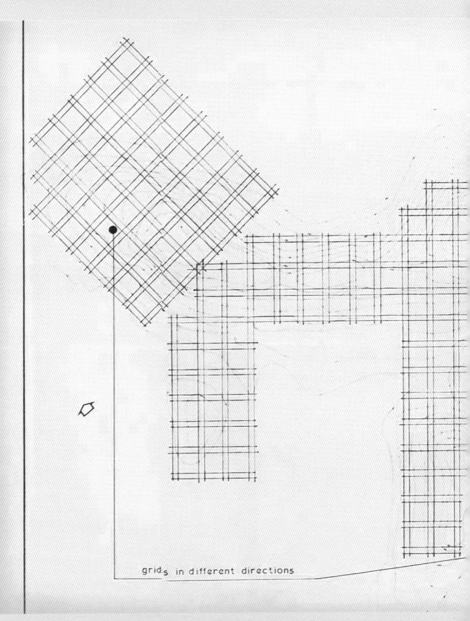

grids in different directions

Fig. 5.13: The basic 26-foot grid developed by Van Embden and associates

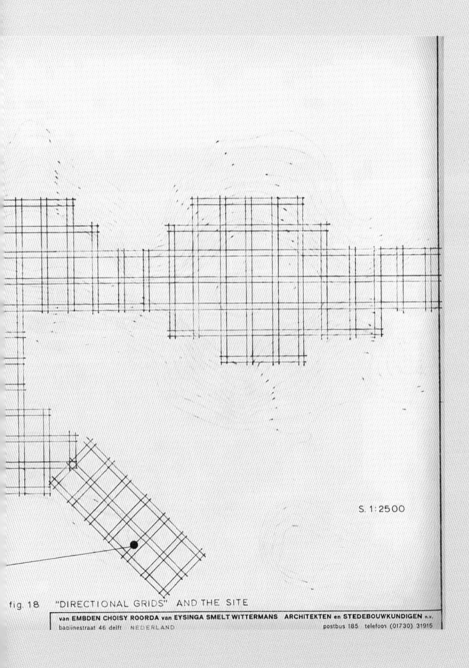

S. 1:2500

fig. 18   "DIRECTIONAL GRIDS" AND THE SITE

van EMBDEN CHOISY ROORDA van EYSINGA SMELT WITTERMANS   ARCHITEKTEN en STEDEBOUWKUNDIGEN n.v.
baaiinestraat 46 delft   NEDERLAND   postbus 185   telefoon (01730) 31915

Van Embden's Masterplan

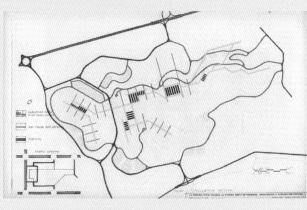

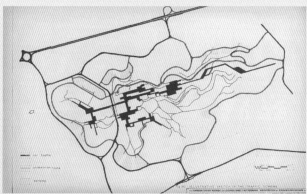

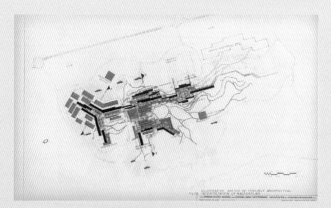

Fig. 5.14: Planning the circulation and build-up of the campus

Van Embden's Masterplan

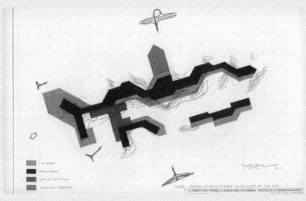

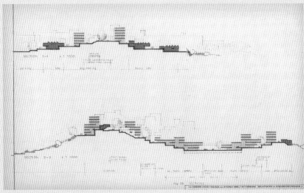

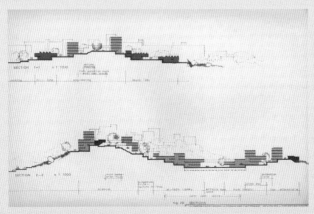

Fig. 5.15: Building heights and densities planned against function and the elevation of the site

every three open grids in both
directions. We also made sure
that access to the lift was never
more than 25m from any point.[99]

According to Meng, the 26-foot grid
solved "90% of the problems" and
allowed for "one middle corridor
with rooms on both sides, or a single
corridor with bigger rooms on the other
side".[100]

Preservation of the natural contours
of the Ridge was all important. Indeed,
Van Embden noted that the site
chosen for the university was "one of
the most beautiful natural assets of
Singapore, with a breath-taking view
over the sea, steep slopes and large
green open spaces" and determined
that "any building on this site should
be subordinate to these qualities"
and "the strong configuration
of the Ridge itself should always be
respected and any building on or near
it should enhance its nature rather than
attempt to dominate it".[101] Meng Ta
Cheang, who was responsible for designing the architecture of the university,
concurred. Recalling his first visit to the
site in December 1970, he said:

> I fell in love with the site
> immediately when I first saw it;
> the hilly terrain reminded me of
> North Italy. So I told the team
> that the hills must be preserved,
> with minimal disturbances to the
> landform and vegetation.

> I thought about how Singapore
> U could be like a hill town.[102]

The Ridge was thus reflected as
the dominant feature on the site.
Consideration was given to the dynamic
changes inherent in university curricula
and buildings were structurally designed
to take an additional floor for minor
upward extension. The buildings were
carefully laid out with adequate land for
future major extensions. This element of
flexibility was further expressed in the
separation of service cores from the main
building. This allowed for adaptability
and change in use of internal space as
the technical facilities (electricity, gas,
water, air-conditioning ducts, etc.) were
located in service cores external to the
main building.

Parking zones in the campus were
decentralized. They were planned on the
lower contours of the site and as near
to the buildings as possible. Separation
of pedestrian and vehicular traffic was
achieved by the provision of overhead
linkages and underpass for pedestrians.
A main pedestrian routing which acts
as a link for the whole university was
incorporated in all the buildings.

It passes through areas where
facilities were used by large crowds such
as lecture theatres, seminar rooms and so
on. Because of the terrain, the route goes
through different levels. This network of
linkages in the various buildings forms a
main connection route and was given its
distinct identity by treatment of double-

Fig. 5.16 (left): Staircase from Kent Ridge Crescent leading up to the plaza in front of the Engineering Faculty, adorned by Sun Yuli's sculpture "Striving". This was one of Edward Larrabee Barnes' focal points and points of arrival. Fig. 5.17: In Van Embden's plan, the main pedestrian routing through campus was identified with dark brown floor tiles and for covered walkways, by a yellow metal ceiling treatment. This coding system is still used today

storey height, yellow metal ceiling and dark brown floor tiles.

Preservation of trees and treatment of open spaces were given special attention: the central green area spreading eastwards along the whole Ridge was left intact; this central green was further complemented by fringe green areas dotting the peripheral of the campus; and small open spaces between buildings were similarly landscaped.

Phase I (1973–77)[103]

Given the urgent need to vacate the Singapore Polytechnic campus at Prince Edward Road, construction of the campus prioritized the newly-created faculties from the Singapore Polytechnic—the faculties of engineering and architecture, and the School of Accountancy and Business

Administration. Phase I of the building works would be carried out in two stages. The first stage consisted of the Faculty of Engineering, Faculty of Architecture and Building, Computer Centre, a canteen and six lecture theatres. The second stage saw the construction of the Central Library, the Administration Block, the School of Accountancy and Business Administration and two more lecture theatres. Other buildings completed in Phase I of the project included the Yusof Ishak House (to house the students' union), designed by Edward Yim.[104] Two halls of residence (student hostels) were also slated for completion in this phase.

The first faculty to move into Kent Ridge was the Faculty of Architecture and Building, which moved from its Ladyhill campus in early June 1976.[105] The Faculty of Engineering complex, which was slated for completion in June

Fig. 5.18: The Engineering Faculty viewed from the walkway down from the top of Kent Ridge towards Yusof Ishak House

Fig. 5.19: Central Library, 1977

Fig. 5.20: View from the Administration Block, 1977

1976,[106] was not completed till October that year.[107] The engineering faculty finally moved to its new premises in July 1977[108] and was officially declared open by Toh Chin Chye on 6 January 1977.[109] The Faculty of Accountancy and Business Administration moved to Kent Ridge in July 1978.[110] With this move, the Bukit Timah campus was left to accommodate only 1,100 law, arts and social sciences and science students in the 1978–79 academic term.[111] These faculties were slated to move to Kent Ridge in 1980 although the law library moved to Kent Ridge in May 1978.[112] The Faculty of Arts and Social Sciences and Faculty of Science only moved to Kent Ridge in 1981.[113]

The first hall of residence to be officially opened at Kent Ridge was the King Edward Hall which was opened by President C.V. Devan Nair on 5

Fig. 5.21: Kent Ridge Building Plan 1975

AL UNIVERSITY OF SINGAPORE
RIDGE CAMPUS

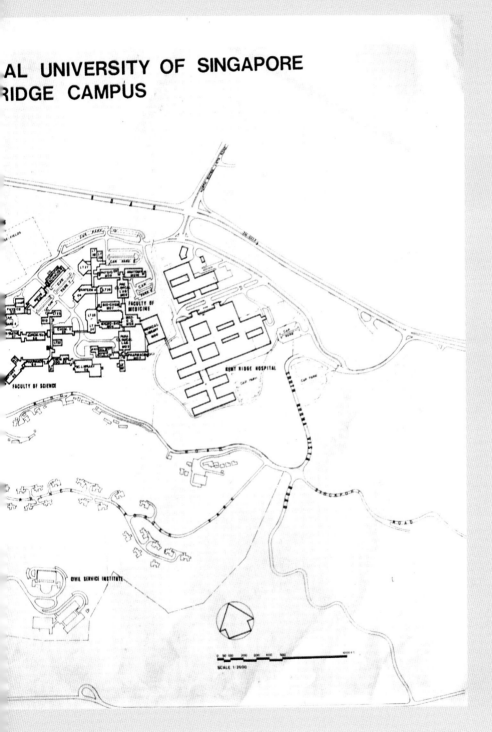

SCALE 1:2500

December 1981. Built at a cost of $4.5 million, it could accommodate 450 students.[114] Towards the end of the Phase I construction, the university announced plans to endow the grounds of the campus with an attractive landscape where small "open spaces and footpaths between buildings will have greenery and plants" and where the overall "green effect will aptly complement the grey buildings".[115]

Phase II (1975–81)[116]

Phase II overlapped Phase I by two years, with the work commencing in 1975. Under this phase, buildings for the Faculty of Arts and Social Sciences, Faculty of Law and a mega Bio-Sciences Complex to house the faculties of science and medicine as well as a bio-medical library, would be added. Another two canteens, eight lecture theatres, a language centre, staff house, sports complex and centre for musical activities would also be built during this phase.

The sports complex at Kent Ridge was not built till 1980.[117] The complex would house an Olympic-size swimming pool, a sports hall, five squash courts, a gymnasium, outdoor running track, soccer pitches and courts for tennis and basketball.[118]

Another important building on the Kent Ridge campus that was built but which was not part of the university's master plan was the new Guild House. Back in June 1978, when it was clear

that the entire university would move to Kent Ridge, the University of Singapore announced plans to build a $600,000 clubhouse on Kent Ridge. The new clubhouse would be built on land offered by the university, and was originally to have been situated next to the academic staff premises. It was Vice-Chancellor Kwan Sai Keong who made the offer of a lease of this 9,600m² land to the Society.[119] Under its original plan, the clubhouse would have a dining hall for 150 persons, two function rooms, a bar, a billiard room, a jackpot room, a health centre, squash courts, a theatre for 150 and a number of meeting and guest rooms.[120] Announcing these plans, Kiang Ai Kim, chairman of the society's building committee, stated that students of the School of Architecture had submitted some 64 drawings for the new building through an academic exercise and four of them had been shortlisted.[121] The final "winner" would be submitted to the building authorities for planning approval.[122] The Kent Ridge Guild House, which cost some $5.3 million to build, was officially opened on 7 December 1984.[123]

Phase III (1981–83)

On 8 August 1980, the National University of Singapore (NUS), incorporating the University of Singapore and Nanyang University, was established. Together with the establishment of NUS, the government decided on an expansion programme for the university to increase total enrolment from 6,700 in 1980[124] to 9,000 in 1982 to 16,000 in 1990. The physical expansion of campus facilities was carried out under Phase III—estimated to cost $174 million[125]—and implemented in two stages. In the first stage, additional floors were added to the buildings housing the faculties of arts and social sciences, accountancy and business administration, Engineering Block 1, and the Language Centre. In the second stage, existing facilities at the Faculty of Medicine (at Sepoy Lines) were upgraded while a new Faculty of Medicine building was being constructed at Kent Ridge. In addition, new buildings were added to the faculties of architecture, law, accountancy and business administration, and arts and social sciences, and science. A new Science Library was built, as was a new School of Postgraduate Medical Studies.

The Faculty of Medicine moved from its long-time home in Sepoy Lines to Kent Ridge in July 1982.[126] In 1975, the university began having second thoughts about building a teaching hospital for its medical faculty as it was feared that the proposed 1,042-bed hospital, which was to also accommodate the School of Postgraduate Medical Studies, would be much too costly and would be unjustifiable given the small population base of its locality. Aid for the building of the teaching hospital was to have been provided by the China Medical Board of New York.[127] These doubts did not linger for long as Singapore plunged headlong with its various development plans. A Kent Ridge Hospital Executive Planning Committee was established under the chairmanship of Edward Tock, Professor of Pathology. In September 1978, he undertook a two-and-a-half-month study tour of teaching hospitals in France and America and developed proposals for the Kent Ridge Teaching Hospital[128] which would be completed in 1985 at an estimated cost of $143 million. Tock explained:

> The Kent Ridge Hospital is planned as a general hospital with various specialties, and as a university hospital for teaching of medicine and dentistry. Apart from providing facilities for research the hospital will house the existing university departments of medicine, paediatrics, surgery, orthopaedic surgery, obstetrics and gynaecology, anaesthesiology, pathology and sociology and public health. The Faculty of Dentistry will also be under its wing, and this comprises the departments of operative dentistry, oral surgery and prosthetic dentistry.[129]

Tock's committee had determined that in view of the many other private and government hospitals being planned, the original 1,042 beds would be reduced to 752. Even so, it would form "part and

Fig. 5.22: Yusof Ishak House in early 1979

Fig. 5.23: Computer Centre, with the Engineering Faculty in the background

Fig. 5.24: Central Library

Fig. 5.25: Administration Block

parcel of the medical facilities for the people apart from providing the basis for achieving a high standard of medical education and research".[130] The hospital would occupy 16 hectares of the campus grounds. The Singapore Government secured a $19 million loan from the Asian Development Bank to finance the Kent Ridge and Polyclinic project, part of which went into the building of the teaching hospital.[131]

One of the last buildings to be put in place under Phase III of the university development plan was the $2.4 million Visitors' Lodge. The 20-room facility, which was designed to house visiting academics, was proposed in February 1984 and completed towards the end of 1985.[132]

Fig. 5.26: By the 1980s, lush greenery had come to define the campus

Second and Third Master Plans: Review by Edward Larrabee Barnes

A second master plan was commissioned in 1991 to give a sense of place to identify the university. The review was undertaken by the well-known American architect Edward Larrabee Barnes (1915–2004) and was intended to consider the development of the campus in view of the projected increase of student population over the next decade. Barnes concentrated his efforts on "focal points" or "points of arrival" and "landmarks" within the campus. Five questions were posed: (1) How do you know that you have arrived at the university? (2) How do you get from one place to another? (3) How do you know where you are as you move about? (4) What is the potential for the preservation of open space? and (5) What is the extent of academic expansion required and how can this be accommodated in the review of the campus master plan?

According to USDU architect Robin Wong, Barnes' review of the campus design—which called for underground connectivity, the connecting of certain roads to create a loop, and a number of eye-catching open spaces, buildings and plazas—was not implemented on account of the high cost involved.[133] Plazas were to have been built in front of the Central Library, at Yusof Ishak House, in front of the University Cultural Centre and at Lower Kent Ridge Road near the Faculty of Science. These were not implemented even though several elements of Barnes' plan bore fruit.

These included connecting the road at Prince George's Park, the building and development of the University Cultural Centre, Kent Vale staff housing and the Prince George's Park hostels.[134] The Barnes plan did not lead to major infrastructural change but rather to cosmetic enhancements of key arrival points, such as the area around the engineering faculty, the Central Library and Administration Block, the roundabout opposite Yusof Ishak House and the National University Hospital (see Fig. 5.16).

In the late 1990s, the university decided to develop yet another new comprehensive master plan—the third master plan—to review and rationalize the university's land use and facilities in view of its expansion and positioning as a premier regional and international university. NUS President Professor Shih Choon Fong charged the director of the Office of Estates and Development (OED), his vice-president for campus infrastructure, Yong Kwet Yew, with the task of leading a small team with officers from both OED & Office of Finance (OFN) to undertake this review. Liu Thai Ker, a prominent local architect, former chief planner of the URA and former chief architect of the HDB, was selected through a shortlist to undertake the campus master plan review in 2000.

Appointed as master planner on 23 December 1999, Liu was expected to review NUS development plans in

light of the 1991 Barnes Master Plan, as well as to propose a new conceptual Campus Master Plan (CMP) and a set of Urban Design Guidelines (UDG) that would support the university's long-term strategic growth and, if required, to study expansion beyond the present campus.

On 10 January 2002, the university successfully presented a conceptual CMP to the cabinet. In-principle approval was given to NUS to expand across the Ayer Rajah Expressway into the land occupied by the Warren Golf Club and Medway Estate. This was, of course, subject to NUS and the ministries of education and national development working out the exact amount of land needed to achieve the NUS Campus Master Plan's strategic intent. Despite several discussions with MOE and URA, the project was eventually held in abeyance pending resolution of issues relating primarily to funding. The opportunity to revisit the expansion of NUS campus into Warren was revived with the new Ministry of Finance initiative to launch and drive the Public Private Partnership (PPP) Framework (all capital projects exceeding $50 million would have to consider using the PPP Framework).

With this new funding model, the Provost's Office revisited some of the earlier academic, pedagogical and planning parameters and evolved a mode of student accommodation that was distinct from the existing traditional hostel as well as the residences at Prince

Fig. 5.27: The 1987 Institute of Molecular and Cell Biology building embodied a new R&D focus at NUS

Fig. 5.28: Kent Ridge campus, before the development of Pasir Panjang port

George's Park. The proposal—which manifested as the University Town (UTown)—consisted of locating 12 residential colleges within a university village. This scheme emphasized residential learning, where curricular teaching and learning occur alongside academic mentoring and informal intellectual activities in residences. These residential colleges would be located amidst a range of social and recreational facilities that provided an environment that supported social, physical and emotional growth.

The University Town, which was officially declared open on 17 October 2013 by Prime Minister Lee Hsien Loong, was touted by NUS President Tan Chorh Chuan as "the campus core that had previously been missing in our otherwise lovely Kent Ridge Campus". The new site offered an innovative model of living, learning and discovering, with its integrated residential colleges, teaching, research and commercial spaces and ancillary recreational facilities. UTown added more than 240,000 m^2 of integrated learning and living space. With a strong research agenda, UTown plays host to the Singapore-MIT Alliance for Research and Technology, the first research centre within the National Research Foundations' Campus for Research Excellence and Technological Enterprise (CREATE). It is also the home of the Yale-NUS College. UTown is linked to the old Kent Ridge campus via

a vehicular and pedestrian bridge across the Ayer Rajah Expressway.

Developments from 2000 to 2015

In addition to acquiring premises vacated by the Warren Golf Club for the building of UTown, the university also successfully canvassed for the return of the old Bukit Timah Campus (BTC) to its fold in late 2005. This made available an additional 38,700 m^2 of space to accommodate the relocation of the Faculty of Law, the Lee Kuan Yew School of Public Policy and other key university research centres and institutes such as the East Asia Institute, Asia Research Institute, South Asia Institute and Middle East Institute. As these institutions shifted out of Kent Ridge, the administrative heart of NUS also moved to the new seven-storey University Hall, which was completed in June 2005. The old Administration Block next to the Central Library has since been allocated for the use of the University Scholars' Programme.

The most significant faculty building constructed in this period was the nine-storey Mochtar Riady Building, which houses part of the NUS Business School. Designed by Philip Cox, the building has an impressive five-storey atrium. It was named after Mochtar Riady, founder and chairman of the Lippo Group, in recognition of the Group's $21 million gift to the NUS Business School.

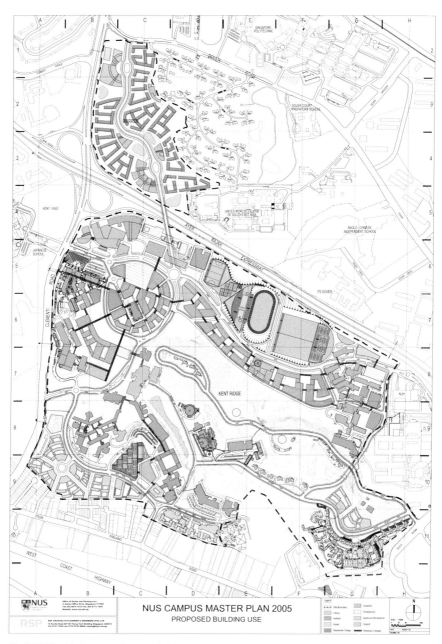

Fig. 5.29: The third master plan provided for expansion of campus across the Ayer Rajah Expressway to what is today's UTown

At the Yong Loo Lin School of Medicine, a new 15-storey building to house the Centre for Translational Medicine was completed in 2011. The Centre is equipped with cutting-edge technologies and facilities such as the Clinical Imaging and Research Centre (CIRC), digital media classrooms for medical and nursing students, as well as a simulated hospital complete with an operating theatre, an intensive-care unit and clinical skills laboratories. The Cancer Science Institute of Singapore and the National Specialty Centres in Cardiovascular Disease and Cancer are also located in this building, together with an expanded Investigational Medicine Unit.

The former Institute of Molecular and Cell Biology (IMCB) Building was renovated and had another floor added, and when it reopened in June 2006, it was renamed the Centre for Life Sciences (CeLs). And in December 2008, the NUS Vivarium, a state-of-the-art, four-storey building was completed. It is the university's central animal holding facility for research and teaching. This facility houses staff and researchers from the current MD1 Animal Holding Unit at Kent Ridge. Another science-related building that was completed in January 2009 was the NUS-Temasek Lab. This was a joint development project between NUS and the Defence Science and Technology Agency (DSTA), and houses the Temasek Laboratories and other university research initiatives.

One of the most appreciated physical changes on campus during this period was the complete renovation of the ever-popular Arts and Social Science Canteen (fondly remembered as "The Spaceship" on account of its shape). The canteen, which used to be a single-storey building with a seating capacity of 966, was transformed into a two-storey food court-styled building with the first non-air-conditioned floor accommodating 1,018 seats and the second storey housing a new 236-seat air-conditioned dining area. It was reopened in August 2007. Three years earlier, in August 2004, a new Student Service Centre was built in the upgraded Yusof Ishak House. Sheares Hall student hostel—which claims to have originated from the Dunearn Road Hostel founded in 1952—moved from its original site in Lower Kent Ridge Road to newly-constructed buildings at 20 Heng Mui Keng Terrace in 2002. In January 2008, a covered walkway was constructed to link the new Sheares Hall to Kent Ridge and to the NUS Business School.

Cultural life on campus received a big boost with the opening of the University Cultural Centre (UCC) by then Deputy Prime Minister and former Vice-Chancellor Tony Tan on 5 September 2000. With the opening of the centre, with its large 1,714-seat hall, university convocations or "commencements" could finally be held on "home ground", something which had not been done since the early days of the University of

Malaya. In addition to the Hall, the UCC has a 450-seat theatre and two function rooms. Housed in an adjacent building to the UCC is the NUS Museum, which had its roots in the University of Malaya Art Museum established in 1954. This museum was closed in 1973 and its collection was moved to the National Museum. In 1980, when the University of Singapore merged with Nanyang University, the latter's Lee Kong Chian Museum (established in 1970) moved to Kent Ridge and, over the next decade, the old University Malaya Art Museum collection was eventually recovered from the National Museum and brought back to Kent Ridge. In 2002, the NUS Museums opened with the collections of the aforementioned collections as well as with material from the Ng Eng Teng collection. In 2006, it was renamed the NUS Museum.

With the UCC and museum in place, a cultural core was developing within the NUS campus and was greatly boosted in October 2006 with the opening of the three-storey Yong Siew Toh Conservatory of Music building, which abuts the UCC and museum. In 2015, after a superhuman fund-raising effort by Professors Leo Tan and Peter Ng, the Lee Kong Chian Natural History Museum opened opposite the NUS Museum, on the site of the old Estate Office. This museum is the permanent home of the precious but not-always-appreciated Zoological Reference Collection (ZRC), which had

almost been lost to the imperatives of development.[135]

Over the years, the size of NUS' alumni has grown dramatically, and to foster better alumni relations, bonding and interactions, a new building—the Shaw Foundation Alumni House—was completed in September 2008. Located right next to the extended NUS Guild House, the Alumni House houses an auditorium, seminar rooms, a multi-function hall as well as several food and beverage outlets.

At the time of writing, the university is embarking on a campus-wide Precinct Master Planning initiative. Starting with the first precinct of Bio-Medical Science Cluster—consisting of the faculties of science, medicine, dentistry and the National University Hospital—and working progressively to the other precincts, this initiative seeks to ensure that the university's physical planning remains relevant and helps NUS remain competitive. The review process will seek broad-based feedback from NUS stakeholders, including faculty and staff, students, alumni and employers, through a series of meetings, charades, focus group discussions and surveys.

Conclusion

When NUS celebrated its 110th anniversary in 2015, it had been at Kent Ridge Campus for almost 40 years. In that time, the university's student

Fig. 5.30: The Visitors' Lodge, which was built in 1985 and demolished in 2018

population had grown from some 5,000 to more than 38,000. Correspondingly, the number of faculties, research centres and support and recreational facilities have grown in tandem. In 2016, NUS was ranked Asia's top university and among the top 13 in the world. These accolades also mean greater pressure on the university to expand its programmes and initiatives to stay competitive and to increase its enrolment as well. This means that space, or the lack thereof, will continue to be a major challenge. If more land cannot be acquired for the university's use, then the temptation for planners and architects will be to build upwards. Can this be done without destroying the beauty of Kent Ridge and maintaining the unity of design that makes the NUS campus so unique?

Fig. 5.31: The NUS campus (not including UTown) as of 2017, built up, but still dominated by the Ridge

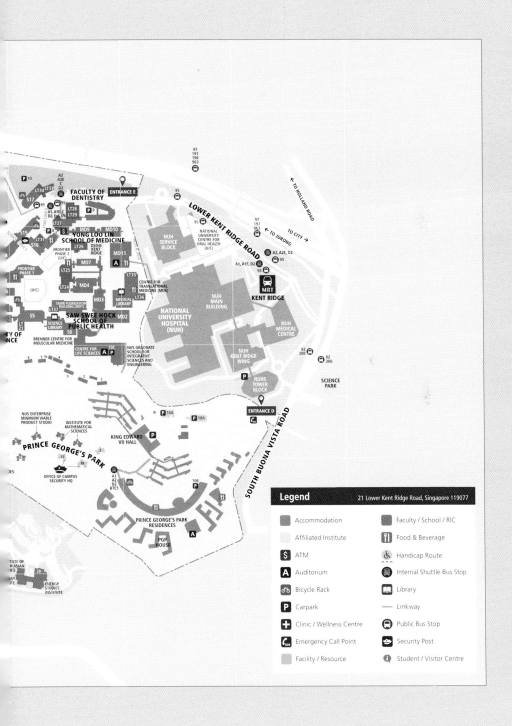

Notes

1. See, generally, Lim Pin Jie, *Positioning the Role of the State in the Kent Ridge Campus Master Plan: An Architectural History of Our University*, MArch thesis (National University of Singapore, Department of Architecture, 2009).
2. "The Medical School", *The Straits Times*, 29 Sept. 1905, p. 5.
3. "Sale of Enemy Property: Government Purchases Mount Rosie", *Singapore Free Press*, 6 Feb. 1919, p. 86.
4. "The Site for Raffles College", *The Straits Times*, 7 Oct. 1921, p. 9; "Raffles College: Report of the Committee Meeting", *The Straits Times*, 11 Feb. 1921, p. 9.
5. See, for example, "New Plea for University: Is Malaya being Sacrificed to Hong Kong?" *The Straits Times*, 4 Feb. 1937, p. 12; "Need for a Malayan University", *The Straits Times*, 5 Feb. 1937, p. 16; "'Malaya is Sufficiently Wealthy to Afford a University', Says Penang Official", *Singapore Free Press*, 28 Sept. 1938, p. 3; "Why Malaya must have a University", *The Straits Times*, 9 Apr. 1947, p. 4.
6. "University College Suggested for City: Fusion of Medical and Raffles Colleges", *The Straits Times*, 14 Dec. 1939, p. 10; "Malaya to have Varsity College", *Singapore Free Press*, 31 Aug. 1946, p. 5; "College as the First Step to University", *The Straits Times*, 31 Aug. 1946, p. 1.
7. This is the old spelling for "Johor Baru" and, for consistency, I have used this variation throughout this article. See "Varsity Plan for Malaya", *The Straits Times*, 28 Dec. 1947, p. 1; "Carr-Saunders Commission Issues Report", *The Straits Times*, 1 May 1948, p. 1; "Johore Bahru Site Ideal for Varsity", *Singapore Free Press*, 3 May 1948, p. 5.
8. "Wants University in Penang", *The Straits Times*, 15 Jan. 1948, p. 5.
9. "Kuala Lumpur Suggested as University Town", *The Straits Times*, 11 Apr. 1947, p. 3.
10. "Johore Bahru Site Ideal for Varsity", *Singapore Free Press*, 3 May 1948, p. 5.
11. Ibid. See also "University Town", *The Straits Times*, 4 May 1948, p. 6.
12. "The University Site", *The Straits Times*, 15 June 1948, p. 8.
13. "1 Million Grant for Malaya's Varsity", *Singapore Free Press*, 27 July 1948, p. 1.
14. "No University Legislation Yet", *The Straits Times*, 18 Oct. 1948, p. 5; and "Abercrombie Coming to Singapore", *The Straits Times*, 23 Nov. 1948, p. 7.
15. "University Bill for Legislative Council Today", *The Straits Times*, 15 Mar. 1949, p. 7.
16. "Singapore Passes Varsity Bill", *The Straits Times*, 30 Mar. 1949, p. 1.
17. "Varsity's First Degrees in July", *The Straits Times*, 30 Mar. 1950, p. 7.
18. "60 Bungalows to be Built for 500 Students", *The Straits Times*, 16 Dec. 1950, p. 5.
19. According to the *Oxford Dictionary of Architecture*, the firm of Easton & Robertson was formed by John Murray Easton (1889–1975) and Sir Howard Morley (1888–1963) in 1919. It was well-known for its work in remodelling the Savoy and Claridge's hotels

as well as the Sadler Well's Theatre. See James Stevens Curl and Susan Wilson, *The Oxford Dictionary of Architecture*, 3rd ed. (Oxford: Oxford University Press, 2015), p. 640. Sidney Edward Thomas Cusdin (1908–2005), who joined the firm in 1930, was the specialist in educational buildings, having been responsible for the buildings of the Medical College of St Bartholomew's Hospital; the Department of Engineering and University Chemistry Laboratories at Cambridge; the Middlesex Hospital Medical School at the University of London; and the Institute of Clinical Sciences building at Queen's University, Belfast. See "Sidney Edward Thomas Cusdin: Doctor of Science *honoris causa* Citation", University of Hong Kong: http://www4.hku.hk/hongrads/index.php/archive/graduate_detail/191 [accessed 1 Oct. 2016].

20. "Malaya wants Best Varsity in the World—Architect", *The Straits Times*, 4 Oct. 1952, p. 8; "University Report Ready by Mille of Next Year: London Architects are Here", *The Straits Times*, 17 Oct. 1952, p. 5; and "Malaya to have Biggest Seat of Learning in SE Asia", *The Straits Times*, 3 Nov. 1953, p. 1.

21. "University Plan Faces Land Poser", *The Straits Times*, 17 Mar. 1954, p. 2 and "Two-University Scheme: $145 Mil Plan may be Dropped", *The Straits Times*, 13 Nov. 1953, p. 1.

22. "Scrap the JB University Plan: Joint Govt Group Say", *Singapore Free Press*, 9 June 1954, p. 1; see also *Report of the Joint Committee on the Future of the University of Malaya* (Singapore: Government Printing Office, 1956). On the failure of this scheme see Lai Chee Kien, *Building Merdeka: Independence Architecture in Kuala Lumpur, 1957–1966* (Kuala Lumpur: Galeri Petronas, 2007), pp. 36–7.

23. "New Town Site", *Singapore Free Press*, 17 Mar. 1960, p. 7.

24. The Faculty of Arts and the Faculty of Social Sciences were combined to form the Faculty of Arts and Social Sciences in 1969.

25. "The Campus Total Goes Up to 2,400", *The Straits Times*, 19 Apr. 1962, p. 16.

26. "University to Build 10-storey Science Tower", *The Straits Times*, 2 Mar. 1964, p. 11.

27. Ibid.

28. "University of Singapore to Get $3 Million Cultural and Sport Centre Soon", *The Straits Times*, 24 Dec. 1967, p. 15.

29. Ibid.

30. "$150 Mil 'New Look' Plan for S'pore Varsity", *The Straits Times*, 5 Dec. 1968, p. 9.

31. *Report of the Preparatory Mission for the Polytechnic and the Technical Education in Singapore* (UNESCO, UNDP: Nov./Dec. 1968) quoted in P. Jonquière, *Singapore: Campus Planning*, UNESCO S/No 2620/RMO.RD/SCT (Paris: UNESCO, 1972). See also Lee Soo Ann, *Report on the Cost Effectiveness of Shifting the Development of the University of Singapore from Bukit Timah to Kent Ridge* (Singapore: Department of Economics, University of Singapore, 1970).

32. *Report of the Preparatory Mission for the Polytechnic and the Technical Education in Singapore*, p. 1.

33. Ibid.

34. Ibid.

35. "Case for a New Campus", *The Straits Times*, 6 Dec. 1968, p. 12.

36. Ibid.

37. Ibid.

38. Chia Poteik, "S'pore Seeks Services of UN Expert to Help Plan a Bigger Varsity", *The Straits Times*, 8 June 1969, p. 2.

39. Ibid.

40. Ibid.

41. "It's Nearly Full House Now at S'pore Poly", *The Straits Times*, 14 July 1969, p. 8.

42. "Best Engineering College in Region to Go Up at Kent Ridge", *The Straits Times*, 13 July 1969, p. 8.

43. "To Pasir Panjang", *The Straits Times*, 15 July 1969, p. 12.

44. Ibid.

45. Francis Rozario, "S'pore Varsity to Get New Home", *The Straits Times*, 15 July 1969, p. 13.

46. "$4.5 Mil UN Aid to Expand S'pore Varsity", *The Straits Times*, 3 Feb. 1969, p. 8.

47. "Unesco Chief Pledges Aid for S'pore", *The Straits Times*, 7 Feb. 1969, p. 4.

48. "$150 Mil S'pore Varsity", *The Straits Times*, 11 Feb. 1969, p. 4.

49. Ibid.

50. One of the proposed uses to which the vacated Bukit Timah campus was put was to accommodate the Singapore Polytechnic. This was disclosed by Minister for National Development E.W. Barker in Mar. 1970. See "University Campus for the Poly", *The Straits Times*, 27 Mar. 1970, p. 5. This plan was later scrapped when it was decided that the Singapore Polytechnic would move to a completely new site at Dover Road, a short distance from Kent Ridge.

51. Ivan Lim, "Low-cost Huts for the University", *New Nation*, 17 Jan. 1972, p. 3.

52. "Nissan Huts House Extra Students", *The Straits Times*, 18 Jan. 1972, p. 3.

53. On Van Embden, see Joosje van Geest, "Sam van Embden, 1904–2000", *Rotterdams Jaarboekje* [Rotterdam Yearbook], 2011, pp. 115–24.

54. According to Meng Ta Cheang, Van Embden was a good friend of Winsemius, who had suggested to the Singapore government that they should invite Van Embden to Singapore on the UNESCO Mission. See interview with Meng Ta Cheang, 14 May 2009, Appendix I of Lim Pin Jie, *Positioning the Role of the State in the Kent Ridge Campus Master Plan*, p. 65.

55. Interview with Meng Ta Cheang, ibid., p. 66.

56. Lim Pin Jie, *Positioning the Role of the State in the Kent Ridge Campus Master Plan*, p. 28.
57. Van Embden, Choisy Roorda van Eysinga, Smelt Wittermans Architects and Urban Planners, *Singapore University on Kent Ridge*, nos 1 & 2 (Delft, 1970).
58. *Report of the Preparatory Mission for the Polytechnic and the Technical Education in Singapore*, p. 2.
59. Ibid.
60. Ibid.
61. Lim Pin Jie, *Positioning the Role of the State in the Kent Ridge Campus Master Plan*, p. 30.
62. Meng Ta Cheang was born in Beijing in 1937 but spent most of his early years in India. After World War II, Meng studied at Cheng Gong University in Taiwan before heading to Aachen, Germany to study with Ernst Neufert. In 1959, he studied under and worked for Samuel Josua van Embden. See interview with Meng Ta Cheang by P.J. Lim and Lai Chee Kien, 14 May 2009, Appendix I of Lim Pin Jie, *Positioning the Role of the State in the Kent Ridge Campus Master Plan*, p. 65.
63. *Report of the Preparatory Mission for the Polytechnic and the Technical Education in Singapore*, p. 5.
64. Lim Pin Jie, *Positioning the Role of the State in the Kent Ridge Campus Master Plan*, pp. 30–1.
65. Ow Wei Mei, "City of Learning at Kent Ridge", *The Straits Times*, 24 July 1970, p. 6.
66. Ibid.
67. Ow Wei Mei, "City of Learning at Kent Ridge", p. 6 and "Remarkable, but it Won't Do, Says Professor", *The Straits Times*, 10 July 1970, p. 6.
68. Ow Wei Mei, "City of Learning at Kent Ridge", *The Straits Times*, 24 July 1970, p. 6.
69. Ibid.
70. Chia Poteik, "First Moves to $100m Campus at Kent Ridge", *The Straits Times*, 12 Mar. 1971, p. 6.
71. Ibid.
72. "Land for New Campus has Yet to Be Acquired", *The Straits Times*, 26 Mar. 1971, p. 11.
73. Ibid.
74. Shen Swee Yong, "Engineering will be Biggest Faculty at Kent Ridge", *The Straits Times*, 4 Dec. 1972, p. 9.
75. Chia Poteik, "First Moves to $100m Campus at Kent Ridge", *The Straits Times*, 12 Mar. 1971, p. 6.
76. "Work to Start Soon on $20m Poly", *The Straits Times*, 30 Nov. 1970, p. 7; "Poly's New $20 Mil Campus", *The Straits Times*, 4 Dec. 1970, p. 15.

77. Chia Poteik, "First Moves to $100m Campus at Kent Ridge", *The Straits Times*, 12 Mar. 1971, p. 6.

78. "Kent Ridge can Be our Brains Centre: Toh", *The Straits Times*, 1 May 1971, p. 32.

79. Masie Kwee, "Expert to Plan Computer Centre", *The Straits Times*, 14 July 1971, p. 27.

80. "World Bank Team Here to Study $100m Loan", *The Straits Times*, 1 July 1971, p. 17; "Bank Men See Plan for Varsity", *New Nation*, 2 July 1971, p. 3.

81. "Bank Men See Plan for Varsity", *New Nation*, 2 July 1971, p. 3.

82. Nancy Byramji, "Second Look at Kent Ridge Varsity", *The Straits Times*, 28 Aug. 1975, p. 28.

83. Soh Tiang Keng, "S'pore Passes Economic 'Test' by the World Bank", *The Straits Times*, 17 Nov. 1971, p. 10 and "$60mil World Bank Loans for Singapore", *The Straits Times*, 16 Nov. 1971, p. 1.

84. *The Straits Times*, 21 July 1974, p. 6.

85. "Sheares to Plant Tree at Kent Ridge Site", *The Straits Times*, 25 Mar. 1972, p. 17.

86. "Dr Toh Sees Kent Ridge as Centre to Draw Scholars from Overseas", *The Straits Times*, 26 Mar. 1972, p. 6.

87. "Tenders for Kent Ridge", *New Nation*, 20 Sept. 1972, p. 6.

88. "Kent Ridge Campus to Be Ready in May 1976", *The Straits Times*, 26 Jan. 1975, p. 8.

89. Shen Swee Yong, "Engineering will Be Biggest Faculty at Kent Ridge", *The Straits Times*, 4 Dec. 1972, p. 9.

90. Lee Tuan Seng, interview with Peck Thian Guan, Judith Holmberg and Edgar Liao, 15 Dec. 2010.

91. Ibid.

92. Ibid.

93. Ibid.

94. Ibid.

95. Meng Ta Cheang, interview with P.J. Lim and Lai Chee Kien, 17 June 2009, Appendix II of Lim Pin Jie, *Positioning the Role of the State in the Kent Ridge Campus Master Plan*, p. 76.

96. Lee Tuan Seng, interview with Peck Thian Guan, Judith Holmberg and Edgar Liao, 15 Dec. 2010.

97. Meng Ta Cheang, interview with P.J. Lim and Lai Chee Kien, 17 June 2009, Appendix II of Lim Pin Jie, *Positioning the Role of the State in the Kent Ridge Campus Master Plan*, p. 74.

98. Tan Liang Seng, interview with Peck Thian Guan, Judith Holmberg and Edgar Liao, 15 Dec. 2010.

99. Ibid., p. 73.

100. Ibid.

101. *Report of the Preparatory Mission for the Polytechnic and the Technical Education in Singapore*, p. 3.
102. Meng Ta Cheang, interview with P.J. Lim and Lai Chee Kien, 17 June 2009, Appendix II of Lim Pin Jie, *Positioning the Role of the State in the Kent Ridge Campus Master Plan*, p. 69.
103. "Kent Ridge Campus to Be Ready in May 1976", *The Straits Times*, 26 Jan. 1975, p. 8.
104. Lim Pin Jie, *Positioning the Role of the State in the Kent Ridge Campus Master Plan*, p. 41.
105. "Building Faculty Moves to Kent Ridge Campus", *The Straits Times*, 11 June 1976, p. 15; see also "Varsity Takes in More this Year", *New Nation*, 8 July 1976, p. 4.
106. "New Kent Ridge Faculty Ready by June", *New Nation*, 1 Apr. 1976, p. 4.
107. "Engineering Faculty will Be Ready Next Month", *The Straits Times*, 24 Oct. 1976, p. 8.
108. Choo Wai Hong, "Engineering School Moves to Kent Ridge in July", *The Straits Times*, 16 June 1977, p. 6.
109. "Dr Toh to Open Faculty", *Business Times*, 15 Dec. 1977, p. 11.
110. Teresa Ooi, "1200 Varsity Students for the Big Shift", *The Straits Times*, 29 Sept. 1977, p. 2; see also "Big Shift Starts Next Month", *New Nation*, 4 Mar. 1978, p. 2.
111. "Only 1100 Students in Bukit Timah Campus", *New Nation*, 7 Nov. 1977, p. 2.
112. "Law Library to Move", *The Straits Times*, 5 Apr. 1978, p. 5.
113. "2 Faculties to Stay at Bukit Timah till 1981", *The Straits Times*, 7 May 1980, p. 7.
114. "President to Open First NUS Hostel", *The Straits Times*, 1 Dec. 1981, p. 13.
115. "Green Look for Kent Ridge Campus", *The Straits Times*, 29 Aug. 1977, p. 9; and "Wanted: A Landscape Architect", *New Nation*, 1 Oct. 1977, p. 4.
116. "The Kent Ridge Campus", *The Straits Times*, 4 Jan. 1979, p. 8.
117. "Sports Complex for Kent Ridge Campus", *The Straits Times*, 5 Oct. 1979, p. 9.
118. Ibid.
119. Betty Liu, "Clubhouse a Reality Thanks to Dr Kwan", *New Nation*, 11 Dec. 1981, p. 10.
120. "University Society's Plan for Clubhouse", *New Nation*, 10 June 1978, p. 4.
121. "Another Guild House", *The Straits Times*, 28 Feb. 1979, p. 10.
122. "New Guild House at Kent Ridge", *New Nation*, 23 Feb. 1979, p. 3.
123. "Kent Ridge Guild House opens on Dec 7", *Business Times*, 14 Nov. 1984, p. 3.
124. "Varsity's Intake by 1980 will Be 6,700", *The Straits Times*, 19 Mar. 1975, p. 8.
125. "Third Phase of NUS Campus to Cost $174m", *Business Times*, 27 Apr. 1983, p. 1.
126. "Move from Sepoy Lines to Kent Ridge Begins", *The Straits Times*, 12 July 1982, p. 11.
127. Nancy Byramji, "Second Look at Kent Ridge Varsity", *The Straits Times*, 28 Aug. 1975, p. 28.
128. "Prof Back with Ideas for Teaching Hospital", *New Nation*, 11 Feb. 1978, p. 3.
129. "$143 Mil Teaching Hospital", *New Nation*, 16 May 1978, p. 4.
130. Ibid.

131. "$19m ADB Loan for Kent Ridge Project", *The Straits Times*, 20 Aug. 1979, p. 15.
132. Caroline Boey, "NUS Builds $2.4m Residence for Visiting Academics", *Singapore Monitor*, 23 Feb. 1984, p. 4; and "NUS to Build 20-room 'Hotel'", *The Straits Times*, 18 Feb. 1984, p. 37.
133. Robin Wong, interview with Peck Thian Guan, Judith Holmberg and Edgar Liao, 15 Dec. 2010.
134. Ibid.
135. For a history of this collection and the building of the Lee Kong Chian Natural History Museum, see Kevin Y.L. Tan, *Of Whales and Dinosaurs: The Story of Singapore's Natural History Museum* (Singapore: NUS Press, 2015).

Bibliography

"100 of the World's Worst Invasive Alien Species' Global Invasive Species Database". http://www.iucngisd.org/gisd/100_worst.php [accessed 1 May 2016].

Ager, A.P. "Singapore as it Used to Be: Memories of the Easygoing Nineties". *The Straits Times Annual 1937*. Singapore: Straits Times Press, 1938.

Alexander, F.E.S. "The Geology of Singapore and the Surrounding Islands", Appendix I in *Report on the Availability of Granite on Singapore and the Surrounding Islands*. Singapore: Singapore Government Press, 1950.

___. "Observations on Tropical Weathering: A Study of the Movement of Iron, Aluminium and Silicon in Weathering Rocks at Singapore". *Quarterly Journal of the Geological Society* 115 (1959): 123–44.

Avibase. "White-Crested Laughingthrush *Garrulax leucolophos* (Hardwicke, 1816)". http://avibase.bsc-eoc.org/species.jsp?lang=EN&avibaseid=6583F1BCFBBD293B [accessed 25 Apr. 2016].

Baker, Nick. "Red Pacu at Catchment Pond, Bukit Timah Nature Reserve". *Singapore Biodiversity Records*, 2013.

Bertram van Cuylenberg, John. *Singapore through Sunshine and Shadow*. Singapore: Heinemann Asia, 1982.

Binti Yayit, Kartini. "Vanishing Landscapes: Malay Kampungs in Singapore", BA (Hons) thesis. Singapore: Department of Geography, National University of Singapore, 1973.

Bird, Michael I., David Taylor and Chris Hunt. "Palaeoenvironments of Insular Southeast Asia During the Last Glacial Period: A Savanna Corridor in Sundaland?" *Quarterly Science Reviews* 24 (2005): 2228–42.

Boey, Caroline. "NUS Builds $2.4m Residence for Visiting Academics". *Singapore Monitor*, 23 Feb. 1984.

Bogaars, George E. "The Effect of Opening the Suez Canal on the Trade and Development of Singapore". In *Singapore: 150 Years*, ed. Mubin Sheppard. Singapore: Times Books International, 1982, pp. 220–68.

Boo Chih, Sharon Y.J. Chew and J.W.H. Yong. *Plants in Tropical Cities*. Singapore: Uvaria Tide, 2014.

Borschberg, Peter. *The Singapore and Melaka Straits: Security, Violence and Diplomacy in the 17th Century*. Singapore: NUS Press, 2010.

Braddell, Roland. *The Lights of Singapore*. London: Methuen, 1935.

Brandell, Judith and Tina Turbeville. *Tiger Balm Gardens: A Chinese Billionaire's Fantasy Environments*. Hong Kong: Aw Boon Haw Foundations, 1998.

Büdel, Julius. "Die 'doppelten Einebnungsflachen' in den fuchten Tropen" [The "Double Flat" Areas in the Humid Tropics], *Zeitschrift für Geomorphologie* (1957), N.F. 1, pp. 201–88.

Burns, P.L. and C.D. Cowan (eds.). *Sir Frank Swettenham's Malayan Journals 1874–1876*. Kuala Lumpur: Oxford University Press, 1975.

Burton, Buckley, Charles. *An Anecdotal History of Old Times in Singapore*, rpt. Kuala Lumpur: University of Malaya Press, 1965.

Burton, C.K. *Geological Survey of Malaysia, Map Bulletin No. 2 — Geology and Mineral Resource: Johore Bahru-Kulai Area*. Ipoh: Ministry of Primary Industries, 1973.

Business Times. "Dr Toh to Open Faculty". 15 Dec. 1977.

___. "Third Phase of NUS Campus to Cost $174m". 27 Apr. 1983.

___. "Kent Ridge Guild House Opens on Dec 7". 14 Nov. 1984.

Byramji, Nancy. "Second Look at Kent Ridge Varsity". 28 Aug. 1975.

Chen D.X. and N. Sivasothi. "Fauna of Kent Ridge: Spider Diversity and the Identification of Common Spiders". Singapore: National University of Singapore, 2010.

Chew, Ernest C.T. and Edwin Lee (eds.). *A History of Singapore*. Singapore: Oxford University Press, 1991.

Chia Poteik. "S'pore Seeks Services of UN Expert to Help Plan a Bigger Varsity". *The Straits Times*. 8 June 1969.

___. "First Moves to $100m Campus at Kent Ridge". 12 Mar. 1971.

Chiang Ming Shun. "Britannia Rules the Waves? Singapore and Imperial Defence 1867–1891". In *Between Two Oceans: A Military History of Singapore From First Settlement to Final British Withdrawal*, ed. Malcolm H. Murfett, John N. Miksic, Brian P. Farrell and Chiang Ming Shun. Singapore: Oxford University Press, 1999.

Choong, M.F., P.W. Lucas, J.S.Y. Ong, B. Pereira, H.T.W. Tan and I.M. Turner. "Leaf Fracture Toughness and Sclerophylly: Their Correlations and Ecological Implications". *New Phytologist* 121, 4 (1992): 597–610.

Choo Wai Hong. "Engineering School Moves to Kent Ridge in July". *The Straits Times*, 16 June 1977.

Chua, Marcus and Kelvin K.P. Lim. "Leopard *Panthera pardus*". In *Singapore Biodiversity: An Encyclopaedia of the Natural Environment and Sustainable Development*, ed. Peter K.L. Ng et al. Singapore: EDM & Raffles Museum of Biodiversity Research, 2011.

___. "Wild Pig *Sus scrofa*". In *Singapore Biodiversity: An Encyclopaedia of the Natural Environment and Sustainable Development*, ed. Peter K.L. Ng, Richard T. Corlett and Hugh T.W. Tan. Singapore: EDM & Raffles Museum of Biodiversity Research, 2011.

___. "Deer Family Cervidae". In *Singapore Biodiversity: An Encyclopaedia of the Natural Environment and Sustainable Development*, ed. Peter K.L. Ng, Richard T. Corlett and Hugh T.W. Tan. Singapore: EDM & Raffles Museum of Biodiversity Research, 2011.

Chua, Grace. "Population of Wild Boars on the Rise". *The Straits Times*, 19 Mar. 2012.

Corlett, Richard T. "Vegetation". In *The Biophysical Environment of Singapore*, ed. Chia Lin Sien, Ausafur Rahman and Dorothy Tay B.H. Singapore: Singapore University Press, 1991.

___. "Terrestrial Ecosystems". In *Singapore Biodiversity: An Encyclopaedia of the Natural Environment and Sustainable Development*. Singapore: EDM and Raffles Museum of Biodiversity Research, 2011.

Corner, E.J.H. "The Freshwater Swamp-forest of South Johore and Singapore". *Gardens' Bulletin Singapore,* Supplement 1, 1978.

Court, David and Wang Luan Keng. "Golden Orb Weavers Family Nephilidae". In *Singapore Biodiversity: An Encyclopaedia of the Natural Environment and Sustainable Development*, ed. Peter K.L. Ng, Richard T. Corlett and Hugh T.W. Tan. Singapore: EDM and Raffles Museum of Biodiversity Research, 2011.

___. "Jumping Spiders Family Salticidae". In *Singapore Biodiversity: An Encyclopaedia of the Natural Environment and Sustainable Development*, ed. Peter K.L. Ng, Richard T. Corlett and Hugh T.W. Tan. Singapore: EDM & Raffles Museum of Biodiversity Research, 2011.

Davison, Julian. *Black and White: The Singapore House 1898–1941*. Singapore: Talisman, 2006.

Dopps. Inc: Pasir Panjang—34th Sea Scouts. http://doppsinc.blogspot.com/2008/09/pasis-panjang-34th-sea-scouts.html [accessed 14 June 2009].

D'Rozario, Vilma and Lye Lin Heng (eds.). *Trees of Bukit Timah Campus: A Tribute to Old Friends*. Singapore: NUS and Nature Society, 2007.

Farrell, Brian P. *The Defence and Fall of Singapore 1940–42*. Stroud: Tempus, 2005.

Feng, Zengkun. "Attacks Spark Hunt for m=Monkey". *The Straits Times*, 7 Oct. 2011.

Fonseca, Rory. "Planning and Land Use". In *Singapore Society in Transition*, ed. Riaz Hassan. Singapore: Oxford University Press, 1976, pp. 221–39.

Grubb, P.J., I.M. Turner and D.F.R.P. Burslem. "Mineral Nutrient Status of Coastal Hill Dipterocarp Forest and Adinandra Belukar in Singapore: Analysis of Soil, Leaves and Litter". *Journal of Tropical Ecology* 10, 4 (1994): 559–77.

Gupta, Avijit. "Observations on the Effects of Urbanization and Runoff on Sediment Production in Singapore". *Singapore Journal of Tropical Geography* 3 (1982): 137–46.

Hall, Robert. "Hydrocarbon Basins in SE Asia: Understanding Why they are there". *Petroleum Geoscience* 15 (2009): 131–46.

Haughton, H.T. "Native Names of Streets in Singapore". In *Singapore: 150 Years*, ed. Mubin Sheppard. Singapore: Times Books International, 1982, pp. 208–19.

Hooi, Alexis. "Smoking Banned in Nature Reserves". *The Straits Times*, 11 May 2005.

Hone, H.R. *Report on the British Military Administration of Malaya, September 1945, to March 1946*. Kuala Lumpur: Malayan Union Government Press, 1946.

Ho Hua Chew and Clive Briffett. *Kent Ridge Environs: A Proposal for Conserving Nature at the National University of Singapore Campus*. Singapore: Malayan Nature Society, 1991.

Holttum, R.E. "Adinandra Belukar – A Succession of Vegetation from Bare Ground on Singapore Island". *Malayan Journal of Tropical Geography* 3 (1954): 27–32.

Hope, Geoffrey. "The Quaternary in Southeast Asia". In *The Physical Geography of Southeast Asia*, ed. Avijit Gupta. Oxford: Oxford University Press, 2005, pp. 24–37.

Hutchinson, C.S. "The Geological Framework". In *The Physical Geography of Southeast Asia*, ed. Avijit Gupta. Oxford: Oxford University Press, 2005, pp. 3–23.

Jarvis, Erich D. et al. "Whole-Genome Analyses Resolve Early Branches in the Tree of Life of Modern Birds". *Science* 346, 6215 (2014): 1320–331.

Jonquière, P. *Singapore: Campus Planning*, UNESCO S/No 2620/RMO.RD/SCT. Paris: UNESCO, 1972.

Khew, S.K. and Steven S.H. Neo. "Butterfly Biodiversity in Singapore with Particular Reference to the Central Catchment Nature Reserve". *Gardens' Bulletin Singapore* 49, 1 (1997): 273–96.

King, Sam. *Tiger Balm King: The Life and Times of Aw Boon Haw*. Singapore: Times Book International, 1992.

Kohl, David G. *Chinese Architecture in the Straits Settlements and Western Malaya: Temples, Kongsis and Houses*. Kuala Lumpur: Heinemann Asia, 1984.

Krishnan, R. "Tunneling and Underground Projects in Singapore". In *Tunnels and Underground Structures*, ed. J. Zhao, J.N. Shirlaw and R. Krishnan. Rotterdam: Balkema, 2009, pp. 89–96.

Kwee, Masie. "Expert to Plan Computer Centre". *The Straits Times*, 14 July 1971.

Lee, Edwin and Tan Tai Yong. *Beyond Degrees: The Making of the National University of Singapore*. Singapore: Singapore University Press, 1996.

Lee, Kim Woon, Yingxin Zhou, Yam Khoon Tor and Juan Li. *Geology of Singapore*. Singapore: Defence Science & Technology Agency, 2009.

Lee Kip Lee. *Amber Sands: A Boyhood Memoir*. Singapore: Federal Publications, 1999.

Lee Kip Lin. *The Singapore House, 1819–1942*. Singapore: Times Editions, 1988.

Leyden, John. *Malay Annals*. Tr. John Leyden. London: Longman, Hur, Rees, Orme and Brown, 1821.

Lim, Ivan. "Low-cost Huts for the University". *New Nation*, 17 Jan. 1972.

Lim, Kelvin Kok Peng and Peter Kee Lin Ng. *A Guide to the Freshwater Fishes of Singapore*. Singapore: Singapore Science Centre, 1990.

Lim Pie Jin. "Positioning the Role of the State in the Kent Ridge Campus Master Plan: An Architectural History of Our University", MArch thesis. Singapore: National University of Singapore, 2009.

Liu, Betty. "Clubhouse a Reality Thanks to Dr Kwan". *New Nation*, 11 Dec. 1981.

Longhurst, Henry. *Straits Times, the Borneo Story: The History of the First 100 Years of Trading in the Far East by the Borneo Company, Limited*. Newman Neame, 1956.

Lui, John. "Former National Athlete Bitten by Snake in Toilet". *The Straits Times*, 4 Aug. 1993.

Lynch, Kevin. *The Image of the City*. Cambridge: MIT Press, 1960.

Master Plan Written Statement. Singapore: Government Printing Office, 1955.

Matheson Hooker, Virginia and M.B. Hooker. *John Leyden's Malay Annals*. Kuala Lumpur: MBRAS, 2001.

Ming Kai Tan, R.W.J. Ngiam and M.R.B. Ismail. "A Checklist of Orthoptera in Singapore Parks". *Nature in Singapore* 5 (2012). http://lkcnhm.nus.edu.sg/nis/bulletin2012/2012nis061-067.pdf [accessed 20 Apr. 2016].

Ming Kai Tan. "Preliminary Bioacoustics Study of Ensifera (Orthoptera) in and around Bukit Timah Nature Reserve". Singapore: National University of Singapore, 2011.

___. "Orthoptera in Singapore: Diversity, New Species and Predation", BA (Hons) thesis. Singapore: National University of Singapore, 2015.

___. "Orthoptera in the Bukit Timah and Central Catchment Nature Reserves (Part 1): Suborder Caelifera". Singapore: Raffles Museum of Biodiversity Research, 2012, pp. 1–40. http://lkcnhm.nus.edu.sg/raffles_museum_pub/z_2013/caelifera_btnr_ccnr.pdf [accessed 17 Apr. 2016].

Mohamed Ali, Mariam. "Singapore's Orang Seletar, Orang Kallang and Orang Selat: The Last Settlements". In *Tribal Communities in the Malay World: Historical, Cultural and Social Perspectives*, ed. Geoffrey Benjamin and Cynthia Chou. Singapore: Institute of Southeast Asian Studies, 2002, pp. 273–92.

Morton, Julia F. *Fruits of Warm Climates*. Winterville, NC: Creative Resource Systems, 1987.

Murfett, Malcolm H., John N. Miksic, Brian P. Farrell and Chiang Ming Shun. *Between Two Oceans: A Military History of Singapore from First Settlement to Final British Withdrawal*. Singapore: Oxford University Press, 1999.

National Archives of Singapore. "2 Blocks of European Quarters, Pasir Panjang Rd", Building Plan No 217. Owner: New Harbour Dock Co Ltd.

National Parks Board. "NParks Flora & Fauna Web". National Parks Board, https://florafaunaweb.nparks.gov.sg/ [accessed 24 Apr. 2016].

___. "Kent Ridge Park". https://www.nparks.gov.sg/gardens-parks-and-nature/parks-and-nature-reserves/kent-ridge-park [accessed 5 May 2016].

New Nation. "Bank Men See Plan for Varsity". 2 July 1971.

___. "Tenders for Kent Ridge". 20 Sept. 1972.

___. "New Kent Ridge Faculty Ready by June". 1 Apr. 1976.

___. "Varsity Takes in More this Year". 8 July 1976.

___. "Wanted: A Landscape Architect". 1 Oct. 1977.

___. "Only 1100 Students in Bukit Timah Campus". 7 Nov. 1977.

___. "Prof Back with Ideas for Teaching Hospital". 11 Feb. 1978.

___. "Big Shift Starts Next Month". 4 Mar. 1978.

___. "$143 Mil Teaching Hospital". 16 May 1978.

___. "University Society's Plan for Clubhouse". 10 June 1978.

___. "New Guild House at Kent Ridge". 23 Feb. 1979.

___. "Another Guild House". 28 Feb. 1979.

Ng Heok Hee and Heok Hui Tan. "An Annotated Checklist of the Non-Native Freshwater Fish Species in the Reservoirs of Singapore". *Cosmos* 6, 1 (2010).

Ngiam, Robin. *Dragonflies of Our Parks and Gardens.* Singapore: National Parks Board, 2011.

Noble, Sarah. *Feng Shui in Singapore.* Singapore: Graham Brash, 1997.

Norma-Rashid, Y. L.F. Cheong, H.K. Lua and D.H. Murphy. *The Dragonflies (Odonata) of Singapore: Current Status Records and Collections of the Raffles Museum of Biodiversity Research.* Singapore: Raffles Museum of Biodiversity Research, National University of Singapore, 2008. http://lkcnhm.nus.edu.sg/nus/pdf/PUBLICATION/LKCNH%20 Museum%20Books/LKCNHM%20Books/Dragonfly_of_Singapore.pdf [accessed 17 Apr. 2016].

O'Dempsey, Tony and Chew Ping Ting. "The Freshwater Swamp Forests of Sungei Seletar Catchment: A Status Report". In *Proceedings of Nature Society, Singapore's Conference on 'Nature Conservation for a Sustainable Singapore'—16th October 2011,* ed. Leong Tzi Ming and Ho Hua Chew, pp. 121–66.

___. "Singapore's Changing Landscape since c. 1800". In *Nature Contained,* ed. Timothy P. Barnard. Singapore: NUS Press, 2014.

Oldland, Jo. *Shorebird Conservation in Australia,* Birds Australia Conservation Statement No. 14, 2009. http://birdlife.org.au/documents/OTHPUB-shorebirds09.pdf [accessed 10 May 2016].

Ooi, Teresa. "1200 Varsity Students for the Big Shift". 29 Sept. 1977.

Ow Wei Mei. "City of Learning at Kent Ridge". 24 July 1970.

Pascualita Sa-a. "*Betta imbellis* Ladiges, 1975". FishBase, http://www.fishbase.org/ summary/12038 [accessed 28 Apr. 2016].

Pitts, John. "A Review of the Geology and Engineering Geology in Singapore". *Quarterly Journal of Engineering Geology* 17 (1984): 93–101.

Poh Ern Shih. "Temple of Thanksgiving". http://www.pohernshih.org/History(E).htm [accessed 5 May 2009].

Quek, Carolyn and Michelle Neo. "Crushed to Death on Her Walk to Health". *The Straits Times*, 17 May 2007.

Rahardjo, H., X.W. Li, D.G. Toll and E.C. Leong. "The Effect of Antecedent Rainfall on Slope Stability". *Geotechnical and Geological Engineering* 29 (2001): 369–97.

Ramli, Dol. "History of the Malay Regiment 1933–1942". *Journal of the Malaysian Branch of the Royal Asiatic Society* 38, 1 (1965).

Redding, J. and J.B. Christensen. *Geotechnical Feasibility Study into Rock Cavern Construction in the Jurong Formation*, report. Ove Arup & Partners International Ltd and Norconsult International A/S, 1999.

Report of the Joint Committee on the Future of the University of Malaya. Singapore: Government Printing Office, 1956.

Rozario, Francis. "S'pore Varsity to Get New Home". *The Straits Times*, 15 July 1969.

Russel Wallace, Alfred. *The Malay Archipelago: The Land of the Orang-Utan, and the Bird of Paradise. A Narrative of Travel, with Studies of Man and Nature*, vol. 1. London: Macmillan and Co., 1869.

Savage, Victor R. "Landscape Change: From Kampong to Global City". In *Physical Adjustments in a Changing Landscape: The Singapore Story*, ed. Avijit Gupta and John Pitts. Singapore: Singapore University Press, 1992, pp. 5–31.

Savage, Victor R. and Brenda S.A. Yeoh. *Toponymics: A Study of Singapore Street Names*. Singapore: Eastern Universities Press, 2004.

Scrivenor, J.B. "The Geology of Singapore Island: With a Geological Sketch Map". *Journal of the Malayan Branch of the Asiastic Society* 2 (1924): 1–8.

Shen Swee Yong. "Engineering will Be Biggest Faculty at Kent Ridge". *The Straits Times*, 4 Dec. 1972.

Sheppard, Mubin C. "The Malay Soldier from a District Officers' Point of View". *Straits Times Annual 1939*. Singapore: Straits Times Press, 1940.

___. *The Malay Regiment 1933–47*. Kuala Lumpur: Department of Public Relations, 1947.

Sim, J.W.S., Hugh T.W. Tan and I.M. Turner. "Adinandra Belukar: An Anthropogenic Heath Forest in Singapore". *Vegetatio* 102, 2 (1992): 125–37.

Singapore '73. Singapore: Ministry of Culture, 1973.

Singapore Free Press. "Municipal Commissioner". 18 Dec. 1856.

___. "Squatter's Rubber Trees". 20 Sept. 1917.

"Sale of Enemy Property: Government Purchases Mount Rosie". 6 Feb. 1919.

___. "Malaya is Sufficiently Wealthy to Afford a University, Says Penang Official". 28 Sept. 1938.

___. "Malaya to have Varsity College". 31 Aug. 1946.

___. "Johore Bahru Site Ideal for Varsity". 3 May 1948.

___. "Scrap the JB University Plan: Joint Govt Group Say". 9 June 1954.

___. "New Town Site". 17 Mar. 1960.

Singh, Rajpal s/o Santokh Singh. "Street Naming and the Construction of the Colonial Narrative in Singapore: 1819–1942", academic exercise. Singapore: National University of Singapore, 2002.

Sodhi, Navjot S. and Hugh T.W. Tan. "Report on the Ecosystem Study of the Proposed Site for the Nature Area at the NUS Kent Ridge Campus", internal report. Singapore: National University of Singapore, 2003.

Soh Tiang Keng. "S'pore Passes Economic 'Test' by the World Bank". *The Straits Times*, 17 Nov. 1971.

Song Ong Siang. *One Hundred Years' History of the Chinese in Singapore*. London: John Murray, 1923.

Sopher, David. *The Sea Nomads*. Singapore: Singapore National Museum, 1977.

"Species Profile". Global Invasive Species Database. http://www.iucngisd.org/gisd/species.php?sc=53 [accessed 1 May 2016].

Straits Times, The.

___. "Government Gazette". 14 Nov. 1864.

___. "News of the Week". 19 Nov. 1864.

___. "Game Preserver". 5 Dec. 1874.

___. "Notices". 21 Mar. 1883.

___. "Lands for Military Purposes". 8 June 1896.

___. "Highway Robbery". 25 May 1898.

___. "Legislative Council". 8 Nov. 1898.

___. "Lawless Pasir Panjang". 5 Dec. 1899.

___. "To Contractors". 14 May 1900.

___. "The Volunteer Camp". 27 Jan. 1903.

___. "Daring Gang Robbery". 15 Aug. 1903.

___. "The Medical School". 29 Sept. 1905.

___. "Sport in Singapore in 1905". 2 Jan. 1906.

___. "Betrayed by a Helmet". 30 May 1906.

___. "Hockey". 4 July 1906.

___. "Burglary at 'Labrador Villa'". 3 Dec. 1906.

___. "Hockey". 17 Dec. 1906.

___. "Hockey". 9 Jan. 1907.

___. "Extension of the Railways". 21 Jan. 1907.

___. "Changes in the Garrison". 28 Jan. 1908.

___. "Singapore Government Bungalows". 14 Aug. 1909.

___. "The Ramlila". 15 Oct. 1910.

___. "The Third Brahmans". 11 Jan. 1911.

___. "Volunteer Inspection". 11 Dec. 1911.

___. "SVC Orders". 7 Mar. 1912.

___. "Notes in General". 31 Oct. 1912.

___. "Brahman Murdered". 23 Feb. 1914.

___. "The Murdered Brahman". 24 Feb. 1914.

___. "The Relief of the 3rd Brahmans". 24 Mar. 1914.

___. "Brahman Murder". 2 Apr. 1914.

___. "Pasir Panjang Murder Trial Opened". 9 June 1914.

___. "Ejected Squatter's Claim: Kim Seng Land Co Sued for $3,000". 17 Sept. 1917.

___. "Raffles College: Report of the Committee Meeting". 11 Feb. 1921.

___. "The Site for Raffles College". 7 Oct. 1921.

___. "Malayan Breweries Limited". 21 Mar. 1932.

___. "A New Industry for Malaya". 5 Apr. 1932.

___. "Modern Brewery for Singapore – Nearing Completion". 5 Apr. 1932.

___. "Notes of the Day". 3 Nov. 1933.

___. "Kim Seng Land Company Limited v The Rural Board [1935]". 7 Mar. 1935.

___. "Second Infantry Regiment in their New Home". 1 Apr. 1936.

___. "New Plea for University: Is Malaya being Sacrificed to Hong Kong?" 4 Feb. 1937.

___. "Need for a Malayan University". 5 Feb. 1937.

___. "Diluted Beer: Two Chinese Convicted". 18 Mar. 1939.

___. "Cycling Speed Trial Postponed". 14 Apr. 1939.

___. "Gurdial Singh Wins Gap Hill Climb". 15 May 1939.

___. "Beer Taken to Court". 17 Feb. 1940.

___. "New Military Hospital Now Open". 28 July 1940.

___. "Hill Climb Attracts Good Entry". 31 July 1940.

___. "New Company to Run Brewery: Former German Concern Has Been Sold". 27 Jan. 1941.

___. "Malayan Breweries Profit Almost Doubled". 14 Mar. 1941.

___. "College as the First Step to University". 31 Aug. 1946.

___. "Why Malaya must have a University". 9 Apr. 1947.

___. "Varsity Plan for Malaya". 28 Dec. 1947.

___. "Carr-Saunders Commission Issues Report". 1 May 1948.

___. "Peng Han Builds 4 Cars for Hill Climb". 23 Oct. 1948.

___. "Singapore Passes Varsity Bill". 30 Mar. 1949.

___. "Brewery's $750,000 Scheme". 27 May 1949.

___. "Breweries Make a Profit". 2 Oct. 1949.

___. "Varsity's First Degrees in July". 30 Mar. 1950.

___. "Brewers' Tails were 'in the Air'". 6 Oct. 1950.

___. "60 Bungalows to be Built for 500 Students". 16 Dec. 1950.

___. "Report is Wanted on Race Crash". 28 May 1952.

___. "Malaya wants Best Varsity in the World—Architect". 4 Oct. 1952.

___. "University Report Ready by Mille of Next Year: London Architects are Here". 17 Oct. 1952.

___. "Malaya to have Biggest Seat of Learning in SE Asia". 3 Nov. 1953.

___. "Two-University Scheme: $145 Mil Plan may be Dropped". 13 Nov. 1953.

___. "University Plan Faces Land Poser". 17 Mar. 1954.

___. "100-M Cycle Race Today". 23 Oct. 1955.

___. "Jaffa First in Gap Race". 31 Oct. 1955.

___. "Singapore-Malacca Cycle Race Shortly". 18 May 1958.

___. "Leading Drivers, Rider for this Year's Grand Prix". 23 June 1961.

___. "The Campus Total Goes Up to 2,400". 19 Apr. 1962.

___. "Salleh First". 22 July 1963.

___. "University to Build 10-storey Science Tower". 2 Mar. 1964.

___. "University of Singapore to Get $3 Million Cultural and Sport Centre Soon". 24 Dec. 1967.

___. "$150 Mil 'New Look' Plan for S'pore Varsity". 5 Dec. 1968.

___. "Case for a New Campus". 6 Dec. 1968.

___. "$4.5 Mil UN Aid to Expand S'pore Varsity". 3 Feb. 1969.

___. "Unesco Chief Pledges Aid for S'pore". 7 Feb. 1969.

___. "Best Engineering College in Region to Go Up at Kent Ridge". 13 July 1969.

___. "To Pasir Panjang". 15 July 1969.

___. "It's Nearly Full House Now at S'pore Poly". 14 July 1969.

___. "University Campus for the Poly". 27 Mar. 1970.

___. "Work to Start Soon on $20m Poly". 30 Nov. 1970.

___. "Land for New Campus has Yet to Be Acquired". 26 Mar. 1971.

___. "Kent Ridge can Be our Brains Centre: Toh". 1 May 1971.

___. "World Bank Team Here to Study $100m Loan". 1 July 1971.

___. "Nissan Huts House Extra Students". 18 Jan. 1972.

___. "Sheares to Plant Tree at Kent Ridge Site". 25 Mar. 1972.

___. "Dr Toh Sees Kent Ridge as Centre to Draw Scholars from Overseas". 26 Mar. 1972.

___. "Gerry Wins Fastest Time of the Day Award". 24 Sept. 1973.

___. "Choon Kiat Wins Gap". 17 June 1974.

___. "Kent Ridge Campus to Be Ready in May 1976". 26 Jan. 1975.

___. "Rahman Fails by a Wheel to Win Tour of Singapore". 17 Mar. 1975.

___. "Varsity's Intake by 1980 will Be 6,700". 19 Mar. 1975.

___. "Building Faculty Moves to Kent Ridge Campus". 11 June 1976.

___. "Engineering Faculty will Be Ready Next Month". 24 Oct. 1976.

___. "Green Look for Kent Ridge Campus". 29 Aug. 1977.

___. "Law Library to Move". 5 Apr. 1978.

___. "The Kent Ridge Campus". 4 Jan. 1979.

___. "$19m ADB Loan for Kent Ridge Project". 20 Aug. 1979.

___. "Sports Complex for Kent Ridge Campus". 5 Oct. 1979.

___. "2 Faculties to Stay at Bukit Timah till 1981". 7 May 1980.

___. "President to Open First NUS Hostel". 1 Dec. 1981.

___. "Roads that Make Some Riders Go Round the Bend". 18 Apr. 1982.

___. "Move from Sepoy Lines to Kent Ridge Begins". 12 July 1982.

___. "NUS to Build 20-room 'Hotel'". 18 Feb. 1984.

Tan, Hugh T.W. *The Natural Heritage of Singapore*. Singapore and New York, NY: Prentice Hall, 2010.

Tan, Hugh T.W., B.C. Soong and T. Morgany. "Plants". In *A Guide to the Mangroves of Singapore Volume 1*, ed. Peter K.L. Ng and N. Sivasothi. Singapore: Singapore Science Centre, 1999.

Tan, Kevin Y.L. *Of Whales and Dinosaurs: The Story of Singapore's Natural History Museum*. Singapore: NUS Press, 2015.

Tan Khoon Yong. *The Secrets of the Five Dragons: Feng Shui and Singapore's Success*. Singapore: Times Books International, 2001.

Taylor, David, Oh Hwee Yen, Peta G. Sanderson and John Dodson. "Late Quaternary Peat Formation and Vegetation Dynamics in Lowland Tropical Swamp; Nee Soon, Singapore". *Palaeogeography, Palaeoclimatology, Palaeoecology* 171 (2001): 531–8.

Teh Joo Lin. "256 Bush Fires Break Out in the First 40 Days of this Year". *The Straits Times*, 12 Feb. 2005.

Teo, R.C.H. and S. Rajathurai. "Mammals, Reptiles and Amphibians in the Nature Reserves of Singapore: Diversity, Abundance and Distribution". *Gardens' Bulletin Singapore* 49, 1 (1997): 353–425.

The Singapore and Malayan Directory for 1940. Singapore: Printers Limited, 1940.

Thomas, G.S.P. "Geology and Geomorphology". In *The Biophysical Environment of Singapore*, ed. Chia Lin Sien, Ausafur Rahman and Dorothy Tay B.H. Singapore: Singapore University Press, 1991, pp. 50–88.

Toll, D.G., B.H. Ong and H. Rahardjo. "Triaxial Testing of Unsaturated Samples on Undisturbed Residual Soil from Singapore". In *Unsaturated Soils for Asia: Proceedings of the Asian Conference on Unsaturated Soils: UNSAT-Asia 2000*, Singapore 18–19 May

2000, ed. H. Rahardjo, D.G. Toll and E.C. Leong. Rotterdam: Balkema, 2000, pp. 579–92.

Turnbull, C.M. *A History of Modern Singapore, 1819–2005*. Singapore: NUS Press, 2009.

Turner, I.M. and K.S. Chua. *Checklist of the Vascular Plant Species of the Bukit Timah Nature Reserve*. Singapore: Raffles Museum of Biodiversity Research, 2011.

US Fish & Wildlife Service Endangered Species Program. "All About the Peregrine Falcon". http://web.archive.org/web/20080416195055/http://www.fws.gov/endangered/recovery/peregrine/QandA.html#fast [accessed 10 May 2016].

Van Geest, Joosje. "Sam van Embden, 1904–2000". *Rotterdams Jaarboekje* [Rotterdam Yearbook], 2011, pp. 115–24.

Van Linschoten, Jan Huygen. *Itinerario: Voyage Ofte Schipvaert Van Jan Huygen Van Linschoten Naer oost ofte Portugaels Indien 1579–1592*. The Hague: Martinus Nijhoff, 1939.

Wang Gungwu. "Inception, Origins, Contemplations: A Personal Perspective". In *Imagination, Openness & Courage: The National University of Singapore at 100*. Singapore: National University of Singapore, 2006, pp. 3–31.

Warren, Alan. *Singapore 1942: Britain's Greatest Defeat*. London: Hambledon Continuum, 2002.

Wee, Y.C. and R.T. Corlett. *The City and the Forest: Plant Life in Urban Singapore*. Singapore: Singapore University Press, 1986.

Wong, H.F., S.Y. Tan, C.Y. Koh, H.J.M. Siow, T. Li, A. Heyzer, A.H.F. Ang, Mirza Rifqi bin Ismail, A. Strivathsan and H.T.W. Tan. *Checklist of the Plant Species of Nee Soon Swamp Forest, Singapore: Bryophytes to Angiosperms*. Singapore: Raffles Museum of Biodiversity Research, 2013.

Wong Poh Poh. "The Changing Landscapes of Singapore Island". In *Modern Singapore*, ed. Ooi Jin-Bee and Chiang Hai Ding. Singapore: University of Singapore, 1969.

Wyatt-Smith. J. *Manual of Malayan Silviculture for Inland Forest*, Malayan Forest Records No. 23. Kuala Lumpur: Forest Research Institute Malaysia, 1963, Part III, 7.20–1.

Yee, Alex Thiam Koon, Kwek Yan Chong, Louise Neo and Hugh T.W. Tan. "Updating the Classification System for the Secondary Forests of Singapore". *Raffles Bulletin of Zoology* Supplement 32 (May 2016): 13–4, 19, http://lkcnhm.nus.edu.sg/nus/images/data/raffles_bulletin_of_zoology/supplement32/S32rbz011-021.pdf [accessed 7 May 2016].

Image Credits

NUS Press and the editor would like to thank the many individuals and institutions who helped source or granted us a license to publish the images for this volume. They are credited here.

Ang Wee Foong: 3.8, 3.30, 3.32, 3.33

Asian Civilisations Museum: 4.3

Peter Borschberg: 4.1

Amy Choong Mei Fun: 3.12

Marcus Chua Aik Hwee: 3.78, 3.93

Gordon Claughton: 4.19a, 4.19b, 4.21a, 4.21b

Alan Cottrell: 4.17

Flickr user "Junzi", who generously shared these images under a CC-BY license: 1.5, 1.6

Lam Weng Ngai: 3.9, 3.11, 3.15, 3.16

The Lee Kip Lin Collection at the National Library Board, Singapore: 4.6, 4.15a-d

Map by Lee Li Kheng, from PSTA (2009): 2.1

Kelvin Lim Kok Peng: 3.67, 3.68, 3.69, 3.70, 3.71, 3.73, 3.75, 3.76, 3.77, 3.80, 3.81, 3.82, 3.91, 3.92

The Malayan Branch of the Royal Asiatic Society: 4.10

From the collection of Mok Ly Yng: 0.3, 4.7, 4.18

Courtesy of National Archives of Singapore: 1.3, 1.4, 4.11, 4.16

Collection of the National Library Board: 4.7

National Museum of Singapore and Haw Par Villa: 4.13a-d

National University of Singapore: 0.1, 0.2, 0.4, 0.5, 0.6, 1.1, 1.7, 1.8, 1.9, 1.10, 4.2, 4.5, 4.21a, 4.21b, 5.1, 5.2, 5.3, 5.4, 5.5, 5.6, 5.7, 5.8, 5.9, 5.10, 5.11, 5.12, 5.13, 5.14, 5.15, 5.16, 5.17, 5.18, 5.19, 5.20, 5.21, 5.22, 5.23, 5.24, 5.25, 5.26, 5.27

Cerlin Ng Xin Yi: 3.7, 3.14

Peck Thian Guan: 1.4, 4.9, 4.12

Catherine Poh Huay Tan, shared under a Creative Commons license, cropped to vertical, 1.2

Royal Geographic Society, UK: 4.4

Peter Schoppert: 2.2

Tan Heok Hui: 3.72, 3.83, 3.84, 3.85, 3.86, 3.87, 3.88

Horace Tan Hwee Huat: 3.39, 3.40, 3.41, 3.42, 3.43, 3.44, 3.45, 3.46, 3.47, 3.48, 3.49, 3.50, 3.51, 3.52

Hugh Tan: 3.1, 3.2, 3.10, 3.13, 3.17, 3.18, 3.19, 3.20, 3.21, 3.22, 3.23, 3.24, 3.25, 3.26, 3.27, 3.28, 3.29, 3.31, 3.34, 3.35, 3.36, 3.37, 3.38, 3.79, 3.89, 3.90

Kevin Tan: 1.5, 3.3, 3.4, 4.14, 4.20, 5.16, 5.17, 5.18, 5.30

Yeoh Yi Shuen: 3.5, 3.6

Tan Ming Kai: 3.53, 3.54, 3.55, 3.56, 3.57, 3.58, 3.59, 3.60, 3.61, 3.62, 3.63, 3.64, 3.74

Yeo Huiqing: 3.65, 3.66

Index

Note: Page numbers in italics denote figures, images, maps, and tables.